The
Jock
Empire

The Jock Empire

Its Rise and Deservéd Fall

•

GLENN DICKEY

Chilton Book Company
Radnor, Pennsylvania

Copyright © 1974 by Glenn Dickey
First Edition   *All Rights Reserved*

Published in Radnor, Pa., by Chilton Book Company
and simultaneously in Ontario, Canada
by Thomas Nelson & Sons, Ltd.

Designed by Carole L. DeCrescenzo

Manufactured in the United States of America

Library of Congress Cataloging in Publication Data
Dickey, Glenn.
The jock empire; its rise and deservéd fall.

1. Sports—United States.   I. Title.
GV583.D52   796'.0973   74-12277
ISBN 0-8019-5926-8

Foreword

•

Sports are more important to our society than at any time in the history of the country. The signs are everywhere. You cannot turn on the television set without seeing Bob Griese; you cannot go to a banquet without hearing Tom Seaver; you cannot go into the supermarket without noticing a raft of goods endorsed by athletes, some of whom may even have used the product they endorse.

The tone is set at the very top. The President stays awake nights diagramming—unsuccessfully—football plays. He scatters sports references throughout his speeches, and even his subordinates talk blithely of game plans and team spirit. He regularly calls winning coaches and players to congratulate them on their performances. He has games piped into his office on closed-circuit television, and he leads the fight to have home football games televised. He sits in his office watching football games on television when protestors are milling around outside the White House gates, and when he leaves the White House in the early morning to talk to collegiate protestors, he talks about their school football team in an effort to establish some kind of bond.

Sports have replaced the weather as a conversational topic. People of all classes can talk about sports when they can talk about nothing else; it is the common denominator. A man whose chief concern is the preservation of the oil depreciation clause can meet a man whose chief concern is the price of beer, and they can agree on one thing: the Cowboys have a chance to go all the way this year.

People regard pro football as a return to the age of the Roman gladiator, and the popularity or decline of other sports is discussed in sociological terms.

Athletes are ranked with astronauts as our country's heroes, at least one step ahead of politicians. Criticism of star athletes is widely regarded as heresy, and there is far less of it than there is of the President; many remember Jim Bouton's *Ball Four* primarily because of a short bit of criticism of Mickey Mantle.

Sportscasters become national figures solely because they're at so many big sports events and get asked for autographs by fans who recognize them, though most sportscasters are shills who deliberately obfuscate so people will not learn what is really happening. Howard Cosell, an obvious exception, has become a celebrity imitated as much as Cary Grant or James Cagney and sought for parts in movies. His merits and demerits are debated endlessly in bars and around fancy dinner tables throughout the land.

And yet, there are many flaws in the world of sports. Ticket prices continue to rise, and the prices for sports events often rank with those of the opera—and for a clientele which is on the average considerably poorer. Who is to blame? The owners blame the athletes, though owning a pro sports franchise is usually the surest way to profits. Athletes blame the owners, though their own salaries border on the ridiculous. The fan doesn't care who's to blame. All he knows is that he's caught in the middle, with prices rising in good years and bad. In some areas, attendance is already falling off because people can no longer afford to see as many games as they once did, and there is reason to believe that the whole structure of professional sports will one day collapse like a deck of cards.

The gap continues to grow between athletes and fans. Athletes are spoiled from Little League or Pop Warner days. By the time they reach the professional ranks, they've had special treatment for so long, they no longer realize it is special treatment. They regard fans as ignorant and boorish and shun them whenever possible, while fans flock to airports to greet returning teams and pay large sums just to play in golf tournaments with athletes or to attend dinners where athletes are speaking.

Nowhere in society is male chauvinism more rampant than in sports, as we are just beginning to realize. From Little League to professional ranks, sports are a male affair, with women permitted in only as secretaries, as quiet and stupid spectators and as bed partners. Especially as bed partners.

All the problems of society, from drug-taking to racism, are writ extralarge in sports. The Winning Is Everything Syndrome which is the basis of the Watergate affair originated in sports. Nowhere is power politics more blatantly practiced than in the Olympics, which were started as an antidote to politics.

There are rotten spots in the sports apple wherever you look. The Little League program, designed to promote baseball, often has the opposite effect because boys are bored, ruined or heartbroken by the time they're 13. Intercollegiate sports encourage lying and cheating because of the pressure to win and unrealistic rules. Professional sports have problems ranging from hubris to senility. The specter of fixed games hangs over all sports, and many fans seem convinced the exposed cases are only the tip of the iceberg.

This book explores the problems that exist in sports, occasionally by delving into the personalities of some of its leading figures, and even suggests some solutions. Only by an examination of the current excesses can we reach a point where sports occupy a more natural and honest part of our lives.

To my wife, Nancy, and son, Scott; and to Red Smith and Dick Friendlich, who proved that sportswriters could be literate.

Contents

•

The
Jock
Empire

1.

Sex And The Athlete

The following conversation took place on an airplane trip with a professional football team.

Player: How do you rate a town?

Writer: There are a lot of things to consider. The physical beauty of a town like San Francisco gives it an edge, for instance. Then, there are the cultural advantages available, like opera, symphony and ballet. I think the number of good restaurants is important, and the best cities have a generally cosmopolitan air that makes a difference.

Player: Oh. Interesting. The players figure it's a good town if they get laid.

Probably more misconceptions about sex have survived in the sports world than exist anywhere else. Managers and coaches still think it hurts a player's performance, despite the evidence of Joe Namath. Wives think their athlete husbands are celibate on the road. Psychiatrists think all the rump-slapping that goes on is indicative of latent homosexuality. Athletes themselves think they're great lovers because camp followers chase them into bed.

Playboy magazine did a beautiful interview with Joe Frazier before he fought George Foreman, which was published just after Frazier had lost his heavyweight title to Foreman. His comments on sex make him look ridiculous, though his views are hardly unique in boxing.

Frazier was asked if he abstained from sex when he was in training for a fight, and he responded with a number of outmoded clichés. "Yeah," he said.

> I don't know about all fighters, but like I say, I usually go without it for six or seven weeks . . . once I go to camp, that's it. I don't think sex does anything for your body. It takes too much energy out of you, and what you need in fightin' is energy. If you take the energy out of yourself, I don't see how you're gonna be a good fighter, or how you're gonna last long. You'll weaken your mind, you'll weaken your lungs and you'll weaken your heart, I imagine . . .

And masturbation can make you go blind, too, eh, Joe?

It's hard to know where to start with all that, but a good point might be that some doctors consider sex the best exercise of all. It's certainly a lot better for a person than boxing. I'll guarantee Frazier that his mind and lungs and heart will all be in far better shape if he gets laid 50 times than if he fights George Foreman 50 times.

Frazier went on to say, "Once I go into camp, man, I get meaner. I don't talk much. I don't smile very much."

Neither does his wife, I would imagine.

Boxing has always been the worst of sports in its attitude toward women. It's traditional for a fighter to be locked up for a few weeks away from the temptations of the flesh before a fight. Why? The theory is that it enables a fighter to concentrate on the upcoming fight without distraction. In truth, it probably works just the opposite. It has been my experience that sex is much less unsettling to the mind when you are engaged in it than when you are just thinking about it.

Other sports are not without their hangups, either. Pro football players get locked up in training camp every summer so they can concentrate on football. It's a little like an adult YMCA camp, because the athletes are supposedly kept away from women. I say "supposedly" because there are always women in these camps. The only thing the restrictions accomplish is to keep athletes away from their wives. If they must have sex, it will have to be with other women. A great thing for marriages, obviously.

An example of how that works came a couple of years back when Fred Biletnikoff, the Oakland Raiders' fine wide receiver, was attempting a reconciliation with his wife just after the start of training camp. He went to Tom Keating, the club's player representative, and asked Tom to ask coach John Madden if he could stay in a motel near training camp with his wife one night.

"Here was a grown man having to ask me to ask the coach if he could sleep with his own wife," said the disgusted Keating.

Biletnikoff did get permission to stay with his wife that night and it didn't cause him to drop any passes in practice the next day that I noticed. The reconciliation did not take, however, and the artificial atmosphere that surrounds Biletnikoff—as it does any athlete—was at least partially responsible.

Keating has always taken a very jaundiced view of the training camp nonsense. "I call it the monastery," he told me one time. He was single, so he could be a bit more candid than the married players. "It's ridiculous. For seven weeks, we're locked up, away from women, supposedly. During the season, we can get drunk and get laid every day and nobody cares. But in training camp, we have to be pure. I've often thought of installing a girl in the motel next door. What could they do to me?"

Lamentably, Keating never followed through on his threat. What other clubs would have done, I couldn't say, but I know the Raiders, and Al Davis, well enough to know they wouldn't have done anything as long as Keating got to the opposing quarterback with sufficient regularity; he was then the key to their defensive line. The Raiders were a club which tolerated aberrant behavior to an unusual degree. At the time, Davis was trying to get Chip Oliver back from the commune, and later he made every attempt to get Warren Wells, convicted for attempted rape, out of prison so he could continue to catch those touchdown passes.

The attempt to keep athletes away from girls is always an exercise in futility. Training camp could be set up in the Arctic Circle and there would be camp followers hanging around the igloos.

Curfews are supposed to stop some of the action, but they don't. A writer once asked a famous quarterback if the 10 o'clock curfew in training camp held him down. The quarterback thought a minute. "No, not really," he said. "I can usually find one who's willing to come back to the room before then."

Once I was on the road with the Raiders in the unlikely town of East Orange, New Jersey. If you haven't been there, don't make a special trip. The Raiders had played their final exhibition game in Jacksonville, Florida and were to play their first league game in Foxboro, Massachusetts. Instead of coming directly home after the exhibition game, it was decided they would stay in East Orange for the week.

Why East Orange instead of Boston? "There are too many temptations in Boston," Raider executive assistant Al LoCosale explained to me.

I've got news for LoCasale. I happened to be sitting in the hotel lobby one night a minute before the 11 o'clock curfew. Two elevators opened up, packed with giggling girls. The girls walked out the hotel's main door and around to the side where there were stairs to the hotel's three floors. Presumably, they waited until the coaches completed their bed check before going back to the players' rooms.

The Raiders lost to the New England Patriots the following Sunday, which may have been a coincidence.

Baseball players have it best. Their game being no more physically tiring than a fast game of dominoes, they've got plenty of energy left for the pursuit. Also, they spend more time in cities during the season than football and basketball players, so they have more time to investigate, not that they need it.

They also tend to be more straightforward about the pursuit, particularly in training camp, because they have fewer restrictions and more time than either football or basketball players. Some players do not even stay at the team motel, and among those who do, it is not at all unusual to see a player stroll openly through the motel grounds with a girl and head into his room. Since wives are allowed in spring training, sometimes it is his wife. Sometimes, it is not. Envious sportswriters sit by the pool and time them. It is seldom as much as 30 minutes before the couple emerges from the room. Foreplay to a baseball player means picking up a grounder.

It is not just the team sports that have their groupies. Before last year's U.S. Open at Oakmont, Skip Myslenski of the

Philadelphia *Inquirer* published a story about a golf groupie— he called her Annie—and a married golfer, who was not identified by name. It was hardly a surprise to anybody who had been around the golf tour. Golfers are especially good targets because they are alone so much; wives, usually burdened by school-age children, cannot afford to spend much time on the tour.

The camp followers are almost invariably good looking and often striking. They seem to have a most reliable underground telegraph. I have traveled with several teams, and I've noticed they are always there, whether the plane is late or early, whether the arrival was announced or secret.

Usually, their sexual desires are quite orthodox, but there are exceptions. In a football training camp, I once heard of a girl who wanted to go down on everybody in camp, players, coaches and trainers, though she drew the line at sportswriters. She almost made it, too, but her lack of foresight stopped her. She started with the veterans, and some of the fringe rookies were cut and gone from camp before she got a chance at them.

There was another with a toe fetish. She went to a famous kicker and used his big toe to give herself an orgasm. Afterwards, she told him she'd think of that every time she saw him kick a field goal on television. He didn't tell her that he kicked with the other foot.

No doubt, athletes have always had prodigious sex lives, but until recently, that had been kept a secret from the general public. Thus, the reputation of Joe Namath. Just as it was once considered *de rigueur* for a movie cowboy to kiss his horse but not his girl, athletes were supposed to project a profile of clean living and never talk about their sex lives. Namath admitted he did not often sleep alone, and some have never forgiven him for that.

Bill Glass, a former All-Pro with Cleveland, once criticized Namath and Baltimore quarterback Marty Domres, who had "written" a bit of fluff called "Bump and Run," in which the latter admitted that he both drank and made love. Surprise.

"Sure, you find guys who admit privately that they chase broads and soak up booze, but they are ashamed of it," said Glass. "That's the big difference with the Namaths and

Domreses . . . they seem to be proud of their promiscuous lives."

The image of 270-pound linemen being ashamed of their riotous private lives is a little startling. Whom do they apologize to? God? Their coach? Pete Rozelle?

Glass's criticism made me wonder a little about him, because it seemed almost as if there might be a little jealousy behind his moralistic pose. What difference should it make to Glass? Namath is dealing with adult, consenting females.

In truth, Namath's sex life is probably close to the NFL norm for quarterbacks, though he has gotten more mileage out of it than anybody else. Before the 1969 AFL championship game, when he was between wives, the Raiders' Daryle Lamonica told a press gathering, "I get laid as much as Namath. I just don't talk about it."

Glass was bothered because Namath was supposedly setting a bad example for young boys. Apparently, he prefers the hypocritical heroes of the past, who did everything Namath does but hid behind an All-American boy facade in public. For myself, I think Namath is a good example to kids because he never does less than his best on the field and, presumably, in bed, too. If he wants to ball every night, he's entitled.

For most athletes, the sexual chase is nothing but a game, and they never progress beyond the little-boy-peeping-into-the-bedroom stage in their relationships with women. Thus, the popularity of "shooting beaver" among baseball players.

Ron Mix, seven times an All-AFL tackle with the San Diego Chargers, told me once of a game the Chargers used to play during training camp. A player would tell some of his teammates that he was bringing a girl back to the room at night, and they would hide under the bed, in the closet, in the bathroom and watch and listen. Isn't that a grand game for grown men to be playing? "At least, they never let the poor girl know they were there," said Mix, who personally deplored the game.

Athletes tend to think of themselves as great lovers, although their approach is usually reminiscent of Patton going through North Africa. Typical is a well documented story out of a football training camp a few seasons back, featuring a defensive back and a gorillalike lineman. Since both athletes are married, no names will be used.

As was his custom, the defensive back had picked up a girl and brought her back to his room for some sexual gymnastics. Just as the girl murmured, "Oh, I'm coming, I'm coming," the lineman burst through the window—without bothering to open it first—and shouted, "I'm next!"

While all this is going on, the wives sit at home, wrap their furs tightly around themselves and tell each other that their husbands don't do that. Sometimes, they're right.

Most of the sexual incidents in the sports world remain underground, stories which are repeated whenever athletes, coaches or writers gather but which are seldom passed on to the general public. Not so with the Fritz Peterson–Mike Kekich wife swap. The pitchers themselves broke that story, and everybody was talking about it for weeks.

The natural assumption was that the wife swap was the result of the casual sexual atmosphere that surrounds pro sports, but the natural assumption was wrong. Sex played only a small part in the story. These were not casual liaisons undertaken without thought; the pitchers and their wives were groping for a solution of a common problem. Married young, each husband and wife had grown apart and learned they were more attracted to others. In this case, fate played a hand. Peterson and Kekich were close friends, and being roommates on the road, they brought their families together at home. As Fritz Peterson and Susan Kekich found themselves growing closer, the same thing happened to Mike Kekich and Marilyn Peterson.

When, after much time had passed and much thought had been given to it, the couples split and regrouped, they probably didn't realize how much furor would be raised; they had forgotten what a goldfish bowl athletes live in and how hypocritical people can be. The antediluvians in the press immediately attacked the couples, and even Bowie Kuhn weighed in with some insensitive comments of his own.

Two weeks after the story broke and some of the controversy seemed to be dying down, Kuhn called a press conference to officially deplore the situation, thus making certain that everybody would start talking about it again.

Given the constant sexual maneuvering in sports, Kuhn's attitude seemed hypocritical. I am willing to give him the benefit of the doubt, however; since he has given every indication in other matters that he doesn't really know what's happening in his sport, perhaps he doesn't know about the athletes' sexual activities, either. Whatever, he showed not an iota of human understanding or sympathy in the matter.

The ballplayers themselves made bad jokes about the situation and showed no sympathy to Peterson or Kekich, either. On the surface, that seemed hypocritical, too, but it probably wasn't. Athletes have much the same sexual philosophy as Italian men: the husband can screw around as much as he likes, so long as he doesn't get involved and always comes home to his family. Peterson and Kekich committed the cardinal sin: they got involved. Better they should have settled for a series of one-night stands, for the old wham, bam, thank you ma'am routine. That, their teammates would have understood.

Peterson fared far better than Kekich in the exchange. Susan Kekich came to live with him and his career seemed to move along satisfactorily. But Marilyn Peterson, pressured by her family, decided not to live with Kekich, and Mike was treated rudely by fans and ostracized by his teammates and managers. He hardly pitched for the Yankees before being traded to Cleveland in June.

"It's a funny thing," New York sportswriter Murray Chass said to me the day the Kekich trade was announced. "Peterson seems to be skating along on top of all the publicity, and Kekich had to take all the shit. I guess it's because Peterson won—he came out with a wife and Kekich didn't. New Yorkers don't mind what you do so long as you win."

Finally, there is that one last sexual myth, popular with psychiatrists, that athletes are latent homosexuals. You know, all that rump-slapping. Very symbolic.

Perhaps, but the tendency stays latent. It is true that athletes tend to enjoy each other's company more than that of their wives, but that has nothing to do with homosexuality. It is a tendency that seems common to all male-oriented enterprises, from the military to construction workers.

There have been isolated cases in sports, but the homosexuals don't last long. Maybe it's all those group showers; they get too nervous to play ball.

2

·

The Athlete
As Male Chauvinist Pig

It's always been a wonder to me that the feminists didn't zero in on the sports world first thing. Maybe they just weren't interested, because if there's any area that is more dominated by male chauvinist thinking, I haven't seen it. From playing field to the stands, the ambience is strictly masculine, and you'd better not forget it.

There is no doubt of the attitude of athletes toward women, whether they be wives, girl friends or camp followers: they are sex objects. To hear a group of athletes discussing women or to ride on a team bus through a town is to take an instant trip back to college sophomore days. Athletes are forever talking about sex as if it were a physical contest, i.e., as in "going home to punish my wife's body a little." The phrase is not without accuracy.

Athletes' attitudes remain constant when they marry. Usually, they marry cheerleaders or their equivalents, physical types marrying physical types. I was startled one time when I was interviewing A's pitcher Ken Holtzman when he talked proudly of his wife's intelligence; Michelle was a Phi Beta Kappa in college. It struck me that I had never heard an athlete talk of his wife's intelligence before.

Most of these sports marriages are just loose alliances. Athletes travel so much, it would be impossible to maintain a normal home life. Some of them object to all the travel because they would like to stay home and get to know their families, but the hard fact is that many athletes prefer the traveling. It gives them an excuse not to shoulder the normal responsibilities of marriage and fatherhood.

It isn't much better when they're home. I've known athletes to come off a long road trip and then go out and play golf with each other on their first day home. They prefer each other's company to that of their wives and families, probably because they see more of their teammates than of their families.

Nor is it any better on other levels. I mentioned the football training camps in the first chapter, and it is a fact that coaches are as isolated from their wives during that period as the athletes—and by their own choice. During the football season, coaches are so wrapped up with their Xs and Os as to almost forget they have homes. One time, just short of midnight, I called the home of Raider coach John Madden. His wife, Virginia, told me plaintively, "You should know better than to call here for John. Call the office."

The sports hero has always been a masculine figure in our society, but in fact, there is a great deal more to masculinity than muscles. It takes a real man to shoulder the responsibilities of the home, to spend a lot of time with his family and to recognize that his wife may have talents of her own and the need to develop them. Few athletes or coaches can do this.

The atmosphere surrounding a team is relentlessly male. Only men are allowed on the practice field; only men can coach, and even the front office, except for secretaries, is all male. It is a stifling atmosphere to anybody who enjoys the company of women in more places than bed, but it is satisfying to sports people for a couple of reasons. One is that it allows men to revert to their childhood attitudes, which is certainly necessary for one who hopes to excel at a game. The practice field is traditionally one of those male preserves where men can behave like little boys and talk like naughty ones, swearing constantly without having to worry that a woman might hear them. There is a special irony in that these days because the women, especially the younger ones, know all the words and use them as freely as men do. It is no longer possible to embarrass a young woman by saying "fuck" in her presence, but sports people haven't yet realized that.

There is another reason, which remains subliminal, for the lack of women in a sports organization: if women ever got involved on the executive level, they might let out the terrible secret that these games are not worth all the time and attention given them.

Elsewhere in the sports realm, men have dominated just as extensively. Sportswriting, for instance. The traditional view is that the only women who could write about sports were those who limited themselves to features and emphasized how cute Joe Namath's dimple was.

There are two arguments always raised whenever a woman tries to get into sportswriting: 1) She hasn't played the game and thus doesn't understand it; 2) She can't get into the locker rooms.

The first argument is silly, because there are a lot of men covering sports they didn't play or played only sparingly in their youth. For instance, though I never played football in high school or college, I had no difficulty covering professional football for five years. Sometimes, those who were best at playing a particular game get so involved with the details of the game that you can't tell from their stories what happened.

From my own experiences in locker rooms, I'm not sure the second argument is valid either. Sometimes what you hear there obfuscates the issue instead of illuminating it, because athletes and coaches often offer self-serving rationales for what they did. And it is a rare athlete or coach who says something truly worth quoting; most of them offer the traditional clichés, confident they'll be printed or put on television as if it were the Word from above.

And, it should be noted, men writers cover matches involving women athletes and get adequate quotes and information without invading the women's locker rooms.

Nevertheless, the argument prevails, as Sheila Moran discovered in the spring of 1973. She had covered the Yankees for the New York *Post* in spring training but was succeeded by Vic Ziegel when the season started.

"She couldn't get into the locker room," said Ziegel. "It would have hurt the paper. During spring training, it wasn't as vital, but once the season began, it became crucial."

"I did have some problems catching players who ducked into the locker room where I couldn't follow," said Sheila, "but the players have generally been wonderful to me."

And photographer Pat Carroll mentioned the other side of the coin. "The women have some advantages. Players often tell a man exactly what he can do when they are asked a question they don't like. They are more polite to women and give some answer that can at least be printed."

There was another problem with Ms. Moran: She worked too hard. Spring training is a very soft assignment for baseball writers, who have unwritten agreements among themselves not to work too hard and show up the others. Sheila wouldn't do that; she worked hard, and some of her competitors were embarrassed.

But the principal reason for a lack of women sportswriters was probably that expressed to me by Harry Edwards, the moving force behind the threatened black boycott of the '68 Olympics and now a professor of sociology at the University of California, Berkeley. "Sportswriting is a comfortable profession with a lot of privileges," he said, "and when you get that kind of situation, the writers aren't going to be willing to let blacks and women in."

In the stands and at booster clubs, the male predominance has been equally pronounced. The sports world has always been a cozy little domain for men, a place where they could escape from women—and I mean that quite literally—and be with their own; a place where they could put down women, who could certainly never understand the intricacies of secondary pass receivers, and never mind that neither can some of the starting quarterbacks in the National Football League.

To be a sports fan has traditionally been a sign of virility, but I suspect the opposite is true. Many of these red-hot sports fans distrust, and some fear, women. They're quite different from athletes, who only neglect women until they need them. Athletes know quite well what to do with a woman in a bedroom, but I have my doubts about some sports fans. Ball games and booster clubs have always been places where sports fans could retreat from women and tell dirty jokes and lie about their sex lives, confident they wouldn't be called upon for proof. They didn't have to deal with women or try to comprehend their actions or face the responsibilities of home and family.

Some men brought their wives or girl friends to games, but only under certain conditions understood and accepted by both sides. It was quite permissible for the woman to be utterly baffled by a first down, but she was never to say anything like, "Why did Sonny Jurgensen call a reverse when the weak-side safety supports so well against the run?" A question like that was instant grounds for divorce.

Things are changing now, but slowly. More women are becoming interested and involved in sports. I even see a few, other than the ritual pretty faces to sell raffle tickets, when I go to booster club meetings. There is a question why women would even want to go to booster club meetings, but that is another matter. There are still those condescending "Football for the little woman" radio shows around, but their audience is dwindling. And, most important of all, more women are playing sports and being taken seriously. This has been the toughest battle of all.

It has always been considered acceptable for a girl to be interested in sports until puberty. Her parents would concede ruefully that they had a "real tomboy" in the house. Once in her teens, however, she was expected to forget all that and concentrate on the Junior Prom. Playing sports just wasn't feminine, and woe to the girl who defied that dictum. Girls were supposed to be passive, not competitive, and were supposed to learn to cook and sew and otherwise defer to the boys who would eventually become their husbands. It was a terrible misreading of human nature.

There have always been girls and women who played games despite the obstacles, but it hasn't been easy. Not for them the athletic scholarships that a good boy athlete could expect, nor the lucrative pro tours and team sports. Only recently have the women's tennis and golf tours started paying enough to make them enticing. There is no way of measuring how many potentially good women athletes were simply discouraged by the prevailing discrimination and gave up on sports before or shortly after puberty.

Those girls who continued to play sports have always faced the sexual stigma, i.e., the belief by many men that a woman athlete is automatically a lesbian, which is ridiculous; playing sports makes a girl neither more nor less feminine. If you've ever watched boys and girls in infancy, you know girls are as competitive as boys, and sports is a natural way of expressing that competitiveness. And women athletes tend to be as attractive as the general run of women, some more, some less; their games-playing certainly makes no difference.

All these attitudes are changing, as I said, slowly, under the pressure of the times. It is a hard world for the male chauvinists these days. Women are invading their clubs and insisting on being eligible for jobs that have always been marked "Men Only." Now, they are insisting on equal rights in the sports world. The next thing you know, one of them will want to be President. Talk about uppity.

There is no reason why women should not compete in sports. On the professional level, the only real criterion is entertainment, and the women do very well on that basis. In a way, it makes more sense for men to watch the women than the top men athletes, because the games they play are closer to those of the weekend golfer or tennis player.

Watching Jack Nicklaus in a tournament, for instance, is interesting but of absolutely no help to the average male golfer because Jack has no idea of the real problems in golf, such as what club to use for your third shot on a par-three hole when you are under the trees and still 145 yards from the hole.

Tennis is much the same. Any match between the top men pros comes down to a series of unreturnable services and over-head slams. The women play a much more complete game, one that I find more interesting because it is closer to—though much better than—the game I used to play.

Women's tennis is interesting, too, because I think it's an indication of the direction women's sports are heading. It started from nowhere but has now grown to the point where team tennis is replacing the scattergun tours.

The women have been lucky because they've had one player—Billie Jean King—who has been willing to be out front taking the abuse that goes with that position to accomplish her goal. Though Billie Jean talks freely and honestly to anybody who asks, her statements are continually twisted to mean something she never intended, and a public personality is portrayed that is quite at variance with her real one.

Examples of that came before and after the much ballyhooed match between Bobby Riggs and Margaret Smith Court. Riggs had tried to tempt Billie Jean into a match in 1972 and had then backed out when Billie Jean said she'd play. A year later, he tried again, claiming she had said the women players were as good as the men. "Anybody who knows me knows I've never said the women were as good as the men," says Billie Jean. "Of course men are better because they're stronger. All I've ever said was that if we draw as many people, we should get as much money. It's as simple as that."

When Billie Jean turned Riggs down the second time, Margaret Court took up the challenge. Billie Jean thought before and after the match that Margaret's decision was a mistake. When she noted after Margaret's loss that Margaret wasn't accustomed to the pressure involved in such a match, her critics in the media assumed she was criticizing Mrs. Court, which she wasn't. Some were ungallant enough to point out that Margaret had a career edge at the time in her matches with Billie Jean. "That was really the first year Margaret had had sustained pressure like you get on a tour," said Billie Jean. "Before, she'd been in situations like the Australian tournaments, where you don't meet anybody really tough until the finals. She wasn't used to going week after week.

"Margaret played Bobby Riggs strictly for the money, and who can blame her for that? But she had the attitude she was just going to go out there and have fun, and you can't do that. That's kind of an Australian attitude, I think, but she'd have done better if she'd really gone out and figured it would be a tough match and prepared for it that way. I don't think she had any idea of the kind of pressure that would be generated for this match, the weeks of comment and anticipation."

Billie Jean proved she could handle that kind of pressure when, after the Margaret Court loss, she took on Riggs at the Houston Astrodome and beat him soundly in three straight sets. For a lot of the male chauvinists, that was hard to take.

Riggs had been made a favorite by those who had taken note of his easy win over Margaret Court, and they couldn't accept the fact that Billie Jean could beat him. Many of my readers claimed that Riggs had thrown the match because: 1) He was chivalrous; or 2) He had bet against himself.

It was ridiculous but understandable; Billie Jean is poison to a lot of male chauvinists because she's a symbol. That hasn't always been her idea, but she's known it was necessary and she couldn't shirk her duty. "I know it's hurt my tennis," she says. "It's hard to concentrate on my game and the promotion, too. I'll be glad when some of the younger players, like Chris Evert, can step in and do their share of interviews and their share of the promotion. It'll be better for tennis, too, because we need a lot of names, not just two or three, to sell our product."

It's ironic that Billie Jean should have detractors in the press because she's one of the most cooperative athletes I've ever known. She's always been available for interviews, singly or at a press conference, and she's never hidden behind a "no comment." This is due partly to her natural enthusiasm and fondness for people and partly to necessity. One night as I sat with her and Larry at cold Candlestick Park, she explained this to me while waiting for her brother, Randy Moffitt, to come in to pitch for the Giants.

"Look at that press box," she said. "Baseball players don't know how lucky they are. No matter how the writers feel about it, they're out here for every game, and the players know they're going to get the press. We've never had that. I started talking to the press about 1966 to get some publicity for us, but it took quite awhile. For a long time, there just wouldn't be any stories about women's tennis at all. Then, a few small ones started getting in. Now, we're getting good coverage and the stories are so much better, so much more knowledgeable because the writers understand us and the game."

When she was starting out, she couldn't imagine a professional tour for women. Neither could anybody else, because even the men had no regular tour; scattered promotions and an occasional match between the top pro and the latest top amateur to turn pro—as in Riggs-Jack Kramer, Kramer-Pancho Gonzales—were the only professional attractions. Amateur tennis ruled the roost. Now, both women's and men's tennis are thriving professional entities, and their success has created sharper distinctions between professional and amateur.

"It's really a break for us," says Billie Jean. "The professional circuit gives us more freedom. We can't be told where we have to play, like we could when we were amateurs. They'd tell us we had to play in this tournament or that one, just because they had to have a good field. The girls coming up now don't realize how lucky they are, because they didn't have to work for all of it. They just take it for granted."

Along the way, though, Billie Jean's image took a terrible beating. Originally, she was the crowd favorite because of her bouncy, all-out style of play and the fact that she was the cute, girl-next-door type. Now, it is almost always her opponent who is the crowd's favorite. She sometimes pretends to shrug that off, but it bothers her as it would anybody.

She hasn't really changed. She is very outspoken and doesn't hesitate to criticize the press to sportswriters or to tell you what Chris Evert is really like. And of course, she has a mind of her own. A lot of men don't like that in a woman, but they are fools.

She would like to be treated as an athlete, not just as a woman who happens to be playing tennis, and she is defensive about it. At a press conference in the San Francisco Bay Area town of Emeryville, where she lives in between tournaments, she was once asked when she would retire—a strange question to ask of an athlete who was only 28 at the time. "You wouldn't ask me that if I were a man," she said.

She has a lot of iron in her; she's had to have it, just to survive, physically and mentally. She's had operations on both her knees, a year apart, and a less serious athlete would certainly have quit after the second operation if not after the first. She's also had an abortion, because she wanted to continue her career. Typically, she let that news out, fully aware of the abuse she would get, because she thought it would help the cause of other women.

Her travel schedule has been wearing, too, even by contemporary standards in sports. The team tennis situation will ease that, but since the start of the Virginia Slims tours, she's been on the road more than half the year. "We were required to play in at least 75 percent of the tournaments to keep the interest going," she said, but she probably would have played without any requirements because of her sense of duty. She likes to travel, but not on that basis; tennis travel, like travel for any sport, is chiefly from one court to the next, and cities soon blend into each other and become indistinguishable.

Remarkably, Billie Jean has retained a kind of ingenuous quality despite her battles with promoters and players. She doesn't like to get the big star treatment; when people come up to her in the street and ask her if she's really Billie Jean King "I just turn scarlet." In person, she's a charmer, because she's retained a sense of humor and a vitality that make her a joy to watch on the court and a pleasure to talk to off it. And nobody in his right mind would ever question her femininity.

There's no mystery why the male chauvinists don't like her; they can never forgive her for the fact that she's helped build up women's tennis. They feel threatened, and thus feel the need to put her down. But she's really not a threat to anybody. She's only trying to build up women's tennis, not tear down the men's, and in fact, the two have prospered simultaneously. I wish the male chauvinists could realize that.

Though the women's professional tours get most of the publicity, sexual discrimination is probably greater on the high school and collegiate level. *Sports Illustrated* did a series on women in sports. Here are some of their findings:

—In 1969 a Syracuse, New York school board budgeted $90,000 for extracurricular sports for boys; $200 was set aside for girls. In 1970, the board cut back on the athletic budget, trimming the boys' program to $87,000. Funds for the girls' interscholastic program were simply eliminated.

—New Brunswick (New Jersey) Senior High School offered 10 sports for boys and three for girls in 1972, with the split in funds being $25,575 to $2,250 in favor of the boys. The boys' track team was allowed $3,700 one spring while the girls' squad received $1,000—though 70 girls competed and only 20 boys.

—The Fairfield area school district in rural south central Pennsylvania budgeted $19,800 for interscholastic sports in 1972-73, of which only $460 was spent on girls' programs.

—At the University of Washington, 41.4 percent of the undergraduates are women. Yet, the women's intercollegiate budget is $18,000 a year while the men have $1.3 million to spend over and above the income-producing sports of football and basketball.

—The National Collegiate Athletic Association, which governs men's collegiate athletics, has an annual operating budget of $1.5 million and 42 full-time employees. The NCAA's female counterpart, the Association for Intercollegiate Athletics for Women, operates on $24,000 a year and employs one part-time executive and one assistant.

Most likely, similar examples could be found nearly everywhere. High school and collegiate sports programs for girls have always been neglected. This, too, will change as more people become aware of the situation. I frequently give talks to high school and college classes in the San Francisco area, and I notice more and more that questions about women's participation in sports are surfacing, from both girls and boys. Here are some of the questions I get, and my answers. Later, some conclusions:

Are girls good enough to play sports like baseball?

Probably not, as the situation now stands, but that may be more a result of background than anything. Since there is no girls' equivalent of Little League, girls never get a chance to develop their baseball skills. This background is very important, because even a cursory examination of the sports situation reveals that the quality of a sport is directly related to the emphasis on it. One example: there are many good high school football players in Texas because high school football is very important there. No potential football players go undiscovered.

Should girls be allowed to compete against boys in contact sports like football?

The most unrelenting of male chauvinists seem to think golf or tennis is all right for girls—providing they don't embarrass men by playing after they get out of school on a professional tour—but nearly all men and boys draw the line at the contact sports because of the possibility of injury. And yet, women compete in Roller Derby and, in fact, are often the roughest ones on the teams, so perhaps our concern for the girls' health is misplaced.

The obvious fear is that a woman's breasts or sexual organs will be damaged in sports, but in fact, a man is in more danger in that regard. If equipment can be devised to protect men, surely it would be no challenge to devise protective equipment for women.

Basically, I feel that if a girl or woman is physically capable of competing on a level with her male contemporaries, she should be allowed to do so. In other words, she should be given the rights that a boy takes for granted.

If girls are allowed into the Little League program, what would happen if a girl beat out a boy? Wouldn't he be so hurt he would give up on the sport?

This is not a remote possibility. Given the conditioning of our present sports programs, it is almost an inevitability. Most boys and men would feel humiliated if they were beaten by girls or women. And yet, it is ridiculous that the male ego should be so fragile. I think that says a great deal, none of it good, about the overemphasis we put on sports. Boys survive many other disappointments in childhood; why not this? We need to get back to the idea that playing the game is more important than winning.

A letter writer to *Sports Illustrated* posed the hypothetical situation of a young boy being so discouraged when he was beaten out by a girl that he gave up, thus robbing the sports world of a potential 30-game winner.

The implication is that developing 30-game winners is the most important facet of a Little League or any other junior sports program. I disagree, sharply. As a matter of fact, I think it is a good lesson for a boy to learn that at some point in life, somebody will come along who is better than he. The real problems are caused by programs which build up boys to think they are the best and will remain so, which only sets them up for a crushing disappointment at the next level of play.

And finally, we have to break away from the idea inherent in this question that girls and women are second-class citizens. We should be as concerned about the girls' feelings in this situation as we are with the boys'.

Instead of having girls competing against boys, wouldn't it be better to have separate but equal programs?

There is a lot to be said for this concept, but I find two basic flaws in it. One is that it is difficult to make the girls' program equal to the boys', though it has been done in Iowa. The other is that it deprives the truly superior girl athletes of their chance to prove how good they really are. There was an example in the late 1960s in a promotion by Warriors owner Franklin Mieuli, who had girls' basketball teams playing before Warriors' games—to the overwhelming ennui of the fans, it must be added. One of the girls on that team, Denise Long, was a superior player. I'm not suggesting she could have competed in the NBA, but she was certainly better than many boys competing on the college teams in the area. It would have been interesting to see her in that kind of competition, and I'm sure she would have welcomed it, but she never got the chance.

But what happens if girls are allowed to play on previously all-boy teams? Would boys be allowed to play on the all-girl teams? If not, what about the boys bumped off their teams; where would they go to play?

Some high school leagues now officially oppose any participation by boys on all-girl teams. Right now, that's meaningless. Given the status of girls' sports in high school, I doubt that boys would want to compete. But some day, that may be a legitimate question and when it is, there's no reason boys who were beaten out by girls should be left without a chance to play. I think the present system of rigidly sex-segregated sports needs to be replaced by a graded level of competition, much as the boys' programs now have varsity, junior varsity, freshmen-sophomores and so on. There could be one level for the very best of either sex, and then lower levels for the less accomplished. Perhaps it would work out that no girls played on the top level and no boys on the bottom, but everybody should at least have a place to play.

Wouldn't boys be embarrassed if they competed on a team that was mostly girls?

Undoubtedly they would be at first, but I think that embarrassment would soon ease as the artificial distinctions

21

between boys' and girls' sports programs eased. In the end, there would be no more reason for embarrassment than boys now feel if they play on a junior varsity team instead of on the varsity. The game is the thing—or should be.

Wouldn't it be necessary for girls to have women coaches?

To me, there is no more reason for women coaches for girl athletes than there is for women teachers for girl students. We need to get back to the idea that sports are part of the educational process. As this question unintentionally reveals, they are often regarded as separate.

Wouldn't men coaches be inclined to play favorites with girl athletes?

I would think the opposite would be more likely to be true, that the coach would do everything he could to discourage a girl athlete. Coaches are inherently conservative and leery of strange situations, and they would be very uncomfortable with girl athletes. But I think eventually, when girls in sports get to be less of a novelty and as younger coaches come into the profession, they would be treated equally.

What about girls in locker rooms?

This is the type of thing that comes up often in discussions of women in sports, where the details are confused with the principle. These problems can be worked out once you accept the idea that girls will be competing. Obviously, they wouldn't dress together.

Wouldn't there be any problems if boys and girls were competing on the same team when they took trips together?

I wouldn't think so, any more than there are problems when a mixed chorus travels to sing in a musical festival, for instance. High school students can hardly be kept in a hermetically sealed atmosphere away from the opposite sex.

The question remains, is it a good thing for girls and women to compete in sports on as widespread a basis as boys and men? I think the answer should be a resounding yes.

I was reading the story of Peter Pan to my young son one day and laughed out loud at one juncture: Peter had just brought

Wendy and her brothers to his house and was preparing to go out and fight Captain Hook, or whatever. Meanwhile, Wendy was sweeping out his place and sewing his pants. She certainly knew her place.

The only reason left for discouraging girls' competition is custom, which dies hard. Sports programs have always been run by men for other men and boys, and it is not easy for them to change their thinking.

But if there are lessons to be learned in sports, and I think there are, they are certainly as valuable to girls as they are to boys. And the exercise alone is a good thing.

Let's face it, men: even if all you want out of a woman is a good bed partner, it's better if she's in good condition.

3

·

The Myth-Making Process: Did David Really Kill Goliath?

I'd like to tell you a little about the myth-making process in sports, but before I do, one question: do you really believe that David killed Goliath? I did, too, until I went to church one day. It's amazing what you can learn in church if you stay awake. The David vs. Goliath story has been a part of Judeo-Christian folklore for centuries, and George Gershwin even celebrated it in the song "It Ain't Necessarily So." That, as it turns out, is a particularly apt title.

The story is there, all right, in 1 Samuel. It's a beautiful little story, about how David went out armed only with a slingshot and a rock and killed Goliath dead with one well-aimed shot. But if you read a little further, 2 Samuel 21:19 says, "Elha'nan . . . slew Goliath the Gittite, the shaft of whose spear was like a weaver's beam." And that simple statement comes just two verses after another that says David's soldiers warned him against going out into battle. They wanted him as their leader and political symbol, not as a dead hero. The second version, say Biblical scholars, is correct; the first one is a fable. Faced with these contradictory versions, the editors of the King James version wrongly "emended" the second version to read "slew *the brother of* Goliath."

This shows how myths are created. It is easy enough to blame the writer who creates it, but it's not a one-way street. Unless the public is willing to believe the myth, it dies immediately. The ancient Hebrews used the fable to disguise what they knew—that David was a great guerilla fighter who would do anything to win. Vince Lombardi would have loved him. He accomplished his purpose of making Israel secure against the attacks of the Philistines, but once he did, his countrymen preferred not to dwell on his methods. Thus, the David-Goliath fable, which obscured the truth. But the man who wrote the fable couldn't let it lie. He sneaked in the correct version. Some writers are like that.

There are other myths from our own history. There is, for instance, little in the history books to suggest that the Puritans and Pilgrims were malcontents who had a very narrow idea of how society should function and did not tolerate dissent. They would have slapped Howard Cosell in leg irons immediately, which might not be a bad idea at that.

When John F. Kennedy was President, many people wanted to believe only the best of him, and thus the Camelot image was fashioned, an image which must have amused Kennedy himself. In any public opinion poll at the time, the qualities most admired in Kennedy were his supposed devotion to wife and family, though anybody who knew him knew this was the weakest chink in his armor.

But it is in the sports world that mythology has really taken hold; it's no coincidence that sports have Halls of Fame. Sports heroes are venerated, and reality seldom intrudes on their images. One example is Babe Ruth. I'm told by those old enough to remember that Ruth's mortality was recognized during his career, but by the time I was growing up, in the 1940s, his image had hardened into legend. No more was it recognized that he was a hard-drinking, gluttonous lecher. Instead, he was painted as a sweet, lovable man who wanted to do nothing but hit a baseball. Occasionally, I saw veiled references to Ruth's appetites, but in my naiveté, I thought that meant his fabled love of hot dogs, the same which was supposed to have caused a massive stomachache in 1925. It was not hot dogs, of course, that caused that stomachache, but rather a disinclination to seek medical references for the women he went to bed with.

And Ty Cobb. In 1961 Al Stump wrote a terrifying story for *True* magazine, later printed in *Best Sports Stories,* in which he concluded that Cobb was a madman, at that time and in his playing days. In one part of the book, Stump quoted Cobb: "In 1912—and you can write this down—I killed a man in Detroit."

Cobb told Stump that three men had jumped him on the street in Detroit one morning. Cobb had a pistol, but the gun wouldn't fire. They cut him up the back and left him in the street, but he chased them, grabbed one and ripped up his face with the pistol. "Left him there, not breathing, in his own rotten blood," said Cobb.

Cobb then caught a train to the ball game, without even seeing a doctor. Reported Stump:

> Records I later inspected bore out every word of it: On June 3, 1912, in a bloodsoaked, makeshift bandage, Ty Cobb hit a double and triple for Detroit, and only then was treated for the knife wound. He was that kind of ballplayer through a record 3,033 games. No other player burned with Cobb's flame. Boze Bulger, a great old-time baseball critic, said, 'He was possessed by the Furies.'

And yet, then and now, Cobb's mania was described as only an "indomitable will to win."

Baseball is probably the best repository of myths because it was the No. 1 sport in this country for so long and because it is inextricably entwined with small-town America, which itself isn't what myths make it out to be, either. But there are plenty of examples from other sports, and football has come up with some in recent years as it has become preeminent.

For instance: The NFL is doing its best to make a saint out of Vince Lombardi, which must make him very uncomfortable if he's in any position to take note of it. Lombardi was a complex person, a driven man and a man of contradictions, sometimes within minutes. He could be very gentle and he could be an unyielding taskmaster. He forced players to play with nearly crippling injuries at times, and yet he had a genuine affection for his players and they for him. But he was no saint.

From my own experience, the most striking example of a myth remains Willie Mays, and it says something for the power of the myth that more people in the San Francisco Bay Area remember a column I did debunking the Mays myth than anything else I've written, though it was done in May of 1971. When introduced to people, I'm often greeted with "Oh, you're the one who wrote about Willie Mays!" I'm beginning to know how Tony Bennett feels when he's asked to sing about the little cable cars climbing halfway to the stars; I want to point out to people that I've done some other things; too.

I saw Mays from a number of angles. For a long time, it was purely from the angle of sports fan. When I was a kid, I had a violent dislike of the Brooklyn Dodgers, one of those irrational impulses that all sports fans whatever their age share. Thus, when Mays did so much to beat the Dodgers in the Giant miracle year of 1951, he quickly became one of my primary heroes.

Mays was really something in those days. To explain what he seemed to be then, I have to go to another field: popular music. I was struck one night listening to Barbra Streisand on the stereo by how much she knew when she made her first record at age 20. She knew instinctively when to sing softly, when to sing fortissimo. She knew when to speed up the tempo and when to slow it down. She could not have learned any of that; it was all instinct. And it was the same with Mays when he came to the Giants in 1951. He did things nobody else even thought about.

I remember one play in particular against the Dodgers. Though I only heard it on the radio and read accounts of it later, it was so real to me that it is almost as if I saw it myself. Billy Cox, a good runner, was on third and Andy Pafko drove a liner to right center. Mays came over to make the catch and instead of doing the conventional—stopping, turning and throwing—he kept going, spinning around and throwing with all the momentum behind him. He threw out Cox and Brooklyn manager Charlie Dressen commented sourly after the game, "I'd like to see him do it again." Or anybody else, eh, Charlie?

By 1958, I had graduated from college and gone to work on a newspaper in Watsonville, 90 miles down the coast from San Francisco. I often came up to watch the Giants and marvel at Mays, who seemed to do something different every game.

Two plays still stick out in my mind. Mays often went from first to third on routine singles to left field—which nobody else does. One day, he did it with Bob Skinner as the left fielder. Moreover, he did it while nearly walking, crablike, from second to third. Skinner stood mesmerized, unable or unwilling—or both—to let the ball go until Mays reached third.

Another time, against a team I cannot remember, Mays was on third when the catcher let a pitch get away momentarily. It went only a few feet, and an ordinary runner on first probably wouldn't have even tried for second. Mays scored somehow, and the play was so startling it even shocked Giants manager Herman Franks into momentary civility.

Mays was so good in those days that he hurt younger ball-players, who tried to emulate him and couldn't. They would try, for instance, to run the bases as he did, always looking to see where the ball was and running half-speed until a fielder had committed himself, and then bursting instantly into top speed. Mays could do it; the others couldn't.

And ultimately, he received the supreme compliment: every good young outfielder who came up—Ken Henderson, Ollie Brown, Bobby Bonds—was billed as the "next Willie Mays." None were. Bonds, the best of the three, is a superb player who can run, field and hit, but even he is no Mays.

That was Willie Mays as a ballplayer, and I had no reason to believe he wasn't the same as a person because my only contact with him was from the stands and through the myth, nurtured in New York, of the happy-go-lucky, "Say-Hey" Kid.

In 1963, I met Mays for the first time. I was assigned to do locker room stories for the San Francisco *Chronicle,* trying to learn what—if anything—the athletes were thinking at crucial moments, and I came to Mays often for statements. I never got anything from him that could be printed.

There is an anecdote in Jim Bouton's second book, *I'm Glad You Didn't Take It Personally,* about Jim Beauchamp's intro-duction to Mickey Mantle that reminded me very much of my early experiences with Mays.

> It turned out that when Beauchamp (pronounced Beechum) was just starting out in the St. Louis organization, he was at the St. Petersburg ball park that was shared by the Yankees and Cards. Mantle was behind the cage during batting practice and Beauchamp went up to him and said, "Hi, Mickey, my name is Jim Beauchamp. I played football with your brothers . . ." And Mantle got that flat, blank look in his eyes, turned on his heel and walked away.

Six months later, Beauchamp ran into Mantle again. He stuck out his hand, started his little speech and Mickey Mantle said, "Who gives a shit?"

"I actually said to myself," Beauchamp said, "that, well, Mickey must have had two bad days and I blundered into both. But it happened a third time. The same damn thing. And you know, I was a ballplayer, not just some fan, and he knew it."

It was the same with me. When Mays couldn't even be civil to me, I thought the fault must be mine, so conditioned had I been by the New York press. Then I noticed that he was that way with a lot of other writers, too, and I began to see a pattern. He had a very definite scale of values. If you worked for a small paper or were a minor reporter on a big one, you had no chance to get a comment. Ron Reid, now with *Sports Illustrated* but then with the San Mateo *Times,* once asked Mays a question and Mays replied, "What paper are you with?" When Reid told him, Mays said, "Shee-it," and walked away.

With those who regularly did game stories, he was more pleasant, though hardly overly cooperative. Bob Stevens has covered the Giants for the *Chronicle* since the Giants moved west in 1958 and if he has written an uncomplimentary word about Mays, I missed it. But he never got a big story from Mays.

When New York writers came around, though, Willie was once again the picture of charm. There would be long columns about Mays in San Francisco papers, with Willie saying things he never said to the local writers. He knew exactly what he was doing, because the New York writers continued to spread the myth.

I began to notice a few other things about Mays, too. His attitude to those seeking autographs, for instance, was cavalier; he sneaked out of the clubhouse whenever he could. Once, he put his attitude into perspective when he was advising Bobby Bonds, as *Saturday Review* writer Peter Schrag stood nearby. "Fuck the fans," he said.

I began to hear stories from blacks about how they had tried to get Mays to appear before their groups and he wouldn't, but he would appear before white groups. I began to notice that when Mays was photographed on his visits to hospitals and playgrounds the kids in the picture were more often white than black.

I began to hear complaints from other players on the team about Mays' preferential treatment. The Giants' managers had two rules for the club, one for Mays and one for the other players, not necessarily by the managers' choice.

Shortly after the Giants finally traded Mays in 1972, I took a trip with the club and was talking to manager Charlie Fox. When Mays was with the club, Fox said all the right things about Willie, but now he could unburden himself. "They should have traded him five years ago," he said. "I'm supposed to be the manager, but I fucking had to come to him every day and say, 'Willie, can you play today?'"

All these things were piling up in my mind, and in the spring of 1971, I thought it was time they were finally written. My column was written against a background of adulatory treatment from the local press. If you'll indulge me for a minute, here is what I wrote:

> At his testimonial dinner (honoring his 40th birthday), Willie Mays told the audience that being a ballplayer is different. It certainly is. It pays better, for one thing, and you can't beat the hours.
>
> That wasn't what he meant. Willie Mays, who has garnered fame and wealth beyond the dreams of most by playing a game, was complaining. He wanted sympathy. It would be funny if it weren't so sad.
>
> Mays is certainly the best and most exciting ballplayer of his generation, but he sheds his greatness like a cloak when he leaves the playing field, the Willie Mays myth not to the contrary.
>
> You know the myth, created in New York: Mays, the "Say-Hey" Kid, a happy-go-lucky fellow with a kind word for everyone.
>
> Try that on an autograph-seeking kid who has been brushed off, a sportswriter who has been cursed, a manager who has tried to exercise authority, a black who has tried to get Mays to speak out against racial inequities, as Hank Aaron, Bill White and Bob Gibson do.
>
> Mays has had an idolatrous press, but that has not made him co-operative. He talks only to the sycophants and those he thinks can help him. Questions from the others are met with obscenities or silence. He is suspicious, say his friends. Of what, pray tell?
>
> Giant managers are hardly more fortunate. They know they must give Mays preferential treatment, or Willie will become fatigued or beset by one of his mysterious ailments.
>
> Leo Durocher started it, spoiling him outrageously. Mays loved it and now he, not the manager, decides when he plays. For sure, it is never when Gibson is pitching.
>
> Some managers have tried to treat Mays as just another player. Bill Rigney, for instance. Rigney got fired. Clyde King told Mays to

play an exhibition when Mays preferred not to. They almost fought in the dugout, and King was gone the next year.

Mays' hypochondria and love of special treatment fused a few years back when he was sent to the hospital after the first of his famed fainting spells. He doted on all that attention and now sends himself to the hospital from time to time. When the Giants are looking for him, they check the hospitals first.

It will be interesting to see what Mays does when his playing career ends, because his very special athletic skills will not help then.

He has said he wants to go into television, but he has done little to further that aim. A local TV show only exposed his lack of preparation and knowledge. Once he asked Lee Grosscup if there would be a bidding war over O. J. Simpson, apparently ignorant of the pro football merger. Maybe Willie was out of town when it happened.

He went on the Dick Cavett show earlier this year and acted like the boor who spills drinks on your rug and burns a cigaret hole in your couch. He continually interrupted and insulted Cavett and fellow guest Jim Bouton. He will not be invited back.

Occasionally, there is talk that Mays will be the first black manager, but he would bring only indolence, an uncertain intelligence and a petulant personality to the job.

Better keep playing, Willie.

After that column, anybody in the San Francisco area with access to a typewriter or microphone had something to say, usually uncomplimentary. Some of the criticism was honest as, for instance, that from Giant announcer Lon Simmons, who genuinely likes Mays as a person. Other criticism was not so honest. All three columnists for the San Francisco *Examiner,* for instance, criticized me, though I had reason to believe they agreed with me. This is a very important part of the sports myth-making process, that those who create the myth often do not believe it themselves. Sportswriters (and broadcasters) feel they are giving the public what it wants.

I can't quarrel with that. My mail ran very strongly pro-Mays and anti-Dickey, and I am still getting letters from fans who admit they don't want to hear anything critical of Mays, even if it's true. Thus, modern sports fans are not really very much different from the ancient Hebrews: they know what they want to hear, and they won't believe anything they don't want to believe, and damn the facts.

Since that column appeared, it has become much more fashionable to criticize Mays, because he had gone downhill as a player. Interestingly, I was criticized for my timing because

Mays was doing so well at the time—he had just broken the National League record for runs scored—though I had planned it that way. I didn't want to wait until he was down and then kick him. That hasn't bothered other writers.

Mays hasn't changed since then. He stalked off the green at the American Airlines celebrity golf tournament in Puerto Rico because his playing partner, Joe Namath, was late, though Mays has been notorious among tournament officials for promising to play and then ducking out.

As a Met, his behavior toward manager Yogi Berra was the same as that towards the Giant managers. He left the club in spring training without consulting Berra. He was fined upon his return; half of the fine, said one writer, was for leaving, the other half for returning. During the regular season, he was on the disabled list early. When he came off—ironically, against the Giants in San Francisco—he spent one game up in the Giants' broadcasting booth with Simmons, instead of on the bench with his teammates. The next week, Berra put his name on the lineup card without consulting Willie. Mays not only didn't play, he went home—again, without permission.

During spring training, I had been talking to Reggie Jackson of the Oakland A's, a player who had been temperamental when he first came up but had matured since then. Reggie told me, "I don't like to be around him because I want to remember him just as a player. He was great, but when you're around him for only a few minutes, he's always whining or complaining about something, and that just tears him down."

There is a postscript to all this. Shortly after I had talked to Jackson, I was talking with Alan Gallagher, then with the Giants.

Gallagher thought Mays had shortened his effective career by refusing to admit he was growing older. "You know, he never took outfield practice," said Gallagher. "He just liked to fool around in the infield, and he knew he could always do the job in the outfield when the game began. But he had a little trouble as he grew older and he needed that outfield practice, but he wouldn't change. I think that hurt him."

And then Gallagher brought up my Mays' column. "You know, there was nothing but truth in that article. All the players know it. It's too bad he's the way he is, but I don't think he could help it. When you're told for 20 years that you're the greatest, it's hard not to believe it."

And, added Gallagher, "Even though it was true, you shouldn't have written that because he was an authentic hero and kids need heroes to look up to."

What are you gonna do?

4

•

The High Cost Of Watching

To travel through the National Football League these days is to
see some of the finest athletic structures since the Colosseum
was built, though, modern construction being what it is, I doubt
the modern stadiums will last as long.

Whenever football writers gather, one of the prime topics of
discussion is always the new stadiums, the fancy new scoreboards which can show instant replays if necessary, the
elaborate press boxes, the creature comforts.

As this is being written, the completion of the New Orleans
Superdome is being projected for late 1974, and that promises
to be the most lavish of all. Until then, my personal favorite—
and the favorite of many other sportswriters—is the Texas
Stadium, home of the Dallas Cowboys.

Texas Stadium is magnificently designed with a roof that
protects the fans but is open over the field so it does not have
the artificial atmosphere of the Astrodome in Houston. The
seats in the stands are as comfortable as any anywhere. There
are private boxes which are extravagantly decorated even by
Texas standards. The people who rent these boxes for the
season spend up to $50,000 to make them comfortable.
Presumably, they are.

Nor do we sportswriters suffer. The chairs in the press box are as comfortable as any in my living room; the whole area is carpeted, and there are Texas belles circulating through the press box to minister to our every need. Well, almost every need.

For all that, the stadium makes me uncomfortable because it is the prime example of a trend in pro football which will ultimately doom the sport unless it is arrested, the tendency to become a sport for the rich only. Poor people are not prohibited from seeing a game at Texas Stadium, but they are certainly discouraged.

The stadium was financed in an unusual fashion: season ticket holders were required to buy bonds, from $250 up, along with their season tickets. Parking is designed so that the more you pay for your seat, the closer you are to the stadium. Those in the boxes park right next to the stadium; those who buy the cheap seats walk up to three-quarters of a mile to get to the stadium. Once in the stadium, your financial standing still counts. Beer is not sold in the stands; if you want anything stronger than Dr. Pepper, you have to belong to the Stadium Club. That, too, costs money.

The Dallas situation is only one extreme example of what is happening throughout football—and other sports, too. It is becoming more and more expensive to see a pro football game. It is almost impossible to buy just one game ticket, for instance; for a good seat to any game, you have to buy tickets to all games. With most teams, that also means buying tickets to the meaningless exhibition games.

The exhibition schedule itself is at the very heart of the fraud worked by pro football. Lawsuits have been brought against teams to try to divorce the exhibition games from the regular season tickets, but as this is being written, none of them have succeeded.

Years ago, when exhibition games were not tied to the regular season tickets, the situation was much different. Teams traditionally played at least part of the exhibition schedule in nonleague cities. The first year I covered the Oakland Raiders, in their Super Bowl year of 1967, they played games in Portland, Oregon and—are you ready?—North Platte, Nebraska.

The reason for this was not hard to find: the owners figured the hometown fans would be too sophisticated to turn out in large numbers for the exhibition games. No doubt they were right, though the crowds on the road were not that large, either. When teams do not tie the exhibition games onto the regular season tickets, the fans stay home. The Baltimore Colts, forced by a newspaper campaign to sell exhibition games differently than regular season games, seldom play the exhibitions at home because they draw so poorly.

Yet, when pressed to have a league policy separating exhibition and regular season games, both Commissioner Rozelle and the owners try to say that people would turn out for the exhibition games even if they weren't forced to. That is rubbish, as the previous examples show. The fact is, the owners are scared to death to have to sell their exhibition games because they know, as does everybody who has paid the slightest bit of attention in recent years, that there is a qualitative difference between exhibition games and regular league games.

Exhibition games can be interesting, particularly to those who are real fans of the team. It's exciting to watch the younger players develop, unless you're a Washington Redskins fan, in which case there are no younger players. But the exhibitions are not really football games. Coaches use them as proving grounds, which they should, trying to find out who can play and who can't. The coaches don't know themselves until they see the films of the game later; it is impossible to tell during the games themselves, because they are often chaotic. Blocking assignments are missed, receivers run the wrong patterns, quarterbacks fumble center snaps. And it doesn't really matter who wins the game, except for the games involving geographical rivals. That takes all the kick out of it. You can only watch individual development so long before you want to watch a real contest.

There are several things that need to be done with the football season format, revolving around the exhibition season and the regular season, too. The first would be to divorce the exhibition games from the regular season games and reduce the prices so they would be more attractive to the fans.

Owners, of course, claim they must have six exhibition games to make money. What they really mean is that they need those exhibition games to make *even more* money. According to the NFL Players Association, the average profit for NFL teams in 1972 was $1.9 million. At a time when grocery stores are operating on paper-thin profit margins and airlines are suffering huge losses, it's almost impossible to lose money with a pro football franchise. It's a lot better than playing the stock market, believe me.

There is a way owners can make just as much money, even with a different exhibition season. First, lengthen the regular season to 17 or 18 games, since football is the only one of the three major American sports which does not have a long enough schedule to satisfy fans. Then schedule a half dozen exhibition games in three weeks, playing two a week, with the provision that no player can play in more than one a week. This would accomplish two things: it would give fans a chance to see the players they want to see, and it would allow coaches to do all the experimenting they want to do. They could play all rookies in one game; then, the next week, they could play a mixture of rookies and veterans.

George Allen? Well, there would have to be a special provision for the Redskins because Allen wouldn't have any rookies to play.

When that is done, I have a more radical suggestion for the regular season games: end all season tickets and sell tickets only in blocks not exceeding four games—and make certain that everybody who wanted to buy those blocks could do so before anybody was allowed to buy tickets for more games. The blocks would have to be set up, of course, with attractive games in each one.

And I would also require 5,000 seats to be sold on the day of the game. Naturally, these would be the worst seats in the house, but at least they'd be available to those who really wanted to see a game and could not afford more than one or two a year.

There is no danger these suggestions will be adopted, because owners like it just the way it is. Season tickets are the greatest thing to hit any professional sports franchise. For openers, it gives the club your money to play with for six months. The money has to be mailed in long before the season starts—and the club deposits it in the bank. Figure it out for yourself: Using the low figures of 50,000 season tickets at $75 apiece, that gives the club $3.75 million to deposit for six months before the season even starts! Nice work, if you can get it.

Season tickets also protect the owners. If a tornado hits the park on game day, the people have still bought their tickets and the money will be banked even if none of them make it to the stadium; if the Houston Oilers are coming to town, it is not necessary to worry about selling the Oilers because the money is already banked; if your team, which was expected to be a contender, loses its first six games, the fans have already paid their money and won't stay home to boycott.

Nevertheless, the season ticket policy is a very shortsighted one. It is getting so expensive to watch pro football that many families are priced out, which is why you see fewer kids at pro football games then at basketball or baseball games. If you can only afford two season tickets, you probably have to take your wife and leave the kids home.

Even if you can afford four season tickets (which will cost you an absolute minimum of $300), so you can bring your two kids, you've still got additional expenses—parking, hot dogs for the kids, beer for you. It's an expensive operation.

Typical is a letter I got from an Oakland fan one day. He had just finished paying nearly $200 for his Raider season tickets, which was only the start. "I figure it costs me over $300 (baby sitter, parking and food) to attend a full season of Oakland Raider Pride and Poise," he wrote. "I think it is time to look at poor attendance figures as due not so much to lack of fan appreciation or bad ballplaying as to the fact that the average fan has run out of money. I would dearly love to go to all the games, but unfortunately, after I have spent $500 to $600 for sporting events, my wife feels she should be equally compensated and has threatened to buy out I. Magnin's."

This fan is obviously not poor, from his reference to I. Magnin, which is a very expensive department store in San Francisco, but he is feeling the pinch. It is even worse for those with less money. By making the game so expensive, pro football is moving away from its chief support base. It is nice to see the society people at the game, but it is the working stiff who has traditionally supported sports, and club owners forget this at their own peril.

The High Cost of Watching

I have used football as my example in this polemic because it is the No. 1 sport, the nation's fad sport, at the moment. It may not always be. I still remember the hysteria that prevailed when the baseball Giants moved to San Francisco in 1958. Although the Giants had to play two years in Seals Stadium, which held only 22,000 fans, they drew well over a million fans both years, averaging within a couple of thousand of capacity for every game. Transistors were everywhere; at the opera, cheers would go up in the middle of the first act because the Giants had scored. At fancy society parties, the men—and often the women, too—would cluster in a corner listening to the ball game. You could stop in any store on Market Street and ask the score and get it. The Giants, I think, felt that situation would always prevail. They made little effort to sell themselves in the Bay Area because they felt it wasn't necessary. But it was. Slowly but surely, the attendance started dropping. The society swells stayed home; Opening Day crowds were once heavily accented by the Beautiful People, but now few of them bother. Even before the A's moved to Oakland, the Giants' attendance was slipping, and the A's presence caused it to slide precipitously. By 1972, the attendance had dropped into the 600,000 range—which is where it was when Horace Stoneham was forced to move out of New York.

The same thing may happen to pro football when it slips as the fad sport, which could happen at any time; despite what the proponents of individual sports may claim, there is no inherent merit in one sport over another, which explains why soccer is a big sport in European and Latin American countries and a minor one here, and why the American sports have virtually defied exportation.

Pro football has one advantage: it can take preventative steps now, while other sports are already out of control. The great appeal of baseball, for instance, used to be that it was cheap; kids could get in for 50 cents and whole families could go to the game relatively cheaply. But the last time I looked, Charlie Finley was charging $4 and $4.50 for the regular seats at the Oakland Coliseum, which may be why the World Champion A's were suffering an attendance decline.

The basketball situation is even more ludicrous, though the owners' stupidity and not their cupidity is mostly at fault here.

The war between the NBA and the ABA has caused salaries to skyrocket, so that quite ordinary players are getting $100,000 a year. In that situation, prices move up just as rapidly and if you get outside areas like New York and Los Angeles, where practically anything sells, pro basketball is in trouble. And high prices probably bother basketball more than any other sport because it is the one major sport that has more than 50 percent black ballplayers and thus a large black audience, few of whom can afford the pro basketball prices with any regularity.

The San Francisco Bay Area provides an excellent example of what is happening in sports. There has always been severe competition for the sports dollar in the area because, though its population is considerably less than the Chicago and Los Angeles areas, it has six professional teams in four sports—and only New York has more.

Given that kind of competition, the sensible thing would seem to be to keep prices as low as possible, but prices have generally risen. Sometimes it's because of taxes, as in the case of the Giants, who had the city add 50 cents to their tickets because of improvements to Candlestick Park which largely benefited the 49ers; sometimes it's blamed on the athletes' salaries, as with the Warriors, who had a team payroll of at least $1.2 million; sometimes it's sheer greed. But whatever, prices have risen as attendance has dwindled.

This is a pattern throughout society. When patronage is less than expected, airlines raise prices. (Though the example of PSA, the economical California intrastate airline, should surely be enough to prove that a reasonably priced ticket is the surest way to a profitable operation.) Mass transit systems, with few exceptions, raise prices as patronage falls off, and patronage then falls off again in a vicious circle.

The pattern has been repeated in Bay Area sports. Finley raised his prices and the A's attendance fell off; the Warriors raised their prices and, though they had an attractive team, the team could not break even until the second playoff series; Golden Gate Fields started a Sunday race program and raised prices because of union costs, and attendance again fell off.

There is no question the fans are still out there, but there is also no question they are becoming selective. Finley scheduled 12 Family Night games, where everybody is admitted at half price, and the results were dramatic. One such night, more than 20,000 fans came to see the A's play the Milwaukee Brewers. The next night, at regular prices, the same teams drew less than 4,000. Golden Gate Fields finally reduced its Sunday prices for the last program of the season and attendance jumped from an average 12,000 for Sundays to 20,000.

That would seem to be an eye-opener for sports management. It is surely better to have 20,000 people in a stadium at half price than 4,000 at full price. But it seems difficult for owners to accept this. The basic problem in all sports is that most owners figure they're doing the fans a helluva favor just letting them in to see their games.

This position is difficult to support under the circumstances that prevail. Owning a pro football franchise, as I noted earlier, is like having a license to steal. It is not much worse for baseball and basketball owners, even with the basketball war. The Warriors, for instance, have been a sick franchise in recent years and were last in NBA attendance for the 1971-72 season. And yet owner Franklin Mieuli has hung on—he bought out some minority partners in 1972—and the franchise is worth far more than when he first bought in during the 1960s. If he wished, Mieuli could sell at a handsome profit. That's with a sick franchise; imagine what it would be like to own a healthy one.

Owners like to point to low profit margins and say it's impossible to make big money these days, but there are two things you should know about that. One is that there are certain systems of accounting which could make General Motors seem a likely candidate for bankruptcy court; the other is that most owners use their clubs as tax write-offs, and even big profits escape taxation.

Bill Veeck pioneered the tax write-off system. Basically, it works like this: when a club is purchased, only a small part of the purchase price, usually $50,000, is set aside as the franchise transfer fee; the remainder of the purchase price is represented as the value of the ballplayers. Then, the new owner sets up a 5 or 10-year depreciation schedule for the players and writes them off. If the club is purchased for $10 million and he uses a 5-year period, that means he has to make nearly $2 million a year before he pays any taxes. That is why owners with losing teams who claim to be losing money can sell their teams for much more than they paid, and that is why corporations are becoming more and more interested in sports teams.

Sometimes, in spite of everything being geared to them, owners still manage to lose money because they screw up so monumentally, nothing can save them. Even then, though, there is a literal escape clause; they know they can move their franchises. And so, the Washington Senators became the Texas Rangers because owner Bob Short made moves that would cause a student to flunk Economics 1A.

The bad thing about all this is that it is being done at the expense of the general sporting public, which is constantly defrauded in ways it knows nothing about.

Sports franchises are financed by fans and nonfans alike. The obvious contribution is by fans at the gate, but even those who never see a game underwrite a team's operation because, with the exception of Texas Stadium, the parks and arenas that teams compete in are built at the taxpayer's expense.

Sometimes, this is legitimate. The indoor arenas have turned out to be very good business for communities because they generate so much nonsports business. Any good arena in a good city gets far more business from things like ice shows, recreational vehicle shows, home shows and entertainment than from sports. Sometimes, the sports teams have to take second place; the Milwaukee Bucks have had to play some playoff games in Madison because their home arena was being used for a home show of long standing.

The football-baseball stadiums, though, are a different matter. Color them white, as in elephant, because they lie fallow when the season is over, except for occasional Billy Graham Crusades or jazz festivals. This is especially crucial in those cities which have built stadiums and end up with just a football team which uses it 10–12 times a year.

The classic bad example is New Orleans and the fabled Super Dome. In a state which is far below the national average in literacy, in average income, in health care and in almost everything, a huge stadium is being built to house a football team. As it was being built, there were hopes a baseball team would also be moved there, but there were no guarantees.

The stadium should be a beauty, but it is prohibitively expensive (estimates for its eventual cost have run close to $200 million) and it is almost guaranteed to run at a loss because of the operating expense, as anybody who has witnessed the Houston Astrodome operations over the years knows. And it is unnecessary. The Saints have been playing in Tulane Stadium, an old but perfectly functional stadium, since their arrival. One of the bad teams in the NFL, the Saints have still averaged over 70,000 a game. In the light of that and the fact that the stadium has been used for the Sugar Bowl and two Super Bowls, it would seem to be adequate to its job.

Sometimes, the voters seem almost eager to be screwed, voting for whatever the owner demands. In Buffalo, after a hassle of many years, the voters finally approved an 80,000-seat stadium. Why 80,000 seats? Because Ralph Wilson, the Bills' owner, wanted them. And why not? If he can fill them only occasionally, it's a lot of extra money. And if, as seems likely, few crowds exceed 50,000, it's no money out of his pocket; the taxpayers are the ones financing 30,000 unneeded seats.

Those on the owners' side of these matters, which by no means includes only those with a financial interest, argue that since teams generate so much business in a community, they should be underwritten by the city. But that's hard to judge. There is no way of guaranteeing, for instance, that every fan who comes to the game is going to eat dinner in the city—or that he would not have come to the city, anyway, even if he were not going to the game. Sometimes the stadiums are located on the fringe of town and thus do not promote business. The new stadiums in Kansas City and Buffalo are examples of this. And even if the teams do bring in business, there are any number of tourist attractions which are not underwritten. In New York, for instance, how many people do you think come to town to see the Statue of Liberty and the Empire State Building, and how many come to town to see the Jets or Knicks? Yet, the sports enterprises are underwritten and the others are not.

Perhaps it is necessary to underwrite stadium expenses for teams because building a stadium by private means is so expensive—though Walter O'Malley seems to have survived with Dodger Stadium in Los Angeles—but at the very least, the taxpayers should have some rights. They should, for instance, have the rights to inspect the books of a sports franchise and to insist both that quite rigid rules and regulations be laid down governing the operation of the franchise and that ticket prices be adjusted to benefit the taxpayers, not just the owners. If we had that kind of operation, owners wouldn't be able to boost prices and point to increasing costs when, in fact, they have just had record financial years.

5

.

Winning Is Everything... Or Is It?

One of the worst things that has happened to sports and society in recent years is the adoption of the dictum, popularized by Vince Lombardi but hardly unique to him, that winning is everything. You see it everywhere; suddenly, to be anything but the very best in anything is to be a failure. Behind the Watergate affair is the thought that anything can be forgiven if you win; the end justifies the means, though one of the supposed differences between a dictatorship and a democracy is that, in a democracy, the end does not always justify the means.

The obsession with winning accounts in great part for our long engagement in Vietnam. Lyndon Johnson spoke of the war as a massive athletic contest; we were going to "nail the coonskins" to the wall. Richard Nixon, too, saw it as a contest. He was not going to preside over a loss. Apparently, neither Johnson nor Nixon considered the moral aspects of our involvement, or what our preoccupation with saving face was doing to our standing in the rest of the world.

I'm convinced this attitude comes from sports. You see the winning-is-everything idea on every level, from Little League to professional.

The one thing I have against Little League above all else is the pressure it puts on 10- to 12-year-olds who are in no way able to withstand it. A boy pitches and loses in the finals of the Little League World Series and he cries for an hour. I defy anybody to tell me that's healthy.

On the high school and collegiate level, you get coaches who apply strict rules—and never mind that the rules themselves are nonsensical—because they think that's the way to win, and again, the end justifies the means. Thus, Woody Hayes of Ohio State and Bo Schembechler of Michigan virtually lock their teams up or spirit them out of town when they are out for the Rose Bowl, though it is the total experience for the athletes which is important about the Rose Bowl, not the winning of the game.

On the professional level, it is even worse. Football coaches virtually say goodbye to their families for at least six months a year because they think that kind of total dedication is necessary to win a championship.

Fans judge players and teams on whether they are winners or losers. The Dallas Cowboys were scorned because for years they were close to the top but couldn't make it to the Super Bowl. Thus, they "choked," though it was never explained how they got as far as they did if they couldn't take the pressure.

Wilt Chamberlain, who is surely one of the all-time great athletes in any sport, was laughed at for years because he wasn't a "winner," which is to say, his team never won the highest championship available. But when Wilt was surrounded by the right kind of players, with the Philadelphia 76ers and the Los Angeles Lakers in 1967 and 1972, respectively, his team won. Did that somehow make him a better player or a better person?

This kind of pressure ultimately affects nearly everybody it touches, some more than others. I have seen pleasant assistant coaches turn into snarling tyrants when their reputations were on the line as head coaches. I have seen otherwise honorable men lie and cheat to win.

This kind of pressure also produces some strange mutants in the world of sports, men like George Allen, Charlie Finley and Al Davis, who must win at all costs, though Finley's version of winning sometimes has more to do with his individual battles with players than with the results on the field.

All this is a terrible misreading of the values and purpose of sport. There is an important lesson to be learned in sports, the importance of doing your best. There is a very real satisfaction to be gained in knowing you have done your best, but this has very little to do with whether you actually win. In team sports, circumstances can defeat you even when you have done your best, and it is important to be able to accept that fact.

Winning is everything? Not by a long shot it isn't. Winning isn't anything unless you've learned the concomitant lessons of good sportsmanship and hard work and humility. In the next three chapters, I'm going to examine the lives of three men—Allen, Finley and Davis—who have not learned those lessons and who are thus, despite whatever success they do have, ultimately failures as human beings.

6
·
Poor George Allen

I pity George Allen. That may sound strange because Allen is near the pinnacle of his profession, but he is a driven man who cannot be truly happy under any circumstances. His kind can never relax because there is always something more—another championship to win or mountain to climb—no single accomplishment is enough in itself.

Allen is in many ways the most fascinating man in football because his philosophy of trading away draft choices for veterans differs so much from that of most other coaches. This hasn't always been the case though; one of the ironies of Allen's career is that when he first came to the Chicago Bears, he was in charge of scouting players for the draft. He was successful at that job, which indicates that he is more flexible than he sometimes seems. Indeed, even now, he often says that he's still interested in draft picks—but they have to be No. 1 choices.

He was not flexible enough, however, to be successful as a college coach. As William Gildea and Kenneth Turan note in *The Future Is Now,* he demanded more of his players than they were willing to give. But on the professional level, he has been a great coach, proving himself first at Los Angeles and then at Washington.

He is a better coach when he is given *carte blanche* to deal with every phase of the operation. He does not work well in concert with other people. There were hints even in his collegiate coaching days that—like Al Davis, whom he resembles in so many ways—he would cut corners if he really wanted a player. His time with the Los Angeles Rams was marred by the bickering back and forth with owner Dan Reeves, who wanted a more active part in the operation than Allen was apparently willing to surrender. At Washington he has been in trouble because in his eagerness to trade he has traded away draft choices that he didn't have.

His career is a model of upward striving. He started at little Morningside College in Iowa and went on to Whittier in southern California, a school which is better known as the alma mater of Allen's highest-placed fan, Richard Nixon. He left collegiate coaching in 1957 to join the Rams' staff and then went on to the Bears, but it was not until 1963 that Allen first gained any kind of national notice. After the championship game that year, won by the Bears, the winning players gathered in the locker room and, on national television, sang:

> Hooray for George,
> Hooray for George,
> Hooray for George,
> He's a horse's ass.

As television executives fainted in New York, the players then presented Allen with the game ball, a highly unusual honor for an assistant coach, because he had molded the Bears' great defense.

In 1966, he signed a contract as head coach of the Rams and George Halas, the crusty old owner of the Bears, instigated court action to hold Allen to his contract. Halas charged tampering. The NFL's position on tampering is a strange one. Theoretically, assistant coaches are not supposed to contact other clubs or be contacted without permission from their employers. This raises two immediate questions: 1) What if the coaches are not given permission? and 2) What if they hesitate to seek it for fear they'll be fired because they are looking around? It is a thorny situation. Some clubs solve it by, in effect, looking the other way. "It doesn't do us any good to have an assistant who isn't happy here," says 49er President Lou Spadia. Halas didn't feel that way. He felt that Allen's loss would severely hurt the Bears, and so he took Allen to court. The judge ruled that Allen's contract was binding, but before the judge could go further, Halas announced that he was relinquishing any rights to Allen's contract, that he had only been interested in proving his point.

Allen was immediately successful at turning the losing Rams into winners—he was later to do this at Washington, too—but he was in almost continual conflict with owner Reeves. There were a lot of reasons. Reeves didn't like Allen's win-at-all-costs philosophy, which allegedly included spying on a Dallas practice once and thus embarrassing the Rams when the deed was discovered, and he didn't like Allen's habit of promising players more than Reeves wanted to pay.

Reeves didn't like Allen's theory about veteran players being more valuable than young ones, because the Rams had traditionally been a club that relied on draft choices to the point of breaking up successful veteran teams. Reeves wanted to run the club away from the field, and some of the front office people, notably Elroy Hirsch, wanted to get rid of Allen and had Reeves' ear. And, perhaps as important as any of the other reasons, Reeves didn't like having a coach he could never drink with—unless he was willing to settle for a couple of shots of buttermilk.

Reeves tried to fire Allen right after the '68 season, and there were reports of a party in the Ram front office when the news broke. But the players backed Allen to the hilt, many threatening to quit if he were fired, and Reeves rehired Allen, as Hirsch left to become athletic director at the University of Wisconsin.

The second time, Reeves' will prevailed, but there was little satisfaction for the owner because he died shortly after that. As he left after that '70 season, Allen told Bill Libby for an article in *West,* the Los Angeles *Times'* Sunday magazine,

> I operated in an atmosphere of hatred. Our whole team did. Reeves hated me. Hating me, he hated the team. He sought to split us so we'd come apart. Somehow, I held the pieces together.

Poor George Allen

> I do not believe any man in the history of sports has had to overcome as much as I have to accomplish as much as I have. I have been like a fine surgeon striving to bring a sick patient back to health, while the patient wished to die. That man wanted me to fail so I might quit or so it would be easy for him to fire me.
>
> Do you realize that wanting me to fail, to lose, he wanted the team to lose, the players to lose, the fans to lose? He was willing to see everyone else destroyed so long as I could be destroyed, too.

The situation was better for Allen from the start in Washington. He was given a contract that approached $1 million for seven years with all the accompanying benefits, and he was given control of the franchise. Given that control, he immediately traded and coached and schemed his way to the Super Bowl in two years.

There are a lot of reasons for Allen's success. His technique of trading for veterans is an obvious one. You have to understand that, at any given time in the NFL, no more than a third of the club managements around the league have any idea what they're doing, and that's probably high. It has come to be accepted wisdom that you build up through the draft. If you know what you're doing, that can be done; Miami was built mainly through the draft, though the trade for Paul Warfield was also a large factor, and Pittsburgh turned into a contender in 1972 with one good draft. But if you don't know what you're doing, the draft is no help. Check Houston and New Orleans, which have had consistently good draft positions because they have been consistent losers.

Allen was going against the conventional NFL wisdom, but he knew what he was doing and those he was dealing with often didn't. He also wasn't leery of taking on "problem children."

Since many of the problems were caused by lack of money and/or recognition—defensive end Verlon Biggs, who felt he had been underpaid and underappreciated by the New York Jets, is a classic example—he felt he could cure those problems by giving players large salaries and showing them in other ways that he appreciated their efforts. He succeeded. Among those he traded for were Biggs, Ron McDole and Diron Talbert in the defensive line, Bill Kilmer at quarterback and Roy Jefferson at wide receiver, and all were key men in the Redskins' drive to the Super Bowl.

By no means content to stop there, Allen traded in the off-season for Houston's strong safety, Ken Houston, perhaps the best in the game, and then gave Green Bay a No. 2 draft choice for 1975 for the right to talk to linebacker Dave Robinson, who had said he was going to retire. It was a steal.

Allen wanted Robinson to strengthen the left side of the Redskin defense. "He doesn't make any mistakes," said Allen. "He'll smell out the play-action pass. Robinson knows when to commit himself to the run, and he knows when to fall off to get that running back who's usually the target on play-action."

"He can string a play out, too. He uses his good hands to fence with blockers if it's a run. They don't get to his legs. He can also shed a running guard and often bring down the runner by himself. When he doesn't, he's stringing out the running play to give our whole defense time to get in on the action."

Robinson was only 32, a mere stripling by Allen's standards, but he insisted he was going to work for the Schlitz Brewery in Milwaukee as director of minority affairs, a position created for him. He told Allen that when George called and called and called—about a dozen times in all—between February and June.

But in June, the situation changed. "When I talked to Robinson," said Lee Remmel of the Green Bay *Gazette,* "I knew he had had a change of heart. He was watching some of his old Packer teammates working out in Milwaukee, and he said, 'And I began to get that old feeling. They're getting in shape while I'm getting fat.'"

Robinson also began thinking about the salary Allen had offered—$90,000 a year for three years, compared to one in the $40-50,000 range at Green Bay. He called Allen and told him he'd play, and George then sweetened the deal by getting Robinson an off-season job as a minority affairs official for the Marriott hotel-restaurant chain. George never misses a trick.

But getting the players is only half the battle, if you don't know what to do with them. Allen does. He is a great coach, however you measure it. Tactically, he proved his defensive soundness in 1963, and that remains the strongest part of his technical game. His teams tend to be conservative offensively, but since defense is what wins games in the NFL, particularly at the championship level, that hasn't often hurt him.

He works very hard at his job. When he told a reporter one time that he believed a man should schedule his leisure time to coincide with the 5–6 hours a night he slept, he wasn't kidding. He has signs on his office wall to remind him to call a coach every day, just on the off chance he might learn something. He doesn't relax even in the off-season. Raider coach John Madden remembers the time when the coaches were meeting in New York. After the meeting, Allen wanted to go out and have some ice cream, of course, and talk some more.

He can't imagine anybody not being just as concerned with the Washington Redskins as he is. After the Redskins had lost to the 49ers in the NFL playoffs in 1971, Allen referred to the great difficulties the team had had to overcome, which was a reference to the many serious injuries the Redskins had suffered. "What difficulties are you talking about?" asked David Kleinberg, doing a story for Associated Press. Allen glowered. "I guess you haven't been following the Washington Redskins closely this year," he said, with the air of having delivered the ultimate insult. Kleinberg bore up very well under it.

Allen understands that the clichés are important to football players, whose sophistication is often only skin deep at best. When he talks about a 47-man squad, including those on the taxi squad, he means it; other coaches merely pay that concept lip service.

A lot of what he does seems terribly corny. There are the team cheers in the locker room, the "prayer meetings" complete with a team chaplain. But the players like that. The ones who don't are quickly traded.

He is a master at setting up the "us against them" syndrome, usually using the press as a vehicle. In 1972, when there was a question whether Billy Kilmer or Sonny Jurgensen would be the quarterback, he accused writers of trying to stir up a controversy, thus taking the attention away from the difficult decision he had to make.

Before big games, he often seems to have a run-in with the local writers, thus encouraging his players to feel that everybody is against them but him and they must work all the harder because of the forces of evil aligned against them. It is the same technique used so successfully by Joseph Stalin with the Russian people.

He did the same thing in the Super Bowl in 1973. At one of his daily press conferences, he told the assembled writers, "I hope the questions will be better this time." More than one writer grumbled back, "I hope the answers will be better, too."

That Super Bowl is an excellent example of the way Allen operates. He professed to be upset because the team had to come out a week early to reap the publicity bonanza that accrues to the Super Bowl and he complained of missing a coaches' meeting. In both cases, many thought he was merely talking for propaganda purposes.

He told the wives of the players to stay home, which benefited the Ma Bell monopoly because the players spent tremendous amounts phoning home. "I love all the Redskins' players' wives," he told the press. "When does he get the time?" wondered some.

Finally, he was so meticulous in his preparation for the game that he even sent a man to chart the path of the sun at the Memorial Coliseum for the time when the game would be played.

All these are factors in his success, but he has one trait that is most important: He realizes that one compliment is worth a ton of criticism. You would be surprised how many coaches—and bosses in other fields, as well—do not understand that elemental key to human nature.

John Madden told me once about his first encounter with Allen, when Madden was an assistant coach at San Diego State and Allen was in his first year with the Rams. "I visited training camp and I was talking with George just before the end of practice," said Madden, "when he excused himself. 'I have to go put some presents in the players' lockers,' he said. I thought he was kidding, but he wasn't. He really did that. Not all the time, but just often enough to keep everybody happy. That's George's technique. He wants to be liked. Not just respected, but liked."

With the Redskins, Allen has refined that technique even further—having a cake delivered after practice. Corny, but it works.

For all these reasons, George Allen is a great coach, but he pays a price for it. He has to carry around tablets of Maalox to chew for his nervous stomach, and he has even given his wife a nervous stomach. "But it's all worth it," she says, "when you succeed."

Is it? I doubt it.

Allen has quite literally devoted his life to football. He has no other interests. He works very long hours, seldom seeing his family during the season, and all for a game.

It is probably true that anybody with reasonable intelligence and aptitude can succeed at a job if he is willing to work as hard as Allen has. But the true success is the man who keeps his life in balance, who works hard at his job and enjoys it, but still has time to enjoy his family and friends and to pursue other interests away from his job; the kind of man who realizes that sometimes the most important thing you can do is watch an especially pretty sunset or read to a child.

George Allen can never understand that. Poor George Allen.

7

.

Charlie Finley: Applause Meter In The Bedroom?

Charlie Finley is unique in baseball, and probably in all sports, an owner who involves himself totally in all facets of the operation, and yet does things that can only be called counterproductive. There are men in sports who will do anything to win; Finley will do anything to get his way, even if it hurts his club. Only Gussie Busch of the St. Louis Cardinals shares this robber baron attitude. Busch traded away Steve Carleton for petty, personal reasons; Finley released Ken Harrelson and impeded Vida Blue and Reggie Jackson, who had been the hottest gate attractions in the American League. But even Busch doesn't have Finley's outsized ego. There is a temptation to dismiss Finley as a buffoon for the things he does; it is almost as if he needs an applause meter in the bedroom. Everything he does seems geared to keep him in the public eye.

Examples abound. There was the time in spring training when he was riding with baseball writers Ron Bergman and Jim Street and ordered them to stop to pick up a young hitchhiking couple. Finley immediately asked the couple if they knew who he was. They didn't, so Finley produced a copy of *The Sporting News* which had his picture accompanying an article by

Bergman. Presumably, the young people were properly impressed.

When the A's won the World Series in 1972, he danced on the dugout top with his wife and manager Dick Williams and his wife before the capacity crowd in the Cincinnati stadium and the millions watching on national television. Let nobody forget who owns the Oakland A's.

If the headlines are a little slow in coming, Charlie knows he can get them by shopping his team around. When the A's were in Kansas City, he promised to move them to Louisville, Seattle and Oakland at different times, before finally getting to Oakland. Once, he even signed a contract for a stadium in Louisville. He made one mistake: he had forgotten to get permission from the other American League owners, and he never did get it. Since he's been in Oakland, there have been recurrent rumors that he will move the club to Toronto, to Washington, D.C., to Dallas–Fort Worth. The Oakland Coliseum executives claim they have an ironclad contract, but if there is a way out, Finley will find it.

He did the same while he had the Seals. While trying to get the National Hockey League to buy the club back at his asking price, he apparently promised Indianapolis civic officials that he would move the Seals there. Again, he had failed to get permission from other league owners. He tried later and failed, which I'm sure he realized he would, but he had gotten the desired effect: attention. There is no better way, as Charlie knows. Towns without major league sports franchises are always eager to get them, and he gets a hero's welcome. Fans are inclined to think that the stories they've heard about him are false. They learn, later.

Finley works the publicity coming and going in situations like the one with Indianapolis. First, he goes into the new town; whether or not he signs any contracts, he knows a story will break that he is moving a team there. When the story breaks, he denies it, which gives him another day with his name up there in headlines. Sometimes, he gets so enthusiastic, he even promises to buy a home in the new city, a promise he has made in Kansas City and Oakland, while keeping his home in the same place it's always been, La Porte, Indiana. Maybe he can't find a reliable real estate agent.

Nothing is too gross for the man if it attracts attention. Some year, *Esquire* magazine is going to have to devote its entire Wretched Excess issue to the man. He was one of the first to go for colored uniforms in basebell, and the A's uniforms are still the most garish around. Finley's basic principle is that if one splash of color is good, two splashes are better and three are best. He wants orange baseballs, orange bases and God help the players if he ever learns their athletic supporters are white.

The A's home opener in 1973 was typical Finley. He was in the forefront of those seeking to use the POWs for their own means; he had Lieutenant Commander Everett Alvarez Jr. throw out the first ball—a gimmick which Finley pushed all week—and naturally, the ball was orange. A chapter could be written on why it is poor taste to exploit Alvarez's suffering to promote a baseball game, but you might start with Samuel Johnson's dictum that patriotism is the last refuge of a scoundrel.

Aside from Alvarez, there were the usual Finley touches at that opener—that damnable mule, the orange baseballs, the lighted matches during the playing of the National Anthem. The mechanical rabbit of past years was long gone, fortunately, but that was the only bright spot. The world championship flag was big enough to be used as a tarp for the infield, and some thought it might cover the entire state of Rhode Island. It made the American flag beside it look the size of a postage stamp. Poor Betsy Ross: she never Thought Big. During the game itself, Finley even had his organist play, "God Bless America." (See preceding remark by Samuel Johnson.)

All in all, it gives you an idea what Sen. Stuart Symington meant when he said, as the A's were moving from Kansas City to Oakland, "Oakland is the luckiest city since Hiroshima."

None of this would really matter if that was all there was to Finley, but there is a great deal more. He has feuded with players, managers, front office staff, sportswriters, announcers—and even other millionaires. He can be a very charming person if you do things his way; if you don't, watch out, because he means to get his way, and rules are for other people, not Charlie Finley.

"There are two people on this club with more ability than anybody, and I mean ANYBODY," Sal Bando told me in spring training in 1973. "Vida Blue and Reggie Jackson." And, significantly, Blue and Jackson have felt the cutting edge of Finley's wrath more than anybody else. In each case, he built them up, but when they threatened to overshadow him, he cut them down. Nobody overshadows Charlie Finley.

Jackson had a sensational year in 1969, his second with the A's, finishing with 47 home runs although he tailed off in late season because of the pressure. At one time, he had been ahead of the paces set by Babe Ruth and Roger Maris. He was the hottest gate attraction in the American League—which badly needs gate attractions—and Finley showcased him whenever possible. But Reggie made two mistakes the next year—he held out for more money and, when he signed, acted as if his will had prevailed over Finley's. Charlie cannot tolerate that.

When Reggie got off to his usual poor start in the spring, complicated by his lack of a complete spring training period, Finley told manager John McNamara to bench him. By July, Jackson was so frustrated, he refused to come to a party Finley threw for the team at his farm in La Porte (after a game in Chicago) and made intemperate remarks about Finley. Finley threatened to send him to the minors unless he got a public apology. He got it, but the sulking Jackson played poorly the rest of the year, his worst.

The next year, Finley had apparently forgotten all about his feud with Jackson, but Reggie never has. For public consumption, he says things like, "Charlie Finley should be executive of the year in baseball." Privately, his talk is different.

I talked with him in spring training, shortly after he had come from a parade in San Francisco for which Finley was the Grand Marshal. Finley had asked Jackson and some other A's to come, and they did. When the Emperor beckons . . .

Reggie grimaced at the thought. "You have to play his games," he said. "You have to do it his way. You can't expect Charlie to bend for you. Life is too short and I've got too much going for me now to let that son-of-a-bitch spoil it for me. I know there are certain things we have to put up with in Oakland that we wouldn't have with other clubs. I know I'd probably be a $100,000 ballplayer with another club and I'm earning about $20,000 less here, but those are the circumstances that prevail and I have to put up with them."

Significantly, when Blue had problems with Finley in 1972, Jackson spoke up for him, though somewhat obliquely. "When people are hurt," he said, "they do things that might not be understood, especially if they haven't been through these things before." It takes no great insight to realize what Jackson meant by "these things."

But it was in the Blue case that Finley really showed his ability to foul his own nest. The nation's sports fans know of the protracted contract negotiations that ruined Blue's 1972 season, but the problem had its roots in Vida's early career. Vida is black and proud of it. He is no separatist and gets along fine with whites, but he is very sensitive to racial slurs. Finley is not. He does not realize how black men think and feel, and he thus blunders into errors.

Finley first irritated Blue by trying to persuade him to change his name to "True," a typically gross Finley suggestion. Vida was named after his father and is proud of his name. "If Finley likes that name so much," he said, "why doesn't he change his name?"

The rift became wider during Blue's great season of 1971. Vida's salary of $14,750 was very nearly the major league minimum, and some thought Finley would tear up the contract and give Vida a new one after his fantastic start. Instead, Finley made another typical move: he gave Blue a blue Cadillac, with "BLUE" license plates and credit cards to buy gas, and he had the car presented to Blue at a ball game. The move enraged Vida. He did not want to be associated with the image of a successful black driving a Cadillac. He was not asked in advance if he wanted the car, nor did he like the car's flamboyance. He could not drive anywhere without being recognized; that, of course, is a problem with which Finley could never sympathize. But most of all, Blue did not like the idea of Finley figuratively patting him on the head and telling him that since he had been such a good boy, he would get a present. "Why didn't he just tear up my contract and give me a new one?" asked Blue. "He got more than the Cadillac cost him in publicity."

In the spring, Vida was determined to get the money he thought he was worth, with the assistance of attorney Robert J. Gerst; the two had been introduced the preceding year by Blue's roommate, Tommy Davis.

The negotiations were a farce. Gerst set a bargaining position of $115,000; Finley set an absolute limit of $50,000 and would not budge. Blue based his demand on drawing power. In 1971, nearly 1/12th of the fans who had come to all American League games had seen him pitch. Finley could have written an attendance clause into Blue's contract, which would not have obligated him in negotiations the next year, but he would not.

During the negotiations, as Gerst lined up a job for a steel-making firm and movie appearances for Vida, Tommy Davis was released, though he had won nine games for the A's with his pinchhitting the year before and had figured in six more wins. There was speculation that Davis had been cut because he had introduced Blue to Gerst. "I hate to think of anybody being that petty," said Davis, "but I did hear through the grapevine that Finley was pissed off."

Not until commissioner Bowie Kuhn stepped in was the matter resolved. Who won? Neither did. Blue was in poor condition when he signed and even after he got into shape, showed only flashes of his previous style, finishing with a 6-10 record. His pulling power at the gate suffered accordingly, and the A's again fell below a million fans, a figure they certainly would have surpassed easily if Vida had retained his gate appeal.

And Blue was permanently embittered. "He treated me like a damned colored boy," he told Ron Bergman.

Vida had some sharp words for Finley again during the American League playoffs. A's manager Dick Williams had first announced that Blue would pitch the fourth playoff game in Detroit if the A's were leading the Tigers in the series. That made sense—Tiger Stadium is a great park for lefthanded power hitters because of the easy accessibility of the right field stands. The pitching strategy is always to keep the left-handed hitters from pulling the ball, and there is nobody better suited to that than a fast left-handed pitcher. Vida Blue, in other words. Yet, when that fourth game came around, with the A's leading the series, 2-1, Williams went with right-hander Catfish Hunter, and he followed Hunter the next day with another right-hander, John (Blue Moon) Odom, in a game eventually saved by Blue's four scoreless relief innings.

Why didn't Blue start? Vida thought he knew. "Finley didn't want me to start," he said, "because if I made a good showing in the playoffs, I might be able to ask for more money next year."

As a result of all this, Vida felt less than a part of the team, and he intentionally missed the post-Series celebrations in Oakland. "I know there are going to be parties and things for the players," he said right after the A's seventh game win, "but I'm not going to any of them." He kept his word, appearing at neither the civic victory parade nor Finley's private party.

"I don't care if anybody knows how I feel," said Finley. "It sickens me to think that some players on the club didn't have enough red blood in their veins to come to the parade. What bothers me is showing a lack of appreciation. I don't pay salaries; the fans pay salaries."

Strange that he should say that, because when Blue had held out and based his salary demands on his drawing power, Finley had told him, "The fans don't pay your salary; I do."

In the spring of 1973, Blue was still a confused young man. His fastball was no longer the consistent blazer it had been in 1971, and he was struggling to find a new style of pitching to accommodate that fact. More than that, he was still trying to forget his problems with Finley. "You have to just push that out of your mind when you go out between the white lines," said Jackson, "but Vida hasn't learned to do that yet."

Blue had changed, inevitably. Early in his great year, he had been very cooperative with fans and press. He had had trouble later, but he was great in the American League playoffs that year. After he lost to Baltimore, he sat patiently on a trunk in the dressing room for 45 minutes, explaining why.

But by 1973, he had withdrawn from press, fans and players. He answered questions, but usually briefly and noncommittally. And he was no longer the fans' favorite; when he was introduced before the home opener, he was booed. It was sad to see but probably inevitable, considering the way Finley had maneuvered.

There was speculation in the press that Blue might be traded, and apparently the Texas Rangers had made a firm offer. But Finley wasn't ready to trade. As in the case of Jackson, his animosity to Blue had disappeared because he had won. And besides, he had another problem: Dave Duncan.

Duncan had disliked Finley for years, and his rage crested when Finley ordered manager Williams to catch Gene Tenace instead of Duncan in the late stages of the '72 pennant race. It hardly helped Duncan's feelings when Tenace went on to become the hero of the World Series.

There was an emotional scene on the A's plane going from Detroit to Cincinnati after the American League playoffs. Jackson had hurt his leg scoring the winning run and was out of the World Series. Duncan, his closest friend, was sitting with him and crying, over and over, "I know you shouldn't play, but you've got to. The son-of-a-bitch won't let me do it, so you've got to do it for me."

And when the A's returned from their World Series win, Finley stopped by Duncan and put his hand on his shoulder. "I know you, Dave Duncan," he said.

"No you don't," said Duncan. "You've never taken the trouble to."

The next spring, Duncan got his job back by default when the A's traded first baseman Mike Epstein and shifted Tenace to first base. Seeing his bargaining power, Duncan asked for $50,000—$20,000 more than he had received in 1972.

As usual, Finley set himself up as the white knight at the expense of his players, saying that he wouldn't give in because he didn't want to raise ticket prices—though, interestingly, he had already done so.

This time, though, his strategy failed. Duncan is a very stubborn man who would have quit baseball rather than give in. "I've been giving it a lot of thought," he admitted to me before the trade. "I still really like baseball, but I'm getting tired of all this shit that goes on away from the game. I'd miss baseball, but, yes, I think I could walk away from the game if I had to."

Finley finally realized that and traded Duncan to Cleveland. He doesn't usually like to do that. He prefers to have his players stay and suffer.

How can Finley get away with the way he treats ballplayers? Partly because he has a surprisingly uncritical press. Many sportswriters, not known for their social consciences, rationalize that Finley may be ruthless with others but he's great copy. With those he likes, Finley will talk and talk. In the days when he was still talking to me, I called him one day when Campy Campaneris was holding out. Finley gave me the exact figures on Campy's present, past and future salaries and then chuckled. "I gave you more than you expected, didn't I?" he said. He calls up one San Francisco columnist frequently, and this columnist writes a column about Finley and the A's almost every time, though his paper circulates almost entirely in San Francisco, where there are few A's fans.

There are sportswriters critical of Finley and for them, it is another story. Ron Bergman wrote an article for *The Sporting News* that had one line saying the A's announcers would be better if they didn't have to spend so much time praising Finley. Charlie would not allow Bergman to fly on the A's chartered plane (though Bergman's paper pays his expenses) and called the hotel in which the A's were staying in Minneapolis to cancel Bergman's reservations. There is no detail too small for Charlie when he is angry.

On another occasion, there was a rumor that Williams was about to be fired. Jim Street of the San Jose *Mercury-News* talked to Finley and later gave some of his quotes to Bergman, who had not been able to reach Finley; since the San Jose and Oakland papers are not circulation rivals, there was no conflict. The next morning, Finley had Bergman's story read to him and immediately knew where Bergman had gotten his quotes. He then called Street's boss and told him what had happened.

Finley and I have not talked for some time. I wrote a column critical of his announcers and then had reason to call him the next day on another matter. Spacing his words as he does when he wants to make certain he's understood (some think it's so the reporters are able to get it all down), Finley told me, "Mr. Dickey, you have the most unmitigated gall of anybody I've ever known. I never want to speak to you again."

"Did you get that in writing?" Jackson wondered, when I told him about it.

Another element to Finley's power is his relative indifference to money. In both the Blue and Jackson cases, he cost himself money at the gate but that did not bother him. He claims to have made money every year he's had the A's in Oakland, but it doesn't matter. His insurance business is so profitable, he can afford to write off any losses he might incur with the A's.

But the main ingredient of Finley's power in his disputes with players is the reserve clause. Ballplayers are tied to the club, no matter how they feel. If he sometimes treats them like indentured servants, it is not without cause. They are, though well-paid ones.

Even for the nonballplayers who work for Finley and are not tied by a reserve clause, life is not rewarding. The turnover in his office staff is amazing. Even secretaries do not last. It is a terrifying experience to work for him because Finley calls frequently to make sure that everybody is at his desk. It is, indeed, hard to imagine Finley living in the pretelephone era. One former employee described Finley's phone technique to me: "He called me one time and talked for six hours. I had to go to the bathroom one time. I just put the phone down and went, and when I came back, Charlie was still talking."

Finley's insistence on running the show caused him to fire Frank Lane early, though the two are now good friends, with the comment, "I know more about baseball than he does."

When he first came to Oakland, Finley hired Bill Cutler, then assistant to the president of the American League, as "administrative assistant." Cutler soon learned to his dismay that there is no such thing as an administrative assistant in a Finley organization. He was fired and sued Finley, eventually losing. "Charlie just didn't keep his word," said Cutler.

Bob Bestor was the public relations director for the Oakland Seals hockey team when Finley bought it. He immediately started looking for another job. "I had talked to several people who had worked for Finley," says Bestor, "and I had never heard such unanimity. They all said he was impossible to work for."

Bestor worked only three months for Finley, but that was enough. "We had a clipping service that cost us about $10–15 a month," he says. "I thought it was a good public relations tool. Finley called one night about 6:30 when I was the only one left in the office and said, 'What is this clipping service shit? As of Monday morning, that shit stops. I've been in this business too long to get nickel and dimed to death. We don't need some newspapers that aren't fit to wipe your ass on.'

"There was," says Bestor, "absolutely no input from me at all. He never asked me my opinion of the service. It was that way in conferences, too. He made a big thing about involvement, about having everybody together to make decisions, but I noticed that one guy would offer plan A, another plan B, another plan C—and then Charlie would say, 'We'll use plan D.' "

Frank Sanchez, who followed Bestor as public relations director for the Seals, had his problems, too. Once, Finley bawled him out for an inconsequential matter—and insisted that the rest of the office staff stay on the line to hear it. That especially distressed Sanchez because he had felt earlier that he could work with Finley. "When I have something I want," he told me, "I call Finley, but I put the important item maybe fifth on my list. I go down the other things to find out what kind of mood he's in. If it's a good mood, I hit him with it. If he's in a bad one, I say goodbye and try another day."

Mike Haggerty, who served just under a year as Finley's public relations man with the A's, left after Finley tried to shift the blame for a horrendous public relations gaffe. Setting up the press headquarters before the American League playoffs in 1971, Finley decided on the Mark Hopkins in San Francisco, since the list of great hotels in Oakland has yet to get a first name on it. Nobody in the American League was happy with that, because San Francisco is the National League headquarters. Finley then moved the press headquarters to the Edgewater Hyatt House in Oakland and said the earlier decision had been Haggerty's. That fooled no one, because it was obvious that nobody in the A's office had the power to decide anything more important than when to make a trip to the bathroom, but it so disgusted Haggerty that he quit.

There is no better example of the fear Finley creates in his front office employes than an incident in the spring of 1973. I had written a column critical of the Giants' decision to force players to wear short hair. Finley, who is proud of the A's image as the hairiest team in baseball (it started, typically enough, with one of his promotions—Moustache Night), called up the A's office and ordered Art Popham, then working in public relations, to buy 35 copies of the *Chronicle,* clip out the column and send it to each of the A's in spring training. Having done that, Popham sat there wondering what to do with all those papers. He was afraid that if he threw them away, Finley might call later and want them, and nobody else in the office wanted to make the decision to throw them away, either. Finally, the switchboard operator bit the bullet and threw them away. Are you starting to get some idea what it is like to work for Finley?

Popham went to work for the Denver Rockets two months later and his relief at being out from under Finley's thumb was evident. During his time in Finley's employ, he had never commented on anything I had written because much of it was critical of Finley. "Now, I can finally tell you," said Popham just before leaving, "that I really enjoy your columns."

It is apparently not much easier working for Finley in the broadcast booth. Only Monte Moore survives, and that may be because Finley uses him as a pipeline to the players; he once had to establish a mandatory $1,000 fine for any player who hit Moore.

In addition to Moore, Finley had seven broadcasters in his first six years in Oakland. One of them, Bob Elson, said, "Charlie has this one little weakness: He doesn't treat people like human beings."

Another, Red Rush, was fired after the '71 season—but not until the major league broadcasting jobs that had opened up in the off season were all filled. It cost Finley money, because he had to pay Rush for his year of idleness.

Finley's control over the A's extends often enough to the field itself, which is why he has had 12 managers in 12 years, though he counts only 11, since Hank Bauer served two separate terms. His first manager in Oakland, Bob Kennedy, wanted to play Ted Kubiak at short and move Campy Campaneris to left. Campaneris, one of Finley's favorites, phoned Charlie to complain and Finley overruled Kennedy. John McNamara was told when to play Jackson in 1970 and when to bench him.

Dick Williams had more authority for a time, but he had his problems, too. Among other things, Finley advised Williams to rotate his second basemen in 1972, pinch-hitting as each came to bat and then putting a new one in the field the next inning; it almost cost the A's the pennant when they wound up with Gene Tenace there in the fifth playoff game against Detroit and Tenace made a costly error. Finley told Williams when to pitch

Blue in the playoffs, and earlier he had ordered singles-hitter Matty Alou to be batted third because he had just traded for Alou and wanted to spotlight him.

It got worse for Williams in 1973. More and more, players would arrive before Williams had been told they'd been acquired in a trade or brought up from the minors. One of these, Allen Lewis, continued to be the sore spot he had been with McNamara, but Finley was enamored of Lewis because he had once stolen 116 bases in a minor league season. With the A's, however, he was an expensive luxury because he could be used only as a pinch-runner, and not a very good one at that. Finley called Lewis "The Panamanian Express"; after he had been thrown out repeatedly trying to steal, Oakland writer Herb Michelson renamed him "The Panamanian Local" because he always stopped at second.

Williams made up his mind to quit after the '73 season (apparently he made his decision right after the All-Star game break). He was determined to stick it out until the season was over and bit his lip to keep from criticizing Finley publicly. When Jackson was injured and unable to play in the field in late season, he wanted to be used as the designated hitter to protect his league lead in home runs and RBIs. It was a logical move, since designated hitter Deron Johnson was locked in a slump, but Williams did not make it. Pressed by Jackson to explain why, Williams finally said it was on orders from Finley. "I've had it with Finley's interference," he told Jackson and Joe Rudi, indicating that he would quit after the season (he had earlier told Sal Bando).

In the World Series, Finley topped himself. Reserve infielder Mike Andrews charged that Finley had pressured him into signing a statement that he was physically unable to play (after Andrews had made two critical errors) and sent him home, an order later countermanded by baseball commissioner Bowie Kuhn in a rare decisive moment.

After that incident, Williams told the entire A's team that he would resign after the Series. When the news became public, Finley said he would let Williams go (the A's manager was on the first year of a three-year contract), said he considered Williams a very good friend and wished him well. Shortly after, Finley changed his mind and said he would not release

Williams from his contract unless he were compensated. So much for good friend Dick Williams.

Interestingly enough, despite Finley's erratic behavior, those who have close contact with him for the first time choose not to believe the stories, which is a tribute to Finley's salesmanship.

A typical case was his purchase of the hockey Seals. Competing with an Oakland group headed by Raider part owner Wayne Valley and Roller Derby impresario Jerry Seltzer, he won the other NHL owners over with his sales pitch. The Seals were soon a disaster area. Finley quarreled with and lost his one competent front office man, Garry Young; he fired and rehired his coach, Fred Glover; he lost most of his best young players to the World Hockey Association; and he cut ticket prices in half at midseason, which horrified the other owners.

From that point, the owners resolved to get Finley out even if the league had to buy the franchise. It would have been far easier to deny him entry in the first place, but some people have to learn the hard way.

8

·

Al Davis:
Sammy Grown Up

"For what shall it profit a man, if he shall gain the whole world, and lose his own soul?"—Mark 8:36.

"I'm not interested in winning a popularity contest."—Al Davis.

By the summer of 1973, Al Davis seemed to have accomplished enough for half a dozen normal men. He was one of the five most powerful persons in pro football, a former league commissioner and a member of the NFL's executive committee and the competition committee, the latter the league's most important because it decides on playing conditions and rules. In only two months as AFL commissioner in 1966, he forced a merger between the warring AFL and NFL. As first coach-general manager and then managing general partner of the Oakland Raiders, he turned a franchise that had been the worst in pro football into the one having the best won-lost record in the NFL for the next 10 years. In so doing, he put his imprint on that club in unique fashion. With other successful teams, the coach or star player is the dominant figure. But when you think of the Raiders, you think of Al Davis.

And yet, he has been called the most hated man in football; around the league, he is referred to sarcastically as Honest Al; a picture of him is on the wall in the NFL offices in New York, with irreverent graffiti below; and his partner in the Raiders and the man who originally hired him, Wayne Valley, sued him in February, 1973, alleging Davis had a new contract written for himself without consulting or even telling Valley about it.

What manner of man is this, anyway?

In the forbiddingly martial air of the Oakland Raider headquarters, Al Davis seems quite at home. He should. The headquarters are the outgrowth of Davis' belief that the organization should reflect a single personality; you can make your own guess whose personality. The two-story building is done entirely in silver and black, the Raider colors, and Davis often wears those colors himself. The only window in the building is in his office, and there are no clocks on the wall. Raider employees are not supposed to consider what time it is or even whether it is night or day, until they are certain they are going to win the game on Sunday. "I've told the secretaries," says Al LoCasale, Davis' executive assistant and echo, "that if we lose on Sunday, I don't want them coming in all smiles on Monday morning just because they've met a cool guy and scored over the weekend. We're all in this together."

The organization speaks as with a single voice. The publicity releases always speak of the organization with reverence; they always include the key words, dynamic and Pride and Poise; and they never mention the period before 1963, when Davis first took control of the Raiders' destiny as coach-general manager. It is as if those years never existed.

That attitude has permeated even to the secretarial level. Once when I was doing research for a magazine story on Davis, his secretary told me, "You really shouldn't be doing a story on Al. You should be doing it on (coach) John Madden or the team."

"I really believe he holds classes up there," says Tom Keating, for some time the Raiders' player representative, "to make sure they get Pride before Poise. Everybody acts the same way, mouths the same words."

Seated behind his black desk, Davis does not seem like a man who would arouse such strong feelings. He is an attractive man, but not aggressively so. His front teeth protrude ever so slightly to give him a faint resemblance to Bugs Bunny, and he knows it, which is why he never smiles full out at the camera. His dark blond hair is thinning slightly. "You can see him slowing down when he comes to the Thomas hair restoration ads in magazines," laughs Keating.

He has added a little weight in his chest and stomach, despite workouts in the exercise room he had built on the same floor as his office, but his physique remains on the slender side and altogether unremarkable. In the past, he thought his legs were thin to the point of embarrassment and tried to disguise them by wearing pants so baggy as to be confused with a clown's costume, which only called attention to them. In recent years, he has given up that attempt and begun to wear well-tailored clothes.

He is a man of paradoxes. He can be very charming or rude to the point of boorishness, whichever is more likely to gain his objective. He was reared in Brooklyn and he coached in Virginia, and he mixes Brooklyn and Southern accents. Sharp observers have noted that he talks Southern when he is trying to con you and Brooklyn when he is trying to make a point, but knowing that doesn't help: when he is trying to charm somebody, he is almost impossible to resist, because he knows all the psychological buttons to push. "He lies to you, you know he's lying and you still want to believe him," says Keating.

He is a man almost devoid of a sense of humor and suspicious of anyone who has one. If you laugh or even smile while he is talking, he will stop immediately and ask, "What's funny?" And though he likes to sprinkle sexual terms throughout his conversation in a futile attempt to prove he is one of the boys, he seems to have a minimal interest in women. Pretty girls never distract Al Davis.

He takes pride in his intelligence, but his preparation and thoroughness make him seem smarter than he is. He does not like to be surprised. If you call him, his secretary will always ask, "Can I tell him what this is about?"

Despite his reputation for deviousness, he seldom lies outright, but he has a politician's knack for deflecting questions. Asked something he does not want to deny, he is likely to say, "Do you believe I'd do that?" He is a master of indirection. Perhaps the best example is the year he was trying to sneak wide receiver Drew Buie through waivers. He initiated trade talks with other clubs, talking about wide receivers, and word soon got around the league that Davis was looking for a wide receiver. Buie cleared waivers and Davis quit talking trades.

He takes defeat hard, but it is sometimes difficult to tell when he is truly upset and when he is being melodramatic for the sake of his audience. I have seen him moping in airport terminals after a loss in an exhibition game, though I knew he cared nothing about the game's outcome; the Raiders use exhibition games as proving grounds, and when they win it is almost accidental.

Davis is not an easy man to negotiate with, as his players have learned; he has had at least his share of contractual problems. "Negotiating is a game with him, and he has to win," says Keating. "You wouldn't believe some of the things he tries. He used to drag out this piece of paper when I asked for something and say, 'So-and-so at the same position is making only so much.' Finally, I said, 'Let me see that paper,' but he put it away, saying, 'That's confidential information.' He probably had doodles on it."

In the early years, when the Raiders were not drawing well, Davis used to imply that players would get more later if they sacrificed something at the moment. "That just went in one ear and out the other," says Clem Daniels, a former star running back.

In 1972, middle linebacker Dan Conners became a free agent on May 1 by playing out his option, but Davis refused to trade him and other clubs wouldn't touch Conners because of the "Rozelle Rule," which allows the commissioner to set compensation for the club which loses a player if that player signs with another. Conners finally came back to the Raiders during training camp. "It's his ball," said Conners. "I tried to put on a little juice, but I was the one who got squeezed." At Davis' bidding, coach John Madden then benched Conners, and it wasn't until injuries left a hole later in the year that Conners got back into the lineup.

In 1968, Keating had a season-long dispute over who would pay his contract. He had hurt his Achilles tendon in 1967 and it finally snapped in the league's All-Star game. He was idle the entire 1968 season, and Davis contended it was the league's responsibility to pay Keating because the final injury had come in the All-Star game. He finally won out, but not before there were some interesting negotiations with Keating. "He tried to sign me to a contract for two-thirds pay," says Keating. And the player reports other incentives were offered. "I told him no. I was single and could afford to fight him. If I'd been married, with a family and a house mortgage, I might have had to settle."

Davis is a man who intrigues all who know him, and many have a love-hate relationship with him. Everybody has an opinion, and the opinions are likely to be so divergent, it's difficult to believe people are talking about the same man.

Don McMahon, a pitching coach with the San Francisco Giants, idolizes Davis. Asking McMahon about Davis is like opening a fountain; the words come gushing out. "I first met him in high school in Brooklyn," says McMahon. "He was easy to get to know, very friendly. Everybody liked him. Then, we got together again when he came out to the coast (as an assistant coach at USC). He talked me into buying a house out here, in Garden Grove. I used to go over to his place a lot; he always had the projector on, looking at game films. I liked it best when he was coaching Oakland. I used to stand on the sidelines with him. I wish I had a tape recording of when he sent in plays. I'll bet 99 percent of them were big gainers, oh, yeah. He's a genius."

A more balanced view of Davis comes from George Ross, sports editor of the Oakland *Tribune,* who probably knows Davis as well as anybody. A perceptive man, Ross worked with Davis from the start and admired him, though he recognized early that Davis had a little bit of Sammy Glick in him—that tendency to think of his present job as something that wouldn't be good enough next year. "Al always had a lot of sure-footedness about where he was going," says Ross. "Nobody I know is as well organized as he is, not just in his work but in the life style he established for himself."

Ross worked very closely with Davis in the early days. It was a relationship which benefited both men, and George went into it with his eyes open. "We all started out at the same place in the '60s," he says, "establishing sports on the Oakland side of the bay, so if Al was using me, I was using Al, and I could go along with divergent approaches."

But in the end, Ross has been saddened by what he has seen. "He makes use of everybody around him and thinks he's getting away with it," says George. "The basic element in any human relationship is respect. You can't profess to be a man's friend if you don't respect him, and Al never grants you the courtesy of respect. Al would ask me time and again, 'Is so-and-so loyal?'—meaning, is he loyal to Al Davis above everybody else. I began to wonder, 'Al, are you being loyal to this man?' Where was his loyalty to Wayne Valley or Scotty Stirling? Where was Al's loyalty to me?"

The one thing that everybody, even Davis, agrees on is that he has tremendous drive. "I'm a driven man," he has admitted. "I don't know why, but I've always been that way. I've always known where I was going."

"I don't know what gives him that drive," says Ron Wolf, the Raiders' brilliant talent man. "He's got everything I'd want. If I were in his position, I think I'd take a cruise around the world."

Bob Bestor, for four years publicity director and then business manager for the Raiders, marvels at his enthusiasm. "I'm convinced that enthusiasm—and his intelligence—are what makes him," says Bestor. "You have to see him during the draft to appreciate that. He's just as excited on the 17th round, when everybody else is dragging, as he is on the first. I've heard him say on the 17th round, 'I'm really excited about this guy! If we could get him, it would give everybody a real lift!'"

Davis works at his job in a way almost nobody else does. He seldom gets to the office before noon, but he is often on the phone at home before then; during the season, there are probably not a half dozen nights he leaves the office before midnight. He is always thinking about the job to be done. Most of us have days in which we'd rather just take off and sit in the sun. Al Davis never wants to sit in the sun. He has a lovely wife, Carole, and a teen-aged son, Mark, and a home in the posh Piedmont section of the East Bay, but they are all secondary to the success of the Raiders.

And yet, with all his brilliance and accomplishments, he is insecure. He has shied away from magazine articles for years. The official Raider position was given me by Al LoCasale: "Al doesn't like stories on him because he feels it detracts from John Madden." That you can take with a whole box of salt. Davis' position is much more complex. On one hand, he likes publicity; on the other, he likes to maintain a certain air of mystery. But most of all, he wants to control it. He would be delighted to have a magazine article done on him—if his publicity man could write it and he could edit it. Al Davis is not a man who likes to leave anything to chance.

Davis' insecurity is the root of all his organizational problems. He has said himself, "This has to be a dictatorial system. There has to be fear in the organization."

There can be no doubt there is. "I learned an awful lot from him," says Bob Bestor, "but in the end, that atmosphere of fear drove me out. He could make me afraid. I hate to admit it, but he could. And at the same time, he could make me desperately want to get his approval."

Few have remained close to him over the years. John Rauch was his coaching protégé and Scotty Stirling his front office protégé, but Stirling quit in 1968 and Rauch a year later because of the Davis-induced pressure. During 1969-73, five assistant coaches quit, and with four of them there was a residue of bitterness. Wayne Valley found it impossible to get close to Davis even in the early days, and the situation got far worse later.

But if the insecurity is easy enough to recognize, its roots are not. It isn't poverty. Though Davis likes to talk of being from the ghetto when he is negotiating with blacks, his friend from high school days, Don McMahon, remembers it differently. "He lived in the Irish-Jewish section up the hill. He was in a lot richer neighborhood than I was."

Davis, Jewish on his father's side, often likes to imply that anti-Semitism is behind criticism of him, and he has told of being barred from a fraternity at Syracuse. But Davis never makes much of his Jewishness. Bob Bestor says, "We weren't really conscious in the organization that Davis was a Jew until he had a bar mitzvah for his son in 1968. I never remember him saying anything about it before then."

His lack of a solid athletic background has apparently bothered Davis, who has suggested at times that he was a better athlete in college than he actually was; he never lettered at Syracuse. Wayne Valley once brought out clippings and pictures of himself as a fullback at Oregon State and taunted Davis: "Show me your clippings, Al." But if Davis is troubled by his inability to become a star athlete, he is hardly alone; there may be 50 million American men who feel the same way.

Just perhaps, Davis' insecurity stems from the fact he has always been a short distance from the top in everything he has done. He was no better than second as a Raider coach. He was AFL commissioner and wanted to be commissioner of the merged league, but there was no way he could unseat Pete Rozelle.

He would like to be thought of as the most successful front office man in football but the Raiders have been to the Super Bowl only once, and then as a loser. The Raider corporate approach is that of an encyclopedia salesman and they push the fact that they had the best percentage in football for the 1963-72 period, but there is no escaping the fact that success in pro football means winning the Super Bowl. By that measure, Miami, Green Bay, Kansas City, Dallas, Baltimore and the New York Jets have all been more successful than the Raiders since Davis' arrival.

And finally, Davis is subject to one continuing problem: it isn't easy being Sammy Glick grown up.

Davis' early career is cloaked in obscurity. He went from Adelphi College to Fort Belvoir to the Baltimore Colts to The Citadel to USC, his only public notice coming from his over-zealous recruiting, which got USC placed on probation. But then he became an assistant coach for the San Diego Chargers in 1960; time and fate were beginning to swing to his side. In 1963, he became coach-general manager of the Raiders. Once, in less turbulent times, Wayne Valley explained to me how it all happened.

"We were losing our war with the 49ers," said Valley, "and we had to do something. We needed somebody who wanted to win so badly, he would do anything. Everywhere I went, people told me what a son-of-a-bitch Al Davis was, so I figured he must be doing something right.

"I talked to a lot of people about Davis, and they'd tell me, 'You don't want him. He got USC into trouble and his Army record was kinda funny. But nobody could tell me exactly what it was that he'd done wrong. It all boiled down to the fact they thought he was devious. I figured a lot of it was jealousy. I know from my own experience that some people don't like you because you're too sharp for them. I didn't care whether he was devious or whether he was likable or not; I wanted a winner, and I thought he would be one. I knew he would work 16 hours a day to make sure nobody got ahead of him."

To his later regret, Valley learned that one of the people Davis did not want ahead of him was Wayne Valley.

Valley wondered about Davis' business mind. "I asked him if he could make up a budget. I was talking to him at 11 in the morning and he said he'd get back to me about 4 that afternoon. At 4, he came in with this complete budget. I said to him, 'Well, Al, now I know what the San Diego Charger budget looks like.' That shook him a little. I figure what he did was to hop a PSA jet down to San Diego, talk one of the secretaries into letting him see the budget and just make a few changes to fit what he thought were our needs. Nobody ever told me what happened, but what can you think when a guy can't talk about a budget at all 11 A.M. and five hours later has a complete one, down to the last detail?"

Davis was an immediate success as Raider coach. The team had gone 2-12 and 1-13 in the previous two seasons, losing an AFL-record 19 straight games over two seasons, but he coached the Raiders to a 10-4 record his first season.

"He always had a good eye for talent and he knew which players could really help him," says Scotty Stirling, who was the Raider beat man for the Oakland *Tribune* that first year before Davis hired him as, first, the publicity man and then the general manager. "He had a standard at each position and he kept looking for players who could fill that standard until he got them.

"He was flexible. We always ran sweeps much shallower to one side because (guard) Wayne Hawkins was slow and had to cut the corner. When Archie Matsos was a middle linebacker, Davis made him all-league. Matsos never played at more than 190 pounds, but Davis set up the defense so the other team never got a shot at blocking him, and Archie was all over the field making tackles. Davis started the bump-and-run defense because Kent McCloughan had great speed but no quickness, and this gave him a chance to play." (McCloughan, too, became all-league.)

His next two years were not so successful—5-7-2 and 8-5-1—and then Davis became the AFL commissioner, with a hearty push from Valley, who thought Davis was exactly what the league needed. There are two stories stemming from the time he was appointed that give a clear insight into the Davis character:

—Jack Horrigan, then the AFL public relations director, prepared a release announcing Davis' appointment. Davis read the release and then asked Horrigan if he could make just two changes. "Just put them anywhere," he said. He wanted Horrigan to insert "dynamic" and "young genius."

—The night before Davis' press conference, he had Horrigan fire all conceivable questions at him, so he would be prepared. "I'm not sure he needed that," says Horrigan. "I have never seen Al in better form than he was that day. The press conference lasted for a couple of hours and he was brilliant."

In two months, the leagues merged, partly because of Davis' guerrilla tactics in going after the NFL quarterbacks and partly because of the owners' negotiations which went on behind Davis' back. He was unhappy with the settlement, which forced the Raiders and Jets to pay indemnities to the 49ers and Giants. "We had the NFL on the run," he has said.

He was also bitter because he wanted to be commissioner of the merged league. Valley pointed out the arithmetic of the situation—10 AFL clubs, 16 NFL. Davis said, "I've got friends in the NFL." Valley told him, "Al, you don't even have friends in this league. You couldn't get a majority of the AFL owners now."

So, Davis came back to the Raiders as the managing general partner. He was allowed to buy 10 percent of the club and his salary was set at $30,000, with a provision—which has never been necessary—that if his salary and profits from his share of the club did not reach $50,000 in a year, the difference would be made up by the club.

It was Valley's idea to have Davis back as part owner, though the relationship between the two had already deteriorated. "From the very outset, there was a set of abrasions, some from Davis and some from Valley," remembers George Ross. "Al always felt that though owners were necessary, they should know their place. Professional operators should run the thing."

In private, Valley mockingly referred to Davis as "The Genius," and the two hardly spoke. Piqued because he had not gotten his itinerary in time, Valley yelled at Davis one time on a Raider charter, and Davis yelled back in full view of a planeload of fascinated players and newsmen.

And yet, even then Valley said, "I've never regretted hiring him. There are things I don't like about the guy but I hired him to do a job and as long as he does it, I'm satisfied. It's like a marriage; you have to take the bad with the good."

There is some evidence that Valley misjudged Davis. Wayne told his friends he thought he could persuade Davis to return to coaching. George Ross thought otherwise. "He couldn't see himself moving laterally or backwards," says George. "It was a move forward to go into ownership."

Ross was right. "I had made a vow to myself—and I'm a guy who sticks to things when I promise myself—that when I became commissioner, I was through with coaching," Davis told me once. "I hadn't done all the things I'd wanted to do, like winning a championship, but I'd done enough. I don't care what others think, so long as I satisfy myself."

Most of those who have observed Davis over the years think he was also unwilling to stand up and take the responsibility a coach must take. "He's not a guy who will stick his neck out," says Tom Keating. That unwillingness has cost him a chance to be rated among the great coaches. It has probably also cost the Raiders—who lost three championship games and one playoff game over a five-year period—a chance to get to the Super Bowl with frequency. Football is a coach's game. Davis can only take the team so far from the front office.

"The Raiders have the capability of being a super team, like the Cleveland Browns of the late '40s and '50s, or the Green Bay Packers of the '60s," says Clem Daniels, "but there's always been that missing ingredient. I think Al Davis has the ability to give them that intangible the super clubs have, but he has to actively participate by coaching, and he hasn't done that. John Madden is a good coach, but no coach can relate Davis' system as good as he can, and it is Al Davis' system."

Nobody really knows how much influence Davis wields from the front office, but it is considerable. Certainly, it was his decision to revamp the defense in 1972 by bringing in younger players—a decision that paid off in late season. Almost certainly, his reluctance to change caused the Raiders to stick solely with a man-to-man pass defense long after other teams had gone to the zone—which hurt them.

He has also tried to influence game plans, without taking responsibility for it. He has given his ideas to assistant coaches to suggest to the head coach as their ideas in the coaches' meetings. But because he used John Madden as one of his idea carriers under John Rauch, that system hasn't worked very well since Madden became head coach. One assistant, Tom Flores, found he couldn't even get his own ideas across because Madden suspected everything came straight from Davis.

Davis' problems with Rauch were inevitable. There was an indication that Rauch couldn't take the coaching pressure even before Davis came back to the Raiders. In training camp in 1966, when Davis was still AFL commissioner, Rauch phoned Davis and begged him to take the team back. "It's your team, Al. Everybody knows that."

Rauch tried first to go to the cross-bay 49ers and apparently had signed a contract when the league office stepped in to convince the 49ers that was not a wise move. Finally, after two straight league championships, Rauch quit and took the job as head coach at Buffalo. Davis reacted typically, comparing Rauch's decision to a CIA operative defecting to the Soviet Union. "For $50,000 (Rauch's salary), Buffalo gets our complete system," said Davis bitterly. It didn't make much difference; Buffalo won only seven games under Rauch in the next two seasons.

Madden seems better able to withstand the pressure Davis creates, but the Raider assistants have been unhappy in recent years. One night in 1971, when I was working late at the San Francisco *Chronicle* office, I got a call from Richie McCabe, the defensive backfield coach. "I quit the Raiders two days ago," he said, "but they won't release the information. You've got to write something. I want other teams to know I'm free because I need a job." I did write something, and McCabe was later hired by Cleveland.

Something in Davis rebels at the thought a coach would want to leave the Raiders. Linebacker coach Ray Malavasi learned that when he asked permission in February of 1973 to talk to other clubs. "I was looking for a better-paying job," admitted Malavasi. "I knew I was sitting here with one of the lowest-paid coaching jobs in the NFL."

Malavasi was denied permission to talk to anybody. "He told me no. He didn't give any reasons, just said no. That's the way he is. I had no choice but to resign, since my contract ran to April 1. They took my car away but they paid me to March 15, because that kept other clubs from talking to me."

Meanwhile, Davis charged that Los Angeles had tampered with Malavasi, and the coach, with five children at home, sat idle until he was finally hired by the Rams in June. Pete Rozelle ruled there had been no tampering by the Rams.

Davis is fond of saying, "Everybody wants our people," but, in fact, there has been no spinoff from the Raiders, as there has been with some clubs.

Two examples: Vince Lombardi, Tom Landry and Allie Sherman all graduated from being assistant coaches for Jim Lee Howell with the Giants to being head coaches; Davis, Chuck Noll and Jack Faulkner did the same from Sid Gillman's staff in San Diego. But no Raider assistant coaches have become head coaches with other clubs—though Rauch and Madden moved up within the system to coach the Raiders— and the reason is not hard to see: Davis is unwilling to delegate the kind of authority assistants must have to prepare for being head coaches.

It is the same in the front office. Nobody has left the Raiders to run a club elsewhere. There are, however, some very talented people remaining: Ron Wolf, the talent director, George Glace, the ticket manager, and Tom Grimes, the public relations director, are probably as good at their jobs as anybody in the league, and they all profess admiration for Davis.

"I really think he's got an ability which should be utilized on a league level, not just the club level," says Wolf. "You get tired of hearing the word, but he really is dynamic. If you come in pushing a player, you'd better be ready for questions coming at you from about eight different directions."

"He's not a dictator," says Al LoCasale. "He'll give you the benefit of his thinking, of the way he would do something, but he'll let you make your own decisions. I know when I make a decision, he's right behind me."

Both LoCasale and Wolf have strong feelings of loyalty to Davis. "When I left San Diego," says LoCasale, who had worked with Davis with the Chargers, "he called me from Oakland and told me I could use his credit card to call for jobs."

"I really feel if it had been anybody else as coach-general manager the first couple of years or if he hadn't been so involved in everything else, from the football team to sweeping out the stadium, I'd have been gone," says Wolf. "I'd be back in school in Oklahoma or pumping gas in Pennsylvania or something. I feel a loyalty to him because of that. I feel he has patience if he thinks you'll eventually do the job. He's willing to let you set your own pace. I have freedom to do things my way here that I might not have somewhere else."

The picture painted of Davis by former employees is not so kind. Some of it is funny: all have tales of Davis' insecurity causing him to suspect intraoffice plots. Any time he spotted two employees talking together in the hall, he would summon each one into his office separately and ask what they were talking about.

Some of it wasn't so funny. "He'd always second-guess," says Bob Bestor. "I'd try to get him to commit himself on paper, but it never worked. I'd bring in a piece of paper with everything written out and he'd never even look at it. He'd just say, 'Just do what you think is right, Bobby,' and then when it went wrong, he'd ask me why I'd done it that way.

"When I was making out the travel schedule in June, 1968, I asked him whether he wanted to charter a plane to San Diego or take the regular flight, which made a 20-minute stop in Los Angeles. The difference was $1,500 or $2,000. He said we'd go on the regular flight. Then, when we made the trip and stopped in Los Angeles, everybody was unhappy. So, Davis looks around the cabin and says, 'Why the fuck are we stopping here? Who's responsible for this?' I reminded him of our conversation and he said, 'I don't remember that conversation.'"

Davis' insecurity also leads him to an apparent necessity to prove he can make people work for him at low salaries. Through good years and bad, the Raider payroll has remained low. In 1972, John Madden's salary as head coach was $32,000; some assistants around the league were getting as much or more. No Raider assistant got more than $20,000 and some got less. LoCasale, used by Davis as a surrogate son-of-a-bitch in dealings with others, was paid only $19,000—and he was regarded as second-in-command.

His insecurity finally led to the final break with Wayne Valley, too, culminating in a lawsuit filed by Valley in April, 1973. The contract and the lawsuit both had their genesis in the involved case of Warren Wells, the former Raider wide receiver.

Wells was first sentenced for attempted rape on September 19, 1969, and given probation. After several arrests for drunken driving and illegal possession of guns, Wells was sent to county jail on February 17, 1971. He was put back on probation April 15, but after another incident in Beaumont, Texas, in which he allegedly tangled with a girl who later knifed him, Wells was imprisoned on September 3.

Davis wanted him freed, naturally enough, since Wells had caught 36 touchdown passes in the previous three years, and seemed convinced that Valley—a friend of the sentencing judge, Leonard S. Dieden—had the political muscle to get Wells out but would not use it because he wanted to embarrass Davis by forcing a decline of the Raiders.

"Davis never made a flat statement that Valley was to blame," says Tom Keating. "He alluded to Valley's relationship with the judge and said, 'Some people in this organization are racist.' It was silly. Valley's a businessman; Wells could make him money and he wanted him out on that field as much as anybody."

Valley is vulnerable to the racist thrust because he talks roughly, using racial epithets, in public. The talk means nothing—he is, in fact, singularly unconcerned with a man's race or religion if he does the job—but the rumors quickly spread and contributed to a general unrest on the team. Finally, in midseason, 1971, Keating called Valley and said he'd like Wayne to meet with the team and explain the situation. Valley agreed, if Davis were also there and reporters attended. Davis refused.

Wells wasn't released until the following July, and by that time he was through, mentally and physically. The Raiders released him before the end of camp.

Valley, who had been willing to shut his eyes to the other dubious Davis practices, looked on the Wells' case as a moral situation and resolved to try to get Davis removed as managing partner when their partnership agreement expired on January 1, 1976. Realizing that, Davis beat him to the punch and had club attorney Herman Cook draw up a new contract to take effect in 1976. He and the club's third general partner, Ed McGah, signed it; McGah didn't even bother to read it, he admitted later.

"It fit in with Davis' personality, with his long-range view," says George Ross. "He saw that with the expiration of the contract in '75, something had to happen, so he thought he'd make his move now."

The new contract was a beauty. Among other things, it called for:

1. $100,000 salary for Davis for 10 years, with a year added as each year is lopped off, for a maximum of 20 years, when Davis would be 65.

2. The contract cannot be breached by other partners; if it is, Davis gets payment for remainder of contract and suffers "irreparable damage" to his reputation as a football expert, which could be the basis for a suit.

3. The contract cannot be breached by the death of a general partner.

4. Davis has sole responsibility for hiring and running the operation, both on the field and off. He can hire a general manager, at whatever salary he desires; he sets his own expense account, consistent with other clubs in the league; and he is the sole judge of how much time and energy he puts in on the job.

5. If Davis were totally incapacitated for 12 months, the contract could be broken, but he would be paid for its remainder.

6. Davis will have the club's vote at NFL meetings.

7. Davis can engage in any other enterprise that is not in direct competition with the Raiders.

The contract was written in July, 1972. Valley kept hearing comments around the league about Davis taking over the club, but he dismissed them as exaggerations spread by Davis and his friends. Not until February, 1973, did he realize what had happened, when stories about it ran in the Oakland *Tribune* and *The Sporting News.* He confronted Davis in front of an appalled Pete Rozelle—the three were meeting on another matter—and Davis told him to go jump in the lake, or words to that effect.

Though the Raiders are a very small part of his total holdings, they are important to Valley, a lifelong sports fan; in his office are helmets representing the original AFL teams and pictures from Raider games. "I'm not going to let him steal my team," he told friends. And so, he sued—the suit being filed on the first day of the NFL owners' meeting in Scottsdale, Arizona.

It was all sad to those close to the situation. Most of us who had known Davis had been impressed at the start and remained immersed in his aura for some time; it is hard not to be impressed with his record. But the longer you know the man, the more difficult it is to respect him because his insecurity drives him to take advantage of everybody, and that eventually leads to ruin, for himself and for the situation.

Says one who has known him for a long time: "Everything he touches turns to shit."

9

.

Sportswriters: Maintaining The Status Quo

"You're not welcome in this camp, Mr. Schecter, so get out."—Cincinnati Bengals' coach Paul Brown to free lance writer Leonard Schecter, who had written what Brown considered rip jobs on Vince Lombardi, Pete Rozelle and Al Davis, at the Bengals' training camp in 1971.

Sportswriters are probably as responsible for the myths that surround sports as anybody—with the possible exception of the fans, who are silly enough to believe the myths. Traditionally, the sports department has been a world apart. Sportswriters are at once the most envied and the most despised members of the newspaper. They are envied because many newspapermen cannot imagine anything better than being paid to watch a baseball game or a football game or whatever. Some spend more time in the sports department checking scores than they do at their own jobs. Yet, sportswriters are despised because the rules that apply to writing in other sections of the paper don't seem to apply in sports. The worst sportswriters twist the language, root openly for the hometown team in print and in person and commit any number of egregious errors.

Some of the best newspapermen have started in sports, but the sports department also produces more than its share of the worst. The suspension of writing rules gives more freedom to the good writer to do his best, but it also allows the bad writer to do his worst.

Sportswriters also tend to be enthusiasts, in direct contrast to other reporters. A court reporter has his job because he was assigned to it, not necessarily because he likes lawyers or judges. A police reporter is likewise where he is because of a direct assignment, not because of an affinity for policemen. But a sportswriter is almost always a sportswriter because he likes sports. Many are frustrated athletes, and they remain convinced to the end of their working days that the best possible life is that of an athlete. It is too much to expect that you will get objective reporting from anybody with this set of mind.

There are other problems. Proximity is possibly the main one, again as opposed to other departments of the newspaper. If film critic and author Pauline Kael pans a movie or criticizes an actor, she does so with the knowledge that she need not see anybody she has criticized. A sportswriter may have to go to an athlete he has criticized for a story the next day. Only a political writer has the same kind of problem, and his is eased by the fact that few politicians are in condition to scare him physically. The average athlete has no trouble scaring the average sportswriter.

Athletes have traditionally held the view that the only good sportswriter is an uncritical one. A writer could commit virtually every offense imaginable to the English language—and some have—but as long as it was in praise of an athlete, the athletes couldn't care less. A writer ignores this premise at his own peril. It has not been very many years, for instance, since Earl Lawson, a Cincinnati baseball writer, was getting punched around regularly by the Cincinnati players. Two years ago, Bucky Walter of the San Francisco *Examiner,* a mild-mannered man who has not intentionally criticized a living soul in at least 20 years, was threatened by Gaylord Perry because he had written that Perry had had a cortisone shot when Perry, in fact, had taken the medicine orally. That, please note, was not even criticism.

Even if a reporter doesn't fear physical violence, there is always the danger that he is alienating his sources. This was Schecter's problem, as the epigraph to this chapter illustrates. It has also been mine from time to time. Once, after writing critically of the Raiders' Al Davis, I tried to reach him for a story. After being brushed off none too subtly by his secretary, I called him at home. The conversation follows in its entirety:

"Hello."
"Hello, Al."
"Who is this?"
"Glenn."
"I've got a long-distance call coming in."
"Bull—
(click)
"—shit."

The beat system that most papers employ—one guy covering a team all year, and often for several years—also causes a lot of problems. Some newspapers are beginning to recognize this fact and make a partial retreat from it by having one writer cover a team for half a season and another writer for the second half. On the *Chronicle,* managing editor Gordon Pates has tried to break up the beat system by using the best writers to cover as many different events as possible. Naturally, that has been resented by the lesser talents who had become beat men because of their seniority.

The beat system has one big advantage: a writer who has been paying attention knows whom to approach when a story breaks. On any team, there are some players who can be trusted to know what's happening and tell a writer about it and some who cannot. For instance, during the spring of 1973, Sam McDowell—then still with the Giants—went on a radio program and assured the audience that Jim Ray Hart would soon be the starting third baseman, when he got in condition. Under any circumstances, that was a debatable proposition; this time, it was demonstrably false because Jim Ray had just been traded to the Yankees.

But the drawbacks of the system outweigh its virtues. The basic problem is that a sportswriter on a beat usually comes to feel closer to his team than to the newspaper he's working for. Perhaps you think that's an exaggeration, but I know it to be true both from my own experience of covering the Oakland Raiders for five years and from talking to other writers. It's not at all uncommon for sportswriters to refer to the team they're covering as "we" and ignore stories that would be harmful to the team.

Why? Part of it is financial. Some teams pay the expenses of writers on the road, and even those who don't, give out Christmas gifts which can be very nice. But that, I think, is a minor danger. It has been my experience that the writers who can be bought by those gifts are already in the club's pocket, anyway. I have seen writers become "homers" within a few weeks of being assigned to a team, without having received any real monetary award.

The big danger again is proximity. When you travel with a team, it is very difficult not to sympathize with the players and management, not to fall into the Us vs. Them syndrome. You become friends, though the friendship is a strange one entirely dependent on what you write. It's difficult to criticize friends. It is especially difficult because you know that if you praise a player or team, you'll get a lot of smiles on the team plane the next time, but if you criticize, you'll get a lot of heat—and either way, you usually hear nothing from your own front office.

In my years at the *Chronicle,* I have never had an unalloyed word of praise from the paper's sports editor, even when I had that most hallowed of newspaper traditions, a scoop. On the other hand, I overheard him apologizing over the telephone one time for something I had written—moments before he came to me and told me he had defended me! That gives one pause.

For these reasons, the biggest problem with sportswriting today is the lack of criticism. What criticism there is tends to be very pallid and always directed at athletes, never at management. For reasons of age—sportswriting is as wed to the seniority system as the U.S. Senate—sportswriters have usually felt much closer to management than to players. It is no coincidence that stories on the football and baseball strikes of recent years have been heavily weighted toward management.

The seniority system hurts in another way; age and time spent working in the department, not ability, are almost always the criteria by which writers are assigned beats. By the time a sportswriter gets a good beat, he is often so worn down by the system that he is content to go along. Not always, of course. I have always admired Dick Young because he stayed a tough reporter during his many years on the baseball beat, but he is a rare one. Most writers, particularly on the baseball beat, tend to go along with the system.

I had an example of this in 1972, when I went on a trip with the Giants around the National League. In St. Louis, after Ron Bryant had been taken out of a game with a lead that had eventually been lost, Bryant told the writers in the dressing room that he was being treated unfairly by manager Charlie Fox. That in itself mattered little because athletes often say these things right after the game; what did matter was what happened later.

The Giants returned to their hotel and Bryant went into the hotel bar, a direct violation of a team rule. He saw Bill Thompson, one of the Giants' announcers, in the bar and came over to say hello. Fox came into the bar and saw Bryant and Thompson there. Instead of staying away and merely telling Bryant later that he would be fined automatically for being in the bar, he came over. Assuming that Thompson had invited Bryant in, he lectured Thompson and then started yelling at Bryant, who yelled right back. It was more action than the hotel bar had seen in months.

After this, Bryant went to his room and called his wife, at home in Davis, California. And after that, he called me and said he wanted to talk to me in my room in about an hour. At that time, he came up and talked to me. By then it was two hours after the Giants had returned to the hotel and three since the end of the game, and Bryant should have been cooled off. He wasn't, and he made it plain that his anger was directed at Fox for everything that had been done during the season, not just during the last game.

Among other things, Bryant was angry because: Fox had several times deprived him of the chance to get a win by taking him out of close games; Fox had no communication with him or any of the younger players; and Fox had a natural tendency to make himself look good at the expense of his players by suggesting that they were losing because they wouldn't listen to him.

Since I had heard some of the same things from other players on the team, I thought it was a good story and wrote it. Fox didn't like it at all, but that publicity forced him to leave Bryant in all the way in his next game—and Bryant beat the Cubs in Chicago. Fox turned it into a joke by salaaming to Bryant in front of the dugout at the end of the game, and Bryant has since then been the Giants' most effective pitcher.

The week after I returned from the trip, I was in the press box at Candlestick, talking to a Giant beat writer who had not been on that trip. "Gee," he said, "Bryant has said these things before but I don't know that he ever wanted them written."

With that kind of attitude, of course, nothing remotely critical ever does get written.

Despite all this pressure, subtle and otherwise, some writers do write critically of sports, and there seems to be a growing tendency in that direction among the younger writers across the country. Obviously, I'm one of them or I wouldn't be telling you all this, and you might be interested in some of the reactions I've gotten from my criticism.

It started early, when I was a sophomore at the Santa Barbara campus of the University of California and sports editor of the college newspaper. The college football team was a bad one, winning only two games that season, but the players—like all athletes everywhere—thought they should still be praised. When I didn't praise them, the team called a meeting to discuss the situation with me. One player asked me if I came out to practice, to see how hard they worked. No, I replied, and added incautiously, "Do you come out to watch me write my column?"

An assistant coach, whose name I've forgotten who had just finished playing two years with the Cleveland Browns as an offensive lineman, said, "No, and it's a good thing we don't because we'd shove that typewriter right up your ass."

So much for honest criticism.

And now we skip to a scene at the Oakland Coliseum many years later. I am just leaving the Coliseum after covering an A's game when Reggie Jackson and John (Blue Moon) Odom come out of the dressing room. Seeing me, they each grab an arm and walk me out of the building, my feet not touching the ground, and ask me why I am writing so critically of the A's. I don't remember what I answered, but it was my most successful speech: they didn't make a wish and pull me apart.

Another incident, this one at the Oakland Raider practice field. Gene Upshaw and Art Shell, who outweigh me by 70-80 pounds each and are both in condition—which I am not—approach me. They are angry with some specific criticism I had of their blocking in a game with Kansas City four weeks before. Against all reason, I decide to take the offensive. "I don't think you have any cause to be angry, Gene," I said, "because I've written an awful lot of good things about you over the years."

"Yeah," replies Upshaw, "but one bad thing outdoes all the good things you've written."

The Athlete's Creed, simply spoken. Fortunately for me, Upshaw and Shell are gentlemen off the field and they didn't, though they were physically quite capable of doing so, stuff me in the nearest garbage can.

These are examples from my days as a regular member of the *Chronicle* sports department. The incidents have greatly increased since I started (in 1971) writing a column which is, in polite language, irreverent. When I wrote the column about Willie Mays, for instance, I had to do a dressing room story only four days later. Naturally, with my luck, the Giants played a double-header, the second game went 13 innings and was won by a home run by (multiple choice time): A) Mao Tse-tung; B) H. R. Haldeman; C) Willie Mays.

I had no great illusions that I would be granted an interview by Mays, so I talked first to manager Charlie Fox in his office, and Fox said all the proper things. Then I talked to pitcher Steve Stone and outfielder Ken Henderson just outside the main part of the dressing room.

And then I started in to the main part of the dressing room, as unobtrusively as I could; there were still no other sportswriters down there to give me cover. As I did, Gaylord Perry, the self-appointed sergeant-at-arms, saw me. "Oh, no!" he screamed across the room. "Look who's here! Get him out of here!" It was a touching display of team spirit by Perry, who disliked Mays himself.

Other players joined in the cry, though I knew—and had it confirmed in private conversations later—that many players agreed with what I had written. The equipment manager, Eddie Logan, told me, "You'd better leave." I agreed. Apart from the physical danger involved, there was no way I could conduct any interviews in those circumstances.

There have been other instances. Once I criticized Red Rush, then announcing for the A's. Rush called me at home and we talked at some length without reaching agreement. That night, I was standing by the batting cage when Rush came up and started berating me at some length and challenging me to fight. I didn't understand what he was trying to say for awhile because I hadn't had a fight since I was a freshman in high school. I didn't have one there, either. Later, I was sitting in the dugout talking to Reggie Jackson and commented, "I don't think he likes me." "He's not alone," said Reggie, solemnly.

The reaction to criticism always depends on whose ox is being gored, as may be seen from several incidents which occurred during the winter of 1973.

Wayne Valley had just sued Al Davis in the Raider ownership battle, and I had written a couple of columns critical of Davis, one of which had appeared the morning of a Warriors' playoff game. As I walked into the game that night with my wife and friends, I saw Al LoCasale, the Raiders' executive assistant. I started to wave. "Don't wave at me you son-of-a-bitch," screamed LoCasale, "or I'll punch you right in the mouth." I wasn't too worried; LoCosale is barely over five feet tall, and my knees were in greater danger than my mouth.

The next day I was cleaning out my desk and found a letter, accompanied by a photocopy of a column by a Kansas City writer, who had criticized me for a column I had done on the brutish Kansas City fans. The accompanying letter joked about how seriously they took everything back there and their need to have more perspective. It was signed, Al LoCasale.

And still later, my wife and I went to a Raider highlight film dinner and LoCosale came up graciously to greet us. He complimented Nancy on her dress and even posed for a picture with us. "That can't be Al LoCasale," said Nancy, who is not as accustomed to these dizzy reversals.

The experience I enjoyed most came at the World Series in 1972 when the A's were playing Cincinnati. It was triggered by a column about the Reds which appeared the day the Oakland part of the Series began. Some excerpts:

> A team of boors, the Cincinnati Reds, are in our midst this week. . . .The boorishness starts at the top, with manager Sparky Anderson. . . . He remains one of the troglodytes of the sport. Anderson is a short-hair freak. He requires that his players have short hair and be clean-shaven. . . . He actually believes that me with short hair are morally superior to those with long. . . .
> Anderson also apparently believes that players do better when their hair is short. It must truly puzzle him that the A's, with their profusion of long hair and moustaches, have beaten his clean-shaven lads two games running. It puzzles his clean-shaven lads, too. The Reds have spent the last few days acting as if they believed the World Series should be awarded them without the formality of playing it.

That started it. Typically, Anderson misunderstood me, thinking I had called him a short-haired creep. That's what happens when you move your lips when you read.

Two days later, I wrote another column, needling the fat cats of baseball who were going around congratulating each other on what a great Series it had been. I mentioned a few things that detracted from it, such as the inane comments by managers (asked about the effect of the twilight on the hitters, Anderson had said, "It's the same for both teams"); the 5:30 start which guaranteed that nobody would see the ball for two hours and also guaranteed record traffic jams; Finley's mule; and the incredible errors by those operating the scoreboard.

I also wrote,

> . . . and they're still playing baseball. The game is basically a dull one, with the rare moments of excitement too often coming from misplays rather than faultless execution. . . . Worse, they've still got baseball players out there, and baseball players generally are the type you wouldn't invite to your home for fear they'd spit on the rug or assult the maid.

That really did it. That morning, I arrived at the Coliseum and a couple of writers told me they'd just as soon I didn't stop near them. Nothing personal, you understand, but they didn't want to be seen talking to me.

"Why don't you wear your name and number on your back?" said Wells Twombly. "Sparky Anderson has been haranguing me for two days because he thinks I'm you." Twombly was miffed because he prefers to be identified for his own hatchet jobs, not mine.

In a radio interview, A's manager Dick Williams referred to me as "that idiot from across the bay."

I sat in the press box during the game, but before the start of the ninth, I left and stood behind the backstop so I could get to the dressing room quicker after the game. Dave Grote, the National League public relations man and a man who believes baseball is no more important than, say, the moon landings, came over to me. "That piece this morning," he said, shaking his head. "Jesus. I believe in the creed that every man is entitled to his own opinion, but . . ."

But not that opinion, right?

After the game, I went down into the Cincinnati dressing room, still protected by anonymity. I had talked to the players and Anderson during the Series, but I had not identified myself; in the crush of interviewers, there was no need to. One player came up to me in the dressing room and asked if I knew Glenn Dickey. I assured him I did, but I hadn't seen him.

I talked to several of the players—Johnny Bench, Pete Rose, Joe Morgan and Clay Carroll—and I was about to leave when I was spotted by Joe Nuxhall, once a pitcher but now a fat radio announcer. Someone had apparently told him who I was, and he screamed at me from across the room. "Get that son-of-a-bitch out of here! That mother fucker doesn't like baseball, so get him the hell out!" The players looked puzzled, but I couldn't forget this had been a club with a reputation for players who hit sportswriters. So, I left, but I couldn't complain. It had been a very interesting day, and the ball game wasn't bad, either.

Most of my sportswriting colleagues can't understand why I would bring this kind of confrontation down on myself. Maybe you can't, either. But it's really not so difficult to understand; it's all a matter of perspective.

Many have accused me of hating sports, which is absurd. I enjoy watching games and writing about them, though my enjoyment is very different from what it was 20 years ago.

That's important, because I don't think anybody can write well about sports over a period of years without enjoying them. There are a few sportswriters who profess to be bored with sports, but they're usually lying, to themselves as well as others.

The problem for most sportswriters, of course, is that they love sports too much; obviously, nobody will accuse me of that. My love of sports is not blinding. I regard sports as part of our lives, ranking in importance somewhere between making love and carrying out the garbage at night. Athletes are basically entertainers and should be regarded as such. When they do well, they should be praised; when they do poorly, they should be criticized. There certainly should be no reason to regard them as being above criticism.

Within sports, there are a lot of pompous men. This seems especially true in baseball. Some of the highest-ranking baseball officials are so full of hot air, they must take great pains not to get too close to sharp objects. These men, and others like them, have never heeded a simple dictum: take your job seriously but not yourself. They take themselves so seriously, they immediately fly into a snit whenever they or their sport is criticized. I take great delight in causing some of these snits.

Basically, I believe in honesty; I want to be able to look at my image in the mirror without flinching. This is a startling concept for most sportswriters, who are accustomed to criticizing athletes within the press box but not in print. Indeed, I often get letters from readers who realize that and ask, "What really happened in such-and-such a situation?"

Obviously, there are always going to be subjects that cannot be fully covered, secrets that have to be held back. It would hardly be ethical, for instance, to watch a football team practice and write about a play that was being put in that week. But I try to reduce such situations to a minimum; as much as possible, I want my writings to reflect what I actually believe about a situation.

Over the years, I have found most athletes respect that—though a lot of club officials do not. When I was covering the Raiders, for instance, I felt I had good rapport with most players because they knew I would be honest. They also knew that I would criticize both coaches and top management, if necessary, and nobody else was doing that.

Even those with whom I have had disagreements over the years often are friendly later. Despite that incident early in his career, I enjoy talking to Reggie Jackson as much as anybody, and I have had several long, amiable conversations with Gene Upshaw since our confrontation. On and off the field, I have a lot of respect for Upshaw, and I'm sure he understands that.

But I must admit my chief reason for writing the way I do is personal. It is marvelous therapy. People who meet me are invariably surprised that I smile instead of growl; I'm fortunate to be able to release all my aggressions at the typewriter. I recommend it highly.

10

·

Howard And Chris
And All Those Swell Guys

It was not until the third quarter of the Rose Bowl game on New Year's Day, 1973, that I realized Al DeRogatis must be as tired of listening to Curt Gowdy, and vice versa, as I was. Gowdy was going into his Anthony Davis spiel for perhaps the 100th time, telling us how great Davis was, as if we could not see for ourselves, when he was interrupted by DeRogatis. Without missing a beat, DeRogatis started talking about a phenomenal young running back, spicing his comments with "as you just said, Curt" several times.

There was only one problem: DeRogatis was talking about Ohio State's Archie Griffin, not Anthony Davis. If these clowns cannot even listen to each other, how do they expect us to pay attention?

This is not a brief against Gowdy and DeRogatis, who are neither the only nor the worst offenders in this area. It is against all the TV commentators who seem to believe the worst offense they can commit is a moment of dead air. It isn't, believe me.

When they are imparting specific information, their dialogue is useful. But they go far beyond that, and they will blather on when they have nothing to say they haven't said a hundred times before. Sometimes it seems like a competition between the play-by-play man and the "color" commentator to get the most words in; one hardly completes a sentence before the other weighs in with his endless expertise. I think if I hear the term "seams of a zone" one more time, I'll go running and screaming into the street.

If the information meant anything at all, even the first time, it would be something, but it seldom does. One could hardly imagine the amount of irrelevant material that can be thrown at a viewer unless you've listened to some of these guys. Possibly the worst I ever heard was a guy named Frank Sims who used to do the Pacific-8 basketball games. Sims was a master at telling you a player was majoring in ceramics glazing as the player in question was breaking down the floor for a layup.

Who needs it?

The obvious solution to this logorrhea would seem to be shutting the sound off, which I understand a lot of people do, particularly with Howard Cosell. But I find that difficult to do, particularly with football. TV football is unsettling enough because dimensions and distances are so difficult to judge; to take away the sound further deprives me of standards by which to judge the game.

The trend to national announcers, which was supposed to have the goal of eliminating "homers," has led to blandness in most cases; obviously, Cosell is the exception. In the best of situations, the national announcer is one who is familiar with both the sport and the teams involved and can give the viewer an unbiased inside look at the game. Offhand, I can think of only one announcer who truly fits that description: Keith Jackson. And Jackson was shunted off Monday Night Football to make room for Frank Gifford, God help us all.

What we get from the national announcers is usually men like Gowdy and Lindsay Nelson and Chris Schenkel, who cover so many events they really know little about any of them. At least with the local announcers, whatever their defects, you get some inside information on the teams. With Gowdy, Nelson and Schenkel, you really get nothing, except the opportunity to feel superior.

And though national announcers are not partial to one team or another, they are partial in another, worse way: they are shills for the game. Even Cosell, who seems like an exception, isn't: he just has his own twist. Howard will tell you a game is bad, horrible, awful—but as he does so, he reminds you to tune in next week for a great game, and be sure to catch him on his weekend sports show or Wide World of Sports or whatever he and the network are pushing that week.

Part of the shilling is inevitable, given the circumstances. In pro football, for instance, Pete Rozelle has the power to ding any announcer he doesn't like. That effectively eliminates any possible criticism of football.

But that is probably irrelevant; announcers wouldn't criticize the game or anybody in it because their function is entertainment, not information. They are pushing the sport they announce because the networks that pay them have paid a lot of money for the privilege of telecasting the games. Thus, all coaches, officials and players are uniformly good—pardon me, great—men, and every event they describe is a momentous piece of history.

This kind of comment leads to two results. The first is the lesson learned too late by Hollywood: when you describe everything as colossal, nobody believes you when it is. When Curt Gowdy says a player is great, I yawn.

And what is left unsaid is the more important. The officials are almost always praised; therefore, if they are not, you know they have blundered. When Texas quarterback Alan Lowry stepped out of bounds on his way to the winning touchdown in the '73 Cotton Bowl and it was not called, Tom Brookshier watched the instant replay which showed Lowry stepping out and could only say it was "very close."

Brookshier was taken completely by surprise when Duane Thomas showed up to be interviewed after the '72 Super Bowl and, in the finest tradition of inoffensive television reporting, didn't dare ask him the one question everybody wanted to hear: why hadn't Thomas spoken to teammates or writers all year? Brookshier's performance was so inept, Jim Brown even chided him by saying, "Are you nervous, Tom?"

Brookshier illustrates another lamentable trend: the use of ex-athletes as announcers, usually color men. Sometimes, the athletes can't talk so good. Ex-49er end Gordy Soltau was the big joke in San Francisco sporting circles for years for his malapropisms on 49er broadcasts. One time he told his listeners they'd have to "go into the argyles" to check on a record. Another time, he urged listeners to send in for the 49er yearbook, which had "biological sketches" of the players. The response from women was said to be unusually heavy.

Frequently, too, the ex-athletes don't really know all that much about the game they're describing. That may seem strange, but not if you know many athletes. Professional sports have become so specialized that players often know little beyond the requirements of their positions.

This is especially true in football, the most specialized of games. The last person you go to for an accurate opinion about a football player is another football player. Sometimes this is because their egos are involved; if you ask one quarterback about another, for instance, you will likely discover the second quarterback is not in the same league with the one you are talking to. Mostly, though, it's because they don't see much of the game. If you ask a wide receiver about the best corner-backs, you are likely to get a pretty good answer. If, however, you ask him about offensive tackles, he's lost; he never watches them, even on film. Nobody does, except for defensive ends.

An example of this came before the playoff game between the Pittsburgh Steelers and Oakland Raiders in 1972. Since Kansas City had played both teams, somebody asked Chiefs' defensive tackle Buck Buchanan which defense was better. Buchanan said Pittsburgh's was. He may have been right, but he was the last person to know. He was never on the field against either defensive team, and he had the worst seat in the house to watch them.

But the worst sin of the ex-athletes is their absolute horror at the thought of criticizing. As Frank Gifford noted in his defense when I had criticized him, "I've been down the road. I know how tough it is." (Howard Cosell is reported to have said later that Frank Gifford hadn't been down any road that couldn't be traveled by a chauffered limousine.)

The only exception I know to this rule is Bill Russell, whose trenchant and expert comments on the game and its players made him such a delight on the ABC pro basketball games. Unfortunately, Russell quit after a year to return to coaching. I thought he was smarter than that.

Being a professional athlete is like being a member of an exclusive club, and it is understood that the members do not criticize each other. In that respect, it is like the U.S. Senate: William Proxmire and Barry Goldwater may never agree politically on anything, but you don't hear public criticism from one of the other.

Occasionally, athletes breach this rule, and then it can be quite comical. During the 1972-73 pro basketball season, Rick Barry gave the opinion that Sidney Wicks was a better forward than Spencer Haywood and that Julius Erving was better than either. He may very well have been right, but it didn't help matters when he had to sit next to Haywood at the All-Star game banquet later that season. It didn't seem to bother Barry—nothing but a foul called against him seems to bother Barry much—but Haywood scowled his way through the banquet, never even acknowledging Barry's presence. The athlete as spoiled brat.

The ex-athlete—and there is no better example than Gifford—feels it is enough just to be a professional athlete, that a man merits respect for that alone. That is hogwash. The athlete's role in our society is overvalued; there is no intrinsic worth to playing a game. Like everybody else, the athlete should be judged on whether he does his job well or poorly.

On athletic ability, I bow to Gifford. I have no illusions: even in my dreams, I cannot block Alan Page or strike out Johnny Bench. But I can give a more accurate appraisal of what is happening on the field because I don't allow myself to be restricted by artificial barriers.

The influx of former athletes into broadcasting has made it almost impossible for the cream to rise to the top. Thus, most of the good announcers in the country are local ones, and many of them are primarily or exclusively radio men. I'm thinking of men like Vin Scully and Al Michaels, who broadcast the Dodgers and Giants baseball games, and Chick Hearn and Bill King, who cover the Lakers and Warriors in basketball. King also covers the Raiders during the football season.

I have known King on both sides of the microphone for some time, and I have always been impressed with the way he does his work. He is very thorough, both before and during a game. He comes very early to games and studies all the necessary information; for his football broadcasts, he memorizes the numbers of players so he doesn't have to consult his board or have somebody do it for him.

He gives you everything that happens. Ron Fell, the program director for KNBR, which carries the Raider games, once described King's announcing style as approaching television because if you listen carefully you know so much it's almost as if you're watching. In basketball, he gives you almost too much; he talks faster than I can listen.

Because he knows the games he announces so thoroughly, King can tell you what's happening before it happens. On the Raider highlight film, there was a play which started with Daryle Lamonica fading back to pass, and King's description of the play was put on the movie soundtrack. Before Lamonica even turned around, King noted that tight end Raymond Chester was open in the end zone; moments later, the pass went to Chester for the touchdown.

And as an added attraction, King can even give you a critique of the officiating. Someday, he'll find an official he likes.

In any logical system, men like King, Hearn, Michaels and Scully would become national announcers. Instead, they are restricted to local markets (King's basketball partner, Hank Greenwald, another fine announcer, got so frustrated he moved to Australia) and mediocrity marches on nationally.

Who are the worst? My choices are Gifford, individually, and Chris Schenkel-Bud Wilkinson as a team.

There is a lot to be said for Gifford as a terrible example. I've already mentioned some of his flaws, such as his absolute horror at the thought of criticizing any athlete anywhere at any time. His lack of color is another flaw, but perhaps his worst shortcoming is his continual inaccuracy. He cannot even learn to pronounce names. He has been known to pronounce Danny Abramowicz's name as if the Saints' receiver were an Irishman—O'Bramowicz. During a 1972 game, he continually mispronounced Hoyle Granger's name, though Granger had been playing pro football for nearly 10 years. It does not seem to be too demanding to ask that Gifford learn to pronounce the players' names correctly.

During one Raider game on Monday night television, he confused Fred Biletnikoff with Charlie Smith on a pass pattern,

though there was long blond hair coming out from under Biletnikoff's helmet and Charlie Smith does not have long blond
hair. Another time, a couple of months after Warren Wells had
been imprisoned, he referred to a Raider formation as having
Wells flanked left. If he were no more accurate than that with
his refrigerator commercials, we'd all go back to using ice-
boxes.

But as bad as he is, Gifford cannot match Schenkel and
Wilkinson. Their performances on the college football games
always leave me grinding my teeth.

There are a lot of things wrong with those telecasts, and
some of them are the fault of the colleges and the NCAA. There
is, for instance, the restriction on how many times a team can
appear nationally, which leads to a lot of meaningless games
and the necessity to use the subterfuge of regional telecasts to
get the good teams on. And there are those little commercials
that the NCAA requires about the academic programs of the
colleges, maintaining the fiction that those in charge at the
football factories are interested in well-rounded students.
Woody Hayes' idea of a well-rounded student is one who can
kick 50 yards and run 60.

But mostly what's wrong with the telecasts is Schenkel and
Wilkinson. Part of the problem is their personalities, or lack of
same. Schenkel always reminds me of the kind of guy you
avoid at cocktail parties, which is one reason he can make an
exciting game seem dull. There are other problems, too.

There is, for openers, Schenkel's verbal inaccuracy. He goes
Gifford one step better with names, often getting the wrong
first name with the right last one. He cannot keep downs and
yardage straight. Even when you can hear the stadium
announcer in the background telling everybody it is second-
and-eight, Chris is telling us it is first-and-ten.

There is Wilkinson's compelling desire to be on both sides of
every controversial play. His standard approach when a
penalty is called is to say, "It'll be interesting to see how they
call that," and when it is called, however it is called, to say,
"That's absolutely the right call." Thanks, Bud, for that inside
information.

For vintage Wilkinson, you'd have to take the situation in the
fourth quarter of the Michigan–Ohio State game in 1972, which

decided which team would go to the Rose Bowl. Michigan had a fourth-and-ten on the Ohio State 37 and Wilkinson forthrightly said Michigan should punt. He apparently frightened himself with such candor because when Michigan went for the first down and failed, he said, "They wanted to win. I like that kind of spirit." The only thing that Wilkinson believes in strongly enough to commit himself is that football is a Good Thing. Thus, when Ohio State supporters started to tear down the goal posts before the end of the game, which Michigan could conceivably have tied with a field goal, Wilkinson described the situation as "tragic." C'mon, Bud, let's get serious here.

The bad thing about Wilkinson is that he should be able to provide viewers with a great insight from his experiences as a coach and, before that, as a player. But his unwillingness to take a stand leads him into discussing such inanities as who has the ball the most time. Sometimes, it appears he is going to award a victory to the team which has the ball the longest, even if it happens to trail on the scoreboard.

Then, there is the Schenkel-Wilkinson vocabulary, which seems to consist entirely of words like nifty, wonderful and golly. Do you ever hear those words anywhere else any more?

But what I dislike most of all, about Schenkel and Wilkinson is the fact they can't even see what's happening on the field. In that Michigan–Ohio State game referred to earlier, a Michigan receiver made a diving catch of the ball. Schenkel thought he had missed it, of course. While the officials were signaling first down, the yards markers were being moved up and the players were coming up the field, Chris was prattling on and on about the hometown of the intended receiver and his goals in life. Not until the next play started did he realize what had really happened.

Another example, same game: just before the end of the first half, when Michigan got a first down on the Ohio State one, a Michigan player called time in full view of the cameras right after the play ended. It was the kind of thing any experienced announcer should have been looking for, but Wilkinson missed it completely and started talking about Michigan getting a break with the first down measurement that would stop the clock.

It's ironic that ABC is the leader among the networks in sports programming and that its visual coverage is excellent—after watching the Monday night telecasts on ABC, the games on other networks seem primitive. And yet, we have ABC to thank for Gifford and Schenkel-Wilkinson in its dedicated Hire the Handicapped campaign, and we also have ABC to thank for Howard Cosell. Thanks a lot, ABC.

It's a sad thing about Cosell. I suppose it happens to all celebrities sooner or later. He's starting to believe his own press clippings.

Howard was never your basically lovable guy. He's reveled in being the guy you love to hate, the guy who would ask those embarrassing questions that nobody else dared to. As such, he performed a valuable function. There is a lot of hypocrisy in sports and a lot of phony balloons going up, and somebody has to prick them. There are far more announcers and sportswriters who are willing to inflate those balloons instead of deflating them, and thus, Cosell's anti-Establishment posture was very welcome. But now he has come to regard himself as an institution and has become part of that very Establishment.

I started out liking Cosell, perhaps because I hadn't seen much of him. I liked his iconoclastic approach, and I found it admirable the way he defended Muhammad Ali, pointing out the inequities in the treatment of Ali at a time when others in the broadcast and print media were strangely silent.

But Cosell has long since used up that credit. He has become increasingly strident, increasingly arrogant, increasingly impatient with the slightest criticism; and he who once accused others of investing sports with the importance of the Nuremberg Trials has done the same himself. He has become a member of the Establishment he once fought. We have seen the enemy, Howard, and he is us.

It is an indictment of the road Cosell has traveled that in the '68 Olympics he defended the black athletes who protested on the victory stand, but in the '72 Olympics, he crucified Stan Wright, the hapless coach who gave the wrong times to sprinters Eddie Hart and Ray Robinson. He tried to say that the sprinters had blamed Wright, but they had not; they were considerably more gentlemanly in their treatment of Wright than was Cosell.

Some claim it is all a put-on, that Cosell puts up an abrasive front to cover a sensitive soul. I find no evidence of that. Those who know him best, his colleagues in New York, talk of backstabbing and make cracks about Cosell walking his pet rat.

Apparently, he wants to be loved, like our President; but like our President, he is basically an unlovable person. Oh, to the right people, he can be ingratiating. Wells Twombly likes him and regards him as great company, but Cosell thinks Twombly is a great talent and Twombly thinks Cosell is likewise. They can spend hours in this kind of self-congratulatory embrace, but what does it prove?

With lesser-known writers, he can be less enjoyable. An example happened before the '72 Monday night game between the San Francisco 49ers and the Los Angeles Rams. Cosell had received a death threat in the mail before the previous week's game, in Miami, and Tim Gartner of the *Chronicle* was told to call Cosell about it. Cosell gave Tim a lecture on journalistic responsibility and threatened him if he wrote anything about it, though Tim was only doing his job, as Cosell well knew. Later, Don Meredith told a reporter that he and Gifford had been in the room when Gartner had called Cosell, and that Howard had done it all for their benefit. That doesn't make him out to be any more decent an individual.

To be sure, Cosell has a human side, which he shows when he is criticized. The man who criticizes everybody else cannot take it when criticism is turned on him. We have all heard many times how Cosell was going to quit the Monday night show after the first season because of the criticism he suffered.

Before the previously mentioned game between the 49ers and Rams, I criticized Cosell in print and then watched the balloon go up. At the luncheon given in honor of Cosell, Gifford and Meredith that day in San Francisco, Cosell spent 30 minutes berating me. It was great theater; I even enjoyed it myself. Since Cosell had misunderstood much of what I had said and my basis for saying it, it was hard for me to realize at times that I was his subject.

It was all very revealing, too. Cosell admitted that Rams' owner Carroll Rosenbloom had told him not to say anything, on the very realistic basis that Cosell was a much bigger name and he would only be giving me publicity, but Cosell was wounded and he couldn't let my criticism go unnoticed.

What set him off? Don Klosterman, general manager of the Rams, said to me at the stadium that night that he thought it was my remarks about Cosell being of the Establishment. "He prides himself as being so anti-Establishment," said Klosterman. "He's always taking the liberal viewpoint on everything."

He's so anti-Establishment that he dines with people like Rosenbloom. Obviously, he has terrorized the club owners with his criticism, right?

I think what's happened to Cosell is that, after putting on his act across the country and becoming a very big name, he has decided everybody should like him. Because he is important, a lot of people defer to him and make him think he's liked.

But do they really feel that way? All I can say is that at the Super Bowl party, two months after my criticism of Cosell, a member of the Rams' front office rushed up to me, shook my hand and said, "Everybody in football thanks you for that column on Cosell!"

Sorry about that, Howard.

11

·

Sports And Society: No More Escape Routes

One problem with the pace of modern life is that there seem to be no avenues of escape. There are ever-fewer places to go to get away from it all; vacation spots are mobbed by people like you and me, trying to find leisure if it kills them.

The movies used to be great as an escape. Remember all those great Mickey Rooney–Judy Garland movies, when they played high school students preparing for the prom? Somebody was sure to say, "Hey, let's get Frank Sinatra to sing at our prom!" Which, of course, he would, having nothing better to do that week.

Now, movies mirror the more depressing aspects of life. In one three-month stretch, I saw "Lady Sings the Blues," the fictionalized story of Billie Holiday, a great singer who killed herself with drugs; "Images," a psychological case study of a woman who kills her husband; and "Deliverance," a story of a canoe trip which results in three deaths, a homosexual rape and a man smashing his leg. I finally resisted when friends urged me to see "Cries and Whispers." If I want to watch a woman die of cancer, I'll go to a hospital and save myself the ticket price.

It is the same in sports. Games used to be a method for blacking out reality for an hour or two or three, which is one of the big attractions they have held for our President. But to do that with sports now requires an almost superhuman effort of the will, because sport parallels politics in an almost frightening way.

When the Watergate scandal first started heating up, the Oklahoma recruiting scandal was in the sports pages. It is not unreasonable to suggest the same idea motivated the men involved in both cases: the thought that winning—whether games or an election—was so important that the ends justified the means.

The Olympic Games were organized as a means of promoting sports for themselves, but in recent years, there has been no better example of power politics at play than the Games. Demonstrators have used the Olympics as a forum because they know so many people are watching, and that situation will not get better.

The complaints of white bigots that blacks are moving too fast into jobs and housing are mirrored in sports, where the same men complain there are too many blacks playing, particularly in basketball.

Once, athletes trailed their contemporaries. When students started demonstrating on college campuses, athletes were conspicuously missing. They are no longer, and more and more professional athletes are involved in political campaigns.

When young men started wearing their hair longer and longer, athletes kept their crew cuts. But now, athletes' hair is as long as anybody's—except on those teams silly enough to demand that hair be kept short. It is particularly startling for me to see quarterback Ken Stabler, who comes from the conservative South, wearing his hair shoulder length.

Athletes' clothes were once conservative, but to travel with a pro sports team these days is to be dazzled by the total variety of available clothing styles. Because athletes often have a lot of money and because they are at an age when clothes are often very important and because they have the bodies to show off clothes properly, standing outside a team dressing room sometimes seems almost like attending a fashion show.

The generation gap exists in sports, particularly in baseball, where men who are aware of what their players are thinking—

like Chuck Tanner of the White Sox—are unfortunately rare.

The drug problem is at least as serious in sports as elsewhere, to the point where demands are being made for urinalysis of players after games. Young athletes are as prone to defy their elders by smoking marijuana as any college students, and stories about athletes being picked up for possession of marijuana are becoming commonplace.

And, of course, athletes are also caught up in the sexual revolution. The Fritz Peterson–Mike Kekich wife swap should hardly be shocking to a society in which swap clubs are ever more prevalent.

This coming together of sports and society has caused a lot of problems within the individual sports. In the next three chapters, I'd like to discuss some of the main problems that beset football, baseball and basketball—the three major American sports.

12

·

Football And
The Hubris Problem

Whenever there is discussion of why pro football has usurped baseball's position as the No. 1 sport, there are a lot of reasons given: 1) Baseball is primarily a rural sport, football an urban one, and our nation has become urban; 2) Baseball is a gentle sport, football a violent one, and we have become a more violent people; 3) Baseball is too slow for the pace of modern life; 4) Football televises so much better than baseball.

I even saw an unusual explanation in *Harper's Magazine* by Anton Myrer, author of *Once an Eagle,* to the effect that baseball was our favorite as long as we were an optimistic people, because the game is never over until the last man is out. Football puts a time element on success; it is much more difficult to be optimistic when you are down by three touchdowns in a football game with four minutes to go than if you are down by three runs in a baseball game with an inning left.

All of these arguments are persuasive, but I still feel the chief reason for football's ascendency is the NFL organization. Commissioner Pete Rozelle is a former public relations man who has never lost sight of the lessons he learned, and his staff is heavily weighted toward public relations men. They have done a great job of selling pro football to the media and to the fans.

Rozelle is a marvel. When he visits a city, for instance, his secretary briefs him on whom he will meet in the area and what writers he will see and what they have just written. Thus, when he arrives in the city, he can greet everybody by his first name with seeming spontaneity and talk about what the person has just done. That is the ploy of a successful politician.

Rozelle and his staff are always accessible to the media. If I put in a call to the NFL offices, I can be sure of getting somebody who can answer my question within 10-15 minutes at the most. This is very important, because the NFL offices can usually turn away wrath with a soft statement. A personal example: once, when the Raiders were scheduled to play the Thanksgiving Day game in Detroit, an onerous assignment which turned out as badly as the Raiders anticipated, Al Davis was grumbling his usual grumbles about getting screwed by the league office. Since I know Rozelle has no great fondness for Davis, I thought that might be a possibility, so I called Jim Kensil, who explained at great length exactly how the schedule had been drawn up for that game for years to come and why the Raiders were playing in it. The story I wrote was thus quite different than it might have been if I had proceeded without that information.

Trying to get this kind of information out of the baseball people is virtually impossible. My head is still reeling from an experience I had in 1971, in the middle of Vida Blue's great year.

I was trying to find out from the American League office whether Blue's contract had been rewritten by Finley, as it should have been, when he gave Vida that abominable Cadillac. League President Joe Cronin was en route to Cooperstown at the time and could not, his secretary said, be reached for the next three days! Finally, I reached Cronin's assistant, Bob Holbrook, but that was no help. Holbrook, who was a newspaperman himself at one time but has largely forgotten what it was like, said, "Are you trying to stir up something here?" He wouldn't answer my question, and that's what passes for public relations in baseball.

The NFL propaganda machine is without parallel in sports. You have to witness it at Super Bowl time, when the machine is at its best, to fully appreciate it. A whole week is devoted to promoting saturation coverage of one game, and there is hardly a misstep the whole time. As it happened, in just over a three-month period (October, 1972–January, 1973), I had the experience of covering a World Series, a Super Bowl and an NBA All-Star game, and the NFL's promotion was so much better as to make the other sports seem as if they were still in the Dark Ages.

Not all the promotion is original. Baseball was the first to show how important timing and location can be with its spring training sites. Spring training has always received far more attention than it deserved for one simple reason: it takes place in the sunshine of Florida and Arizona. Writers from the north are eager to leave the cold and snow of their home areas to get to the warm country, and they file reams of copy to justify their presence.

Benefiting from that example, Rozelle has tried to keep the Super Bowl in warm cities. He did a first-rate job of brainwashing immediately, getting people to think of the game differently so he could put it where he wanted it. Typically, Jets coach Weeb Ewbank was quoted later as saying that it was good for the Super Bowl to be in a neutral site but it wouldn't be fair to the teams' fans to have a championship game moved. The distinction between a conference championship game and the Super Bowl was nonexistent, but Rozelle had planted the seed well.

There have been a few mistakes with the game, though. Going to Los Angeles for the first time was one because the citizens wisely concluded that the Super Bowl would be a bummer and thus stayed away. Los Angeles fans are like that, as Rozelle should have remembered from his time with the Rams. They will support the best in phenomenal numbers but won't touch anything they regard as only No. 2; Avis would hate them. Thus, the UCLA basketball team has sold out every game since Kareem Abdul-Jabbar was Lew Alcindor and the great USC football teams outdraw the Rams, but the good UCLA football teams and good USC basketball teams have played in virtual privacy. And thus, when Super Bowl VII returned to Los Angeles, it sold out because it was by then the best attraction of its kind. The game itself was less interesting than the first Super Bowl, but that made no difference.

Taking the Super Bowl to Miami was a great move, because the city received it well (as a town, Miami is no more sophisticated than Dubuque) and the Dolphins were out of Super Bowl contention. It would have been the best thing that happened to the game had both situations remained that way, because Miami was also ideally set up to handle the game at that time of year, because of its weather and hotel accommodations; unfortunately, the Dolphins got very good very fast under Don Shula and an attorney's suit to get the game on local television made Rozelle decide to move the game around, trying to alternate conference cities.

Other cities have not been so wise a choice. New Orleans has had some cold weather in its two times hosting the game, and the city, though a charming one, does not have the hotel facilities to accommodate the large influx of people at Super Bowl time.

Los Angeles is so spread out, the Coliseum was an hour's bus ride from the press headquarters and the team practice fields, located in Long Beach and Orange County. In fact, for the '73 Super Bowl, *everything* seemed to be an hour's ride away.

The situation won't get any better, either, because of the shortage of cities that meet all the conditions. San Diego, for instance, would be great from the weather standpoint, but its stadium seats barely over 50,000 and hotel accommodations are insufficient. The San Francisco area has been considered, and Stanford Stadium's 90,000 seats would be ideal, but the January weather is usually rainy. Still, as long as Rozelle keeps the game away from Buffalo, everybody will remain reasonably happy.

Everything possible is done for the press during Super Bowl week. For openers, the teams are brought in a week early. At the '73 Super Bowl, George Allen suggested the teams would be better off coming in Thursday or Friday. From a competitive standpoint, he had a point, but Rozelle ignored the suggestion, not even dignifying it with comment. Allen still thinks what happens on the field is most important; Rozelle is concerned with the number of newspaper articles and television interviews.

Rozelle always makes himself accessible during that week. He holds a press conference that is always a classic of its kind. He answers every question that is asked, and there are a lot of them; he laughs, frowns and jokes at all the right times. He plays his audience like a fisherman landing a prize marlin, and he has the politician's knack of turning away tough questions with soft answers. A Rozelle press conference always leaves a writer with plenty of things to hang a story on, but Pete is not giving away any secrets. Every time I've been at a Rozelle press conference, I came away feeling it was really a good one; and every time I have sat down at a typewriter after such a conference, I had to search futilely for something really worth writing a story about. Rozelle has learned that style can often substitute for substance, if the style is good enough.

And even so recalcitrant a coach as Allen is brought in for the ritual press conferences, though kicking and screaming all the way. Allen made no secret of the fact he thought it all a waste of time—and, considering his answers to the questions, it probably was—but he was there.

That is by no means all. NFL publicity is something like the service at great restaurants: it is there even before you realize you need it.

During the Super Bowl week in 1973, for instance, the big story was home television. In response to politicians on every level, even reaching to the Presidency, Rozelle had announced he would allow the game to be televised in the Los Angeles area if all the tickets were sold a week before the game. They were and he did. The NFL office then made available an impressive piece of research on television and its impact on pro football, citing historical precedents and current realities. Few writers have the time or energy to research all this, and therefore, it is much easier just to use the NFL research which, naturally, favors the NFL position.

Nor is the week all work. There are recreations, from golf tournaments to fashion shows, for the wives, and writers who plan ahead in the matter (most do) are never more than 50 yards from a free drink. Each year, the NFL throws a big party for anybody remotely connected with the game, including press. In 1973, there was a party on the Queen Mary; I was mildly surprised that Rozelle didn't arrange to have the ship make one last voyage for our benefit.

I won't pretend I don't like this; being treated like royalty is never a bore. But it bothers me, because it creates an atmosphere in which it is almost impossible to write anything but the company line.

One writer said to me on our way out to the Queen Mary, "You get so excited during this week, you forget how bad the previous Super Bowls have been." Exactly. This is the greatest triumph of NFL publicity: against all odds, it makes everybody think the upcoming Super Bowl will be interesting.

One of the few predictions I care to look back at came in a column I wrote for the *Chronicle* two days before the '73 Super Bowl:

> On the surface, Sunday's game appears to be a very attractive matchup. Miami is trying to be the first 17-0 team in pro football history, and Washington is striking a blow for the senior citizens of the world. But if precedent holds, it will most likely be the kind of game you'd turn off in the second quarter if it were being played in midseason.

It took no great prescience to make that prediction; the Super Bowl has been a bummer most of the time. Most of the games have been lopsided. Green Bay won the first two easily, 35-10 over Kansas City and 33-14 over Oakland; Kansas City beat Minnesota, 23-7, in a game that was much more lopsided than the score; the highlight of the 24-3 romp by Dallas over Miami was Tom Brookshier's noninterview with Duane Thomas after the game; only Garo Yapremian's unsuccessful debut as a passer made the '73 Super Bowl at all suspenseful, and the '74 game was lopsided.

Only twice in the first seven years was there any real suspense. The best was the third game. Baltimore was a heavy favorite and some writers were predicting a final score as high as 44-0, but the Jets, behind Joe Namath, won, 16-7. In the fifth game, Baltimore outlasted Dallas, 16-13, in a game that seemed scripted by Woody Allen. Baltimore lost four fumbles and had three interceptions; Dallas lost one fumble and also had three interceptions. Eleven turnovers in a game supposedly involving the best teams of two conferences!

Why is this game so often a bad one? Part of the reason is physical. The teams that survive are usually the teams with the best defenses, and defensive football is dull football. Fans pay to see touchdowns, not punts.

There is also the fact that the playoff situation makes it possible for the best teams to get eliminated, because a team must win both a playoff game and a championship game, and a bad day can eliminate a good team. Most of the close observers in the American Conference, for instance, thought that Oakland was a better team than Baltimore in 1970 and Kansas City a better team than Miami the following year, but neither team made it to the Super Bowl.

But most of all, the mental pressure has beaten the losers in this game. In the first two games, Kansas City and Oakland were beaten before they took the field because they believed in the superiority of the NFL.

That kind of pressure hasn't existed for the AFL or American Conference since the Jets beat Baltimore—the pendulum has, in fact, swung the other way—but there is still more pressure for this game than for the other major sports championships, simply because it is one game. In baseball, basketball and hockey, a team can recover from a bad game; in the '73 NBA playoffs, the Knicks lost by 30 points to the Celtics in the opener of their playoff series, yet came back to win that series and ultimately the championship. But there is no recourse for a team that has a bad day in the Super Bowl. (Or, as Frank Gifford, Curt Gowdy, Lindsay Nelson, Chris Schenkel et al. would say, "There's no tomorrow.")

The buildup leading to the game is hardly believable. Sometimes it seems every newspaper with a circulation larger than the publisher's immediate family is represented and journalists and TV and radio people besiege the athletes. It is totally unlike anything that happens in the season, even for the biggest games.

A team that has been to the Super Bowl once is better prepared for this kind of pressure the second time around, which is one reason why Green Bay, Kansas City, Baltimore, Dallas and Miami have all won in their second Super Bowl appearances.

It was this which prompted Al Davis, who usually is smarter than that, to propose a best-of-three Super Bowl series, the better to determine the best team. It would do that, but it wouldn't be worth it.

Three Super Bowls? I don't think any of us could stand the strain. Who would want to take the responsibility for the added stress on family life, for instance? Adding two more Super Bowls would seem to be cruel and unusual punishment for the housewives of America. And what if three Super Bowls turned out to be just as dreadful as the one with which we've been afflicted? Could the American sports fan stand it? Could the game of football?

But mostly I think of my own, the sportswriters, who would have to come up with three weeks of what we call rainy day stories, because by the end of football season, everything that can be said about the Super Bowl teams and players has already been said, usually several times. In the seven years of the Super Bowl, there have been only two noteworthy stories that have come out of the week preceding the game: Joe Namath's "I guarantee" prediction and the rumored involvement of Kansas City quarterback Len Dawson with gamblers—a story which was later disproved. Even by the sorry standards of American sports journalism, that's pretty bad.

But since the sportswriters are there, they'll continue to write stories to justify their existence, whether the stories are any good or not. Thus, in a best-of-three Super Bowl series, we'd get three weeks of stories about Billy Kilmer's reputation for living well or George Allen's passion for ice cream. Are you ready for that? I don't know what the answer to the Super Bowl problem is, but I'm sure it isn't extending the Super Bowl to a best-of-three series.

In addition to the seemingly insoluble Super Bowl problem, pro football has other problems, physical and psychological. Physically, it is limited for two reasons: 1) Most teams have to share a stadium with baseball teams, which have priority when it comes to scheduling; 2) The demands of the sport more and more make it a survival of the fittest and not a test of which team is really the best.

Ideally, the football season should end at least three weeks sooner than it does because the December weather in many NFL cities is treacherous; having to play in Buffalo, Green Bay, Detroit, Minneapolis, Boston, New York, Philadelphia and

Chicago in late season is to risk pneumonia. (Having the season end sooner might make it possible to get the playoffs in before Christmas, too, thus taking away Rozelle's image as the grinch who stole Christmas.)

But because of the problems of getting into home stadiums that are shared with baseball teams, it is impossible to start the league season any sooner. As it is, a team which shares a stadium with a World Series baseball team is in bad trouble. The Jets didn't get into Shea Stadium until the sixth game of the '69 season because the Mets won the World Series, and when they finally did play there, the field was in terrible shape because the infantile Mets' supporters had torn great chunks out of it in celebration of the Mets' win.

As players get bigger and bigger, injuries get worse and worse. Hardly a team gets through the schedule without at least one crippling injury. Some are worse than others; when Joe Namath is injured, the Jets' season comes screeching to a standstill. But all injuries are serious because they so often mean that the teams with the least injuries are the ones which succeed, regardless of quality.

There seems to be no halting the injury wave. Artificial turf was trumpeted as the answer once, but if anything, it has made injuries worse, not better. I have yet to talk to a player who likes artificial turf, though owners and coaches sometimes go to great lengths to try to say the players like it. Just before the 49ers moved into Candlestick Park with its artificial turf, they played a game at the University of Washington stadium in Seattle and coach Dick Nolan took a private poll of the players about the artificial turf there. He claimed that virtually every member of the approximately 60-man squad (during the early days of training camp) liked the stuff, but in my conversations with the 49ers then and later, they all complained about it.

The preseason camps that are becoming more and more common in pro football are also adding to the injury danger, and Ed Garvey, president of the NFL Players' Association, was led to complain in the spring of 1973 that these camps were becoming more and more formalized, with coaches demanding that players attend or risk losing their jobs.

Probably the biggest problem from Rozelle's standpoint has been the home television issue. He fought the good fight against lifting the blackout on home games but was on the losing side of the issue. In September, 1973, Congress voted to lift the blackout on games sold out 72 hours in advance.

It was a popular decision but—I think—a bad one. The NFL has prospered because of an intelligent television policy. Games have been televised on the road but not at home, where they would be competition for the product the owners are pushing. Then, too, as Rozelle has said, pro football is in danger of becoming a studio game because it televises so well. In many cases, people can see the game better on television than they can in person, and they do not have the attendant problems of getting to the game, getting parking, getting baby sitters.

The first weekend that the blackout was lifted, the NFL announced that the "no shows" (those who had bought tickets but had not come to the game) amounted to nearly seven percent of the ticket buyers. The prospect was that it would get worse as the weather got worse.

When people who have bought tickets don't come to the games, owners don't get that concession and parking money. It also changes the game materially, as anybody who has watched sparsely attended games knows. The players react to a filled stadium and play better, and fans feel more as if they're in the game.

There is also an implied obligation to the fans who come to the game. Televising home games rewards those who do not come, who have not supported the product, and punishes those who have bought season tickets. No successful business operates that way. As I noted in an earlier chapter, I don't like the system of season tickets and would like to see it changed, but home television of all games is not the answer.

But the biggest problem that faces pro football today is none of these but the arrogance and indifference of the owners. Pro football owners are the fattest of cats right now, and the general attitude of most owners in all sports—let'em eat cake— is magnified in football. These guys know they've got the best operation going, and they aren't about to make any changes.

Their attitude toward the ticket holders is the most obvious, as they continue to raise prices even in the face of record-breaking profits. Their attitude toward the game is just as revealing. They seem loath to make any changes at all, content they have the best game in town.

Part of this inaction is due to the outmoded NFL constitution, which calls for 20 of the 26 clubs to approve any rule change. "The United States can go to war on a simple majority vote of the Congress," says Tex Schramm, president of the Dallas Cowboys and one of the progressive men in the sport. "The Supreme Court knocked down the death penalty by a 5-4 vote. Yet, the NFL can't decide two-point conversions by a majority vote."

Such changes as have been made by the NFL in recent years have been minor. The decision to move the hash marks closer to the center of the field was greeted as an earth-shaking revolution, and nobody thought to ask why they didn't just bring the ball back to the exact center each time, if opening up the field was what they wanted.

There are some areas of the game which could be changed. Simply abolishing the zone defense would make the game at least 50 percent more exciting than it is now. One of the great joys of football used to be watching the great receiver and great defensive back in their individual battles. Now, there is none of that. It is like watching the 440 run on two curves: until the final straightaway, you don't know who's leading, and until the ball arrives, you don't know who's got the pass defense responsibility.

There should be a way out of all the tie games. More and more, coaches are playing first not to lose and then to win the game if they can, though hardly anybody is satisfied with a tie game.

At the April, 1973 meeting of pro football owners, a proposal—backed by Rozelle—was made to have sudden death for tie games to force teams to come to a conclusion. I don't think that's the answer, for a lot of reasons.

What you see is not what you get. Sudden death inevitably reminds fans of the Kansas City-Miami playoff in 1971, or the Dallas Texans-Houston Oilers championship game in 1962. Both were very exciting games because so much was riding on them, and sudden death added an extra dimension to the game.

But what sudden death really means during the regular season is this: picture Philadelphia and New Orleans going into the game at 2-7 and 1-8 and then slogging through to a 13-13 tie in a game that has fans booing in the first quarter and leaving in the third. With a sudden death provision, these teams would have to play an additional quarter.

Who needs that?

There are other problems with sudden death. The injury factor would be much greater. If teams had to play extra time, the chance of injuries would increase geometrically, because far more injuries occur when a player is tired than when he is fresh.

It would unfairly penalize some teams. Imagine a situation in which Cleveland and Cincinnati are tied for the lead in their division and scheduled to play each other in two weeks. Cleveland wins its game in regulation time the week before but Cincinnati is forced to play an extra 24 minutes in its game and suffers a couple of key injuries during that time. Can you imagine the screaming from Cincinnati?

And, sudden death would change the whole structure of the game. Football is geared to 60 minutes, and the game's excitement comes from the fact that time is such an important factor. Sudden death would change this, and you wouldn't have the same game.

I'm flattering the NFL owners by implying they considered all these things carefully and deliberately, and then decided the weight of logic was against the sudden death proposal. No doubt what actually happened is this: they realized the television networks would be upset, looked at their watches and saw they were late for the cocktail hour and thus decided to table the proposal, with no discussion.

The following April, under the pressure of the sudden existence of the World Football League, the NFL did adopt sudden death and several other changes, too, to liven up the game. But they didn't adopt the two-point conversion, which could have helped, because of its fatal association with the old AFL.

Used properly, the two-point conversion adds something to a game because a team that is seven points behind could win with a touchdown and a two-point conversion. But coaches have managed to take away much of the impact of the rule because they won't take the chance of losing a game by going for a two-point conversion when they're a point behind. Coaches are not the greatest gamblers in our society; they'll take the tie every time. Two examples: in a 1971 game with Kansas City, Oakland coach John Madden went for a tying field goal when the ball was inches away from the goal rather than risk going for a winning touchdown; on the last play of the game, Minnesota coach Bud Grant tried for a 45-yard field goal rather than a touchdown in the season-ending '72 game with the 49ers, though a field goal would only have tied the score and done nothing for the Vikings' divisional standing.

There is a method by which coaches would be forced to use the rule more than they would like, however, and that is by doing away with the very concept of a tie game, by making the team which scored the tying point the loser. It would work like this: Suppose Chicago is trailing Detroit by 24-17 with a minute to go and scores when Bobby Douglass, back to pass, runs instead for a touchdown. Now, if the Bears kick the extra point, they would still be the losers. Thus, they would have to try for the two-point conversion, giving them a chance to win—or lose. Under this system, the only games that would be ties would be 0-0 games, a statistically negligible area, and they could be counted half win, half loss, as all ties are now. Coupled with a two-point conversion, that would force coaches into some interesting strategical moves and open up the game.

But don't look for it to happen. Owners and coaches are too convinced they have the best game in the world, and nobody has thought to point out to them that, despite all the hoopla surrounding them, an awful lot of games are just plain dull. But some day, even the fans are going to catch on that the emperor has no clothes, and the best efforts of Pete Rozelle and Co. won't be enough to repair the damage.

13

·

Baseball's Hardening Of The Arteries

Baseball is in real trouble, which will come as no surprise to anybody who has been watching the sport in recent years. Part of the problem is not of the sport's own making, and part of it is, but unless these problems are at least partially solved, the decline that has hit the sport in recent years will accelerate.

The foremost problem not of the sport's own making is the advent of the new stadiums, particularly those with artificial turf. You have only to watch a game at Wrigley Field or Fenway Park to realize what baseball has lost in the new multipurpose stadiums.

At its best, baseball is an intimate game, a game in which fans and players are almost close enough to each other to touch. Unlike football players, baseball players are not totally obscured by warlike uniforms, and they are recognizable to the fans. You watch football; you nearly participate in baseball. Fans can talk to the players almost until the first pitch is thrown, and they talk at them even after the game has started. In extreme cases, there is interaction between fans and players during the game, as in the case of Ted Williams and the Boston fans.

At a place like Wrigley Field, you quickly learn what baseball is all about. It is a comfortable place, built for baseball and nothing else, with the stands so close to the field that it seems fans are almost in the batting box. A fan who yells at a player, manager, coach or umpire is sure to be heard; in the new stadiums, his voice would be lost.

Wrigley Field and Fenway Park can be tough parks to play in, particularly for pitchers, and the creature comforts aren't always what they are in the new parks. Indeed, at Wrigley Field, the players claim there are rats running through the passageway they take to get to the field. But the players still like it; Giants' pitcher Don Carrithers once told me how much he liked the park right after a game in which he had been knocked out as the Cubs went on to score 18 runs, which would surely seem to be the acid test.

"It's like the old days, hearing the fans," Giants' manager Charlie Fox once told me. "At Candlestick, people ask me why I don't make any signs to them when they yell at me, but I can't hear them because they're so far away. At Wrigley Field, you can hear them; boy, how you can hear them. They're really loud, but they know their baseball."

The game is played at a leisurely pace, but in the old parks, nobody cares. Fans sing or clap in time to the music played by the organist, they buy an extra beer or bag of peanuts and just relax. At its best, baseball is a truly relaxing experience. Time doesn't matter for the period spent in the ballpark; only the innings count.

In the old parks, baseball is also an individual game. At Wrigley Field, the fences are easily reached and the direction of the wind is vitally important; if it is blowing out, you can expect a high-scoring game. Even if it isn't, Wrigley Field is a good park for hitters because it has a good background. At Fenway, the Green Monster in left field affects the whole game and changes managerial and pitching strategy, and in both parks, the games are experiences that cannot be duplicated in the next park and town.

The new parks are precisely the opposite. They are cold, unyielding and virtually identical. Unless you look at the scoreboard, it is difficult to tell if you are in St. Louis or Pittsburgh or

Atlanta. The fences are all about the same distance away; the foul area is about the same. It makes for consistency, but it is a dull sort of consistency, and the spurious attempts by management to enliven the operation with exploding scoreboards and other artificial touches can't make up for what has been lost.

The stands are a long way from the field, too, out of necessity; in building the multipurpose stadiums, there has to be extra room to allow for the conversion from sport to sport. That matters little to football, because fans are conditioned to being a long distance from the field. Indeed, it is probably better that way, because it's difficult to see much about a football game if you're too close, particularly if you're low. But for baseball, that distance is fatal because you no longer get the necessary interaction between fans and players.

You don't have the kind of yelling at a baseball game that you have at football games. It is much more restrained, an individual thing, a fan yelling his individual complaint at a player, manager or umpire. If the person being yelled at can't hear the complaint, there is no longer any reason to voice it, and thus the fan's voice is stilled.

And the new stadiums have artificial turf, as I've said before, to my mind one of the biggest con jobs ever perpetrated on American sports. Though many reasons have been advanced for the use of artificial turf, the one prevailing reason is economy: it is much cheaper to install artificial turf because of the immediate and drastic reduction in maintenance costs. But, at the same time, you also change the game in undesirable ways.

Baseball played on artificial turf is a travesty. It eliminates much of the excitement in the game because nobody can take a chance. An outfielder can't take a chance on a diving catch because the ball may bounce right over his head. And you don't get any suspense on whether a ball hit between the outfielders will be a double, triple or even inside-the-park home run because the damn thing usually hops right over the fence for a ground rule double.

Artificial turf has eliminated the smart infielders who compensated for lack of speed with their knowledge—Eddie Stanky would be a striking example—because they can't compensate for their lack of speed on an artificial turf field.

No longer are there distinct differences between the infields in different parks, either. The groundskeeper was once as valuable as a 20-game winner because by delicately shading the baselines in or out, he could make bunts roll foul or stay in, depending on whether his team had good bunters or not. By letting the grass grow a little long, he could help the slow infielders on his team. As an extreme example, Giants' groundskeeper Matty Schwab watered the baselines so heavily in 1962, to keep Maury Wills from running wild, that the Dodgers referred to the area as a lake—and manager Alvin Dark was known as the "Swamp Fox."

Artificial turf is just a further step in the trend to depersonalize baseball which started long ago with the first night game. Baseball is a day game and a summer game, and it suffers because the owners, seeking the immediate nickel at the expense of the future dollar, have turned it into a night game and extended the season so it encroaches on winter at both ends.

Those damnable transistor radios were next, and people soon got so they weren't certain what they were seeing unless they could hear it on the transistor, too. Along about the same time, television invaded baseball and nearly ruined the sport; indeed, a case could be made that television is the worst single thing ever to hit baseball, and not just because TV made certain the virtual demise of the minor leagues. Who would pay to see Class C at home when the majors were on the tube?

Baseball televises very poorly because of the nature of the game. You can get most of the action in a football game simply by watching the ball, but when something is happening in a baseball game, there are at least two areas of action—where the ball is and where the runner is. Television cannot capture that, and you can't talk back to the TV set, either, as you can to a manager or umpire or player.

What we are seeing, then, is no longer baseball as it was but a synthetic imitation that is not nearly so much fun. I can even understand why people say it was more fun watching the old minor league teams than the present major league ones. Even allowing for the blurring of memory by time, they may be right.

In an effort to speed up the pace of the game, which its critics claim is its major problem, owners have gone to ever-greater lengths in their use of the fancy electronic scoreboards and message boards. These haven't worked. The message boards can be a help. In some cities, for instance, the board lists the starting lineups and all the batting averages, and I'm for anything that keeps the fans informed. But on balance, they're bad, for several reasons.

One is that the message board operators are not always the most imaginative people around. At the Oakland Coliseum, the operator seems content to flash such zingers as "Beep beep" for Campy Campaneris, whose nickname is "Roadrunner," and the first names of ballplayers. When Joe Rudi is up, for instance, the board alternately flashes "Joe" and "Go." Clever.

I believe it was Walter O'Malley, bless his mercenary soul, who first started using the boards to promote his business by mentioning the names of all the groups attending the game. "Hi, there, Anaheim Lions Club, and the Senior Citizens of Pasadena." Now, all the clubs do it.

But even if the message boards are used with some imagination, they are bad for the game because baseball does not lend itself to organized cheering. Trying to make it more like football by message board cheers does the game a distinct disservice, but this is what is happening. Fans no longer know when or how to cheer unless the message board flashes it at them. If the boards ever went out for a full game, I fear a dreadful silence would descend over the park for nine innings.

Moreover, the possibilities of message board hypnosis are frightening. Imagine one flashing, "Buy a beer, buy a beer." You might get trampled in the aisles. Or, at the Oakland Coliseum, they may yet flash a sign, "You will love Charlie Finley."

That's going too far.

So much for the problems that beset baseball more or less from the outside. There are just as many others that are entirely the fault of the game's management. Probably the worst thing that ever happened to baseball was being top dog for so long; the second worst thing is that nobody in baseball seems to realize that that situation no longer exists. When you're No. 1, you can do anything and get away with it, but since baseball began its slide, there has been little attempt to consider what the fans really want.

Consider, for openers, the location of the clubs. The attitude of club owners everywhere has been, "Support us or else!" by which they mean that if attendance drops below the level they think good, away goes the team. This is incredible arrogance for a sport that depends on the goodwill of the fans and the tax money of same. They are playing in municipally owned ball-parks (except for O'Malley's Dodgers in Los Angeles) and usually have had roads put in to handle their traffic, not to mention the extra city employees, particularly police, who have to be used on game days. Even so, the owners remain indifferent to the fan.

The worst example is still Milwaukee. When the Boston Braves moved there in 1952, Milwaukee was the great success story of the majors. The people were wild about major league baseball and turned out in huge numbers, setting a National League attendance record, which was later broken by the Los Angeles Dodgers. Then, enthusiasm cooled and, before anybody realized what was happening, the Braves were in Atlanta. Later, Milwaukee got the Seattle expansion franchise, but that was hardly compensation.

There are other cases. The Giants were moved from New York to San Francisco, and now that attendance has fallen off there, rumblings persist that the Giants might move back East, this time to New Jersey.

The Athletics moved from Philadelphia to Kansas City, but that wasn't enough for Charlie Finley, who shopped every city from Louisville to Seattle before settling on Oakland. But attendance has not been good in Oakland, and there are constant rumors that Finley would like to move elsewhere. At this point, the question is where, since baseball has mined out virtually every good location.

When you start detailing the moves, you can get a little dizzy. The Washington Senators became the Minnesota Twins, and another expansion club was moved into Washington. That team eventually became the Texas Rangers, and then the San Diego Padres were sold to a Washington ownership.

A year after the A's were moved to Oakland, there was an expansion team in Kansas City. The St. Louis Browns became the Baltimore Orioles; an expansion team lasted only one year in Seattle and became the Milwaukee Brewers; the Giants moved from New York to San Francisco and the Dodgers from Brooklyn to Los Angeles, and expansion clubs were put in Houston, Montreal and Anaheim. I've probably left somebody out, but it's understandable: since the first move 20 years ago— of the Braves in 1952—14 of the 24 major league clubs have been moved or newly created.

Sometimes the moves have been inevitable and have been made with sufficient forethought. The Browns obviously couldn't stay in St. Louis, and the Braves' first move and the Giants' move were both necessary.

Others, though, have been examples of cupidity or short-sightedness or just plain stupidity, and sometimes a combination of all three. O'Malley moved to Los Angeles because he guessed, quite accurately, that he could make more money there. (Ironically, he gave as his reason that he couldn't continue to compete on equal terms with the Braves because of their fantastic attendance in Milwaukee.) Typically, Walter brought Horace Stoneham along with him and gave poor Horace the short end of the stick. All it takes is a glance at the comparative populations of the Los Angeles and San Francisco areas, and a sideways look at the summer temperature readings, to know which club is more likely to have good attendance figures.

The American League moved into Seattle without giving the matter any thought at all. That is, I assume there was no thought given to it, because anybody who looked at the picture for any time at all would have had to say that Seattle was a poor risk indeed. The city has an ocean on one side and virtually no population on two others, and it is a one-industry (Boeing) town. Typically, the American League moved in at a time when that one industry was in a decline and Seattle was in a definite recession. The Pilots had only rickety old Sick Stadium to play in, and they charged high prices for an inferior team. It's hard to imagine worse planning than that.

Other moves have made little more sense. Consider, for instance, the move of the Washington franchise to the Dallas–Fort Worth (Arlington) area. What the league should have done was to find a buyer for the club and get Robert Short out because the problem with the Washington franchise was more Short than anything else. He had traded away half his ball club for an over-the-hill Denny McLain, he was paying a huge salary to McLain and he also wound up with Curt Flood when the outfielder decided to sue baseball. As a result, the Senators were a bad team and poorly supported, as you could expect. When the club was moved to Arlington, it continued to do poorly on the field and at the gate.

The National League's decision to put an expansion club in San Diego was hardly the smartest, either. San Diego is in much the same position as Seattle—except worse. There is ocean on one side, Baja California on another, desert on a third and Los Angeles on the fourth. Thus, though the city itself is the second largest in the state, the metropolitan area is relatively small and there is nobody to draw from once you get outside that area.

San Diego is also a poor risk town for any sports franchise because there are just too many options available to residents. In January, you can go skin diving, and clubs hope for bad weather on game days so people will stay away from the beach.

With all that, San Diego might have made it with a decent team, but the area has never had anything but expansion teams or teams in newly formed leagues. Adding another expansion team was an insult, and the fans stayed away.

And thus, San Diego owner C. Arnholt Smith, a friend of the President's, sold the Padres to a Washington, D.C. group which wanted to move a club back into the nation's capital. Typical of baseball owners, Smith wanted to just drop out of a stadium lease with the city which had 15 years to run. The city sued, which caused the deal to fall through, and Ray Kroc bought the club and kept it in San Diego.

Owners have never figured the long-range results of all these moves, preferring to make immediate profits. But now, the long-range and short-range results are combining; moving franchises is just pure bad business.

This could have been predicted because baseball—and any sport—is selling vicarious enjoyment. You go out to the park to root for the home team because you care. When teams are moved so quickly and so easily, it becomes a lot more difficult to care. How many Milwaukee fans could develop the enthusiasm for the Brewers they once had for the Braves?

At first, moving a franchise proved to be at least a short-term success because people were so hungry for big league baseball, they'd turn out even for bad teams. But the thrill is gone now. Major league baseball is no longer a novelty anywhere. Even if there has been no team in the area, most fans have been close enough to see a team in another area or have seen it on television. Thus, expansion teams Seattle and San Diego have been abysmal failures; thus, moving to Oakland was no panacea for the A's; thus, moving the Senators to Arlington failed. What next, Bowie Kuhn?

What should be done next is to make an attempt to restore public confidence. It wouldn't be easy because of all the tricks that have already been played, but there are a couple of steps which could be taken. First, the owners should face the fact that there are simply too many teams. Expansion has diluted the product and made too many bad teams, and there are not 24 cities left that can support teams well. Thus, the majors should be cut back to anywhere from 16 to 20 teams. And then, each team should sign a contract that would bind it to a city for at least 10 years, and baseball should have in its bylaws a stipulation that no move will be approved for at least that length of time. Then, fans might redevelop loyalty for their hometown teams.

None of this is likely to happen because there is no leadership at the top. Kuhn is largely a cipher. He smiles a lot and says he loves baseball, and that's enough for the owners. Even if Kuhn were the same kind of man Pete Rozelle is, which he isn't, he wouldn't be able to do what Rozelle can do. The owners make the decisions, not Kuhn. He is only a high-priced lackey. If he should try to exert his authority, he would go the way of William D. Eckert, and he knows it.

When the owners have this kind of power, chaos is inevitable. I don't think football owners are any more rational than baseball—football is, after all, saddled with Bud Adams and George Halas—but they don't have the opportunity that baseball owners have to throw sand into the machinery.

The difference between baseball and football in the handling of labor problems is instructive. When football had its problems in 1970, forcing the cancellation of a part of the training camps, Rozelle stepped in and worked a settlement before any games could be lost. In contrast, when baseball had problems the next spring, nothing could be done before the season started and games were lost. As a result, all teams played an abbreviated schedule and teams played uneven numbers of games; that fact decided the American League East, where Detroit finished a half game ahead of Boston by virtue of having played one more game and won that game.

And the very next spring, baseball had more labor problems, though this one was solved before any games were lost.

Baseball's lack of leadership really hurts in these situations because Kuhn lacks the power to bring the two sides together, and some of the owners dislike Marvin Miller, the players' negotiator, so much they can hardly deal with him. The more extreme owners—such as Gussie Busch—don't want to even recognize the fact that the players have organized. And the owners' negotiator, John Gaherin, has had no authority at all, being forced to go back to the owners to determine their thinking every time something new is proposed. That is guaranteed to force negotiation to proceed at a snail's pace.

This has hurt both sides; even Kuhn noted during the '73 dispute that baseball isn't an indispensable part of American society. The grasp that sports have on the public seems very firm but it is a tenuous grasp, because it is all based on an illusion, not reality. Why should a grown man really care whether the Reds are better than the A's at playing a child's game? Does it really enrich a person or a city to have major league sports available? Chambers of Commerce invariably think so, but it is a fact that San Francisco was major league before the Giants arrived and Oakland has never reached that status with four major league teams.

Why, then, the popularity of sports? Part of it is plain habit. Fans go to games because they've been going since childhood and it does not occur to them not to go. When that habit is broken, the sport suffers—as baseball did during the '72 season.

Even more than that is the feeling many fans have about a sport, the illusion that they are an integral part of it, or the feeling that the best thing in life would be playing a professional sport. Looked at rationally, all this seems rather silly and even sad, but this attitude is the lifeline for sports. When it begins to penetrate that no athlete is playing only for the thrill of it all, when there is more news coming from courts and bargaining tables than from the playing fields, sports are in serious trouble. Baseball is feeling the cutting edge of that now.

There is another problem that baseball faces—it has not adjusted to the temper of the times. This shows particularly in the way it is scheduled, starting much too early and ending much too late.

With the kind of competition baseball faces for the sports dollar, it should be merchandised as well as possible. But it says something for the lords of baseball that they have never followed through on the one aspect that every fan would like to see—interleague scheduling. It is almost criminal that baseball fans in the American League cities never got a chance to see Willie Mays in his prime, nor National League fans to see Mickey Mantle.

The natural rivalries that abound are dismissed, too. The Chicago White Sox and Chicago Cubs, for instance, have not met except in the meaningless exhibition games since the 1906 World Series! The Oakland A's and San Francisco Giants have not met, except in exhibition games, and neither have the California Angels and Los Angeles Dodgers.

The National League has always dragged its feet on interleague play, because the National is the healthier of the two leagues. But it takes no great savant to see that the problems the American League has faced will soon be visited on the National League, too.

Along with interleague play, the leagues should realign on a geographical basis, to get natural rivals into the same divisions or leagues, thus adding spice to a schedule and cutting down on travel costs.

And, finally, baseball should shorten the schedule; instead, the only change in recent years has been to increase it, from 154 games to 162. That way lies madness, and declining interest.

The present schedule guarantees there are going to be a number of games rained out—even snowed out, in Montreal—in the early season, forcing postponement of games to late season. That, in turn, guarantees that the players will be tired and at less than their best in the stretch run, the most important part of the season.

The problem with so many games is twofold: 1) Few of them mean anything, and 2) Nobody can afford to go to all of them, or to any significant percentage. Thus, few tickets are sold in advance. When a fan waits until the day of the game before buying a ticket, he may change his mind and stay home.

A once-a-week schedule, as football has, would never work because a pitcher like Sandy Koufax would make too much difference, but I think it's entirely feasible to limit the games to Friday, Saturday and Sunday and cut the season to about 23 weeks. That would make a 69-game schedule, which would certainly seem to be enough to settle matters.

For the owners, this would be good because it would enable them to cut costs by cutting the roster and eliminating those unprofitable midweek games, when the plant and employee expenses have to be paid even if only 622 people pay to get in.

Each series would present a fresh team and a new look. Fans would be able to see the stars in the other league, and the players should play better because they wouldn't be tired from an overly long and demanding schedule.

The games could be better promoted on an individual basis. Baseball is the most individualistic of the team sports, and each team has at least one individual worth watching. Under this changed schedule, for instance, each city would be guaranteed to see Tom Seaver pitch. Under the current schedule, even if the Mets are in town two or three times during the year, his turn may never come up.

It's something to think about. It's a shame baseball people won't.

14

·

Pro Basketball:
Bent On Self-Destruction

If there was ever a sport that needs professional help, it is pro basketball. Get it up there on the couch, doctor, before it's too late. It's hard to believe anybody is trying to keep the game afloat. The owners are pirates and the players greedy; nobody knows who is playing for whom, or for how long; players' salaries have long since passed the point of credibility, and owners shun moves which could save them. There may be no hope.

The owners are making a grand gesture to wipe out poverty pockets. Of course, they're working in a very circumscribed area, but by the time they're through, there will surely be nobody over 6-6 on welfare. Owners are pressing so much money so urgently on college players, the athletes can hardly find enough pockets to put it all in. Players are signing contracts as casually as autographs. They sign one and then when somebody comes along with a better offer, what the hell, they sign that one, too. Let the lawyers sort it all out later.

College coaches, of course, are horrified, but they don't have much of a case. The school is using the player, far more than the reverse, but they can't match the pros' money. As Al

McGuire said on national television after Jim Chones had signed, "We give them a four-year contract, er, scholarship." The education? Get serious. At most schools, if an athlete gets a good education, it's an accident.

What I don't understand, though, is where all the money is coming from. Is it real money, or something left over from a stage play? Confederate money, perhaps?

Now, I understand that all is not what it seems on the surface. A lot of these figures are inflated by sportswriters who have never seen anything larger than a $5 bill. And a lot of the offers are not in cash; there are annuities and mutual fund arrangements that will supposedly be worth all that money at some future date. But there has to be some money there to start with, and I can't understand it. I keep getting the feeling I've missed something along the way. Why are these people throwing so much money out for pro basketball?

Don't get me wrong: I like the sport. I think pro basketball players generally are the best athletes of any in the major sports, and when they're playing well—as at playoff time—they are a joy to watch. But I don't think my opinion is shared by a significant majority. A lot of sports fans still think basketball players are just skinny goons running around in their underwear. Given this, it's hard to see why owners think they are going to be overwhelmed by patrons in the next few years.

There's another fact: when you have a football or baseball team, you can make a lot of money by selling out, because stadium capacities range from 50,000 to 80,000. But the largest basketball arena holds 19,500, and most are in the 13,000 to 14,000 range. Considering the costs of opening the doors and the players' contracts, teams almost have to sell out every night to make any money.

But still the bidding war goes on and on and on. It doesn't make sense, but I'll tell you one thing: I've got my son out in the backyard shooting baskets every spare moment.

All this money still isn't enough for the players, who jump from team to team and league to league to get still better deals. Rick Barry was the pioneer in this field. At a time when others were staying with one team, Rick was on the move. After two years with the Warriors, Rick jumped to the Oakland Oaks of the American Basketball Association. The Oaks became the

Washington Caps and then the Virginia Squires, and Rick said he wanted to go back to San Francisco. He signed a contract with the Warriors, to start with the 1972–73 season, but then discovered he would have to stay with the ABA team. He made so much noise in *Sports Illustrated* about not wanting his son to speak with a Southern accent that he got traded to the New York Nets.

Once in New York, with all the economic possibilities that were open to him there, Rick didn't want to leave. He signed a contract with the Nets extending past the time he was to play with the Warriors, and up to the day he had to honor his contract with the Warriors insisted that he would stay in New York, either as a player or not. Through intermediaries, Nets' owner Roy Boe offered Warriors' owner Franklin Mieuli $750,000 for Barry's contract and indicated that the price could go higher, possibly to $1 million.

Mieuli stood firm and Barry finally reported to the Warriors, though out of condition, just before the start of the regular season. The subsequent season was both a personal and team disappointment. Barry did not make the All-Star first team and the Warriors finished a badly beaten second in the Pacific Division.

Thus, after his seventh pro season (he sat out one year under a court order while waiting to play for the Oaks), Barry had played for three teams in four cities and two leagues. But, though he was the first to start jumping around, he is by no means the only one; half the Seattle Super Sonics team consists of former ABA players. It is instructive to see what has happened in one of those cases.

Jim McDaniel signed with the Carolina Cougars for another of those seven-figure deals, but soon decided the steering wheel on his Cadillac didn't have the right tilt, or something, and jumped to Seattle. But he was an instant disappointment there, a seven-footer who didn't seem to have the instincts to play center but was not quick enough to play forward. Seattle tried to give him back to Carolina, but the Cougars were smarter the second time around. McDaniel's problems were probably more mental than physical. He had gotten so much money, he couldn't get a perspective, either on himself or the game.

Another famous case was Julius Erving, who for a time was split between three clubs—Virginia of the ABA and Atlanta and Milwaukee of the NBA. Erving was drafted by the Squires while he still had college eligibility remaining, a practice which was then allowed in the ABA but not the NBA. When his college class graduated, Milwaukee drafted him. Soon, Erving decided he'd like to try life in the NBA, and Atlanta signed him, though the Hawks knew he'd been drafted by Milwaukee. NBA commissioner Walter Kennedy declared that Erving belonged to Milwaukee and that Atlanta would be fined for every game in which Erving played, but the Hawks went ahead and played Erving anyway, which is an indication of the regard with which Kennedy has been held throughout the league. Finally, a district court judge in Brooklyn, operating under the naive assumption that contracts mean something, ruled that Erving still belonged to Virginia, and he returned to the Squires. Don't bet that he'll still be there throughout his career, however.

Ironically, despite all this contract jumping, the players have been fighting to get rid of the option clause, which is the only protection the owners have left. The players have been getting so much money for what is basically a fringe human endeavor, they're beginning to think they're really important.

There is a vast difference between the option clause and baseball's reserve clause, which binds a player to one team. The inequities of the baseball situation are so obvious, they hardly need comment. There is a need for the players to have some freedom to escape intolerable situations, even if that means Charlie Finley would lose half his club every year.

But the option clause provides the necessary freedom. A good example is Earl Monroe, who made it plain that he would no longer play in Baltimore. Soon, he was traded to New York, where he had always wanted to play, and he prospered, eventually playing on a championship team.

Obviously, the option clause does not give the players carte blanche, but some control is necessary. If players could go wherever they wanted, most of them would wind up in New York, where the ancillary money is so plentiful. That works against everybody's best wishes because competition is at the bottom of every sport's appeal, and there would be no competition if the best players were all on one team.

You'd think even the players could see this, but they are curiously shortsighted, as they've proved on the salary issue, and by the way they've fought the merger of the NBA and ABA. They reason that a merger would drive down salaries, which it certainly would, but it would also make it possible for everybody to stay in business. The current foolhardy situation can hardly last forever, and where will the players be then? I would think it would be far preferable to making less but having 26 teams operate than to making more for some players but having half the jobs available because so many teams had folded.

But perhaps the players can't be blamed too much, because they're only following the example set by the owners, who have been consistently shortsighted in their practices.

As the NFL has proved, the surest road to financial security is a strong commissioner, but nobody in the NBA seems to realize that. Every time Kennedy has made a strong move, he's been opposed within the league. When he warned the Atlanta Hawks that they'd be fined for playing Erving, they did it, anyway; when he then fined them, they sued him!

The threat of another suit also caused some strange maneuvering in the case of John Brisker and the '73 NBA draft. It started when Philadelphia made Brisker a supplemental choice in a previous draft, after he had signed with the Pittsburgh Condors of the ABA. When Pittsburgh folded, Seattle owner Sam Shulman was there to sign Brisker. Kennedy approved the signing, saying that Brisker was a free agent, but awarded the Seattle No. 1 pick for the '73 draft to Philadelphia. A court then ruled that Kennedy did not have the power to give Philadelphia the Seattle pick; only the Board of Governors (owners) could do that. Kennedy postponed the draft and tried to get the owners to back him up, but Shulman threatened to sue the league and each owner individually and the other owners caved in. Eventually, Philadelphia was awarded a supplemental pick at the end of the first round, instead of Seattle's pick, which came up fourth.

It was no wonder that, midway through his five-year contract, rumors were rampant that Kennedy was about to be forced out as commissioner.

It is also no wonder that the game is in trouble, beset by problems within and enemies without. The one positive angle I find to pro basketball is the 24-second clock, which forces teams to shoot within 24 seconds. Though it is often criticized by those who are not knowledgeable about the game, the 24-second clock has been pro basketball's salvation.

Critics of the game like to say that you can come in two minutes from the end and see the game decided. This is not quite true—what happens in the first quarter often determines what happens in the fourth, though the game may be close to the very end—but the very fact that it can be said at all indicates that the clock is doing its job, which is to try to make the game as interesting as possible. It makes certain the game will always keep moving, which is crucial. Basketball is an action sport, and when the action slows down or stops, it loses its appeal.

The collegians have never learned this lesson. When a team thinks it cannot win by conventional strategy, it invariably tries the stall, known euphemistically as the slowdown. In recent years, this has been most common in games involving UCLA; because the Bruins have been so dominant, teams have been beaten psychologically before they even take the court.

USC, in particular, has tried stall tactics against the Bruins and they've played games in which neither team got to double figures by the midway point in the first half. USF tried the slowdown in the NCAA Regionals in 1973 and was successful for most of the first half, but the Bruins quickly took charge in the second half and breezed to another win.

If memory serves, Cal once held one of the great USF teams to a 33-24 win by such tactics, and Joe Hagler achieved a momentary fame by holding the ball for eight minutes. That is not basketball. Cal coach Pete Newell, a man I've admired in almost every other instance, argued that a coach is bound to use any tactics he can to even up the game. But if he tries tactics of this sort, the public should not be charged admission unless it is clearly understood the entertainment for the evening will be a farce and not a basketball game. (Interestingly, Newell is now general manager of the Los Angeles Lakers and when we talked at the '73 NBA All-Star game, he said that he seldom saw college games any more because he disliked the slowdowns.)

The NBA was forced into the 24-second clock by just such games. Once, the great Minneapolis Laker team was held to an 18-17 win by stall tactics. Clearly, the pros could not afford that, because they do not have the reservoir of student and alumni interest that colleges have.

The 24-second clock keeps a team from sitting on a lead. There is no stalling in the last 5 minutes, which is all to the good. It also forces a team to play its best for 48 minutes, because a team that relaxes for a couple of minutes at any time can lose the game right there.

Critics say it makes the pro game monotonous, that all teams must play the same type of game, but they're wrong. If you have ever seen the Chicago Bulls and Boston Celtics you know just how wrong. The Celtics are a running team, the Bulls a deliberate one.

But much of the good done the game by the 24-second clock is undone by the other facets of pro basketball. The season is far too long, the officiating uneven at best and the competition is terribly imbalanced.

The officiating is a constant problem, and I'm not sure it can ever be corrected. The suggestion has been made that a third official be hired to catch the fouls the other two miss, but that would only compound the problem because there aren't enough good officials now. The defection of referees to the ABA hurt the NBA, and it has not recovered yet. Even the good referees have been hurt because they are less effective working with weak partners. A good referee often hesitates to make a call out of his area or overrule a bad call by his partner, and thus it is the weak partner who determines the quality of the officiating team.

There are other problems with the officiating. Like the players, the officials get tired by the long season and don't always concentrate the way they should. I sometimes suspect they don't see everything, either, because they're a foot or more shorter than the players they're watching.

But the basic problem is that only a small portion of the fouls is ever called, because to call everything would reduce the games to a shambles. The rule of thumb in the NBA is "no harm, no foul." After watching some games, particularly those involving the Chicago Bulls, it seems more like "no blood, no foul."

All sorts of hacking and pushing and shoving are done away from the ball and seldom called. It is common practice for a defensive player to grab the jersey of his man to keep him within reach; that, too, is seldom called. A player shooting a hook shot will stick his elbow out to keep his opponent away; the defensive player will try to stick a discreet elbow in his man's ribs to cause the shot to go off line. Only infrequently, is either of these called. And with so much being ignored, whenever a foul is called, the fouling player reacts with righteous indignation; sometimes, it seems half the players in the NBA are auditioning for movie roles when a foul is called.

And a slight variation in calling fouls can cause havoc. An example occurred in the '73 NBA playoffs. The Warriors had beaten Milwaukee, 4-2, in a very rough series. At one point, Rick Barry and Bob Dandridge got into a fight, right after Dandridge's elbow had decked Jim Barnett; nobody was ejected.

In the next series, against the Lakers, the officiating was suddenly much tighter. As a result, the Warriors were in constant foul trouble and the games were almost all decided at the free throw line. In one game, Barry fouled out and the other two Warrior forwards, Clyde Lee and Cazzie Russell, had five fouls each, though none of the three normally have trouble with fouls.

The one good factor in the officiating situation is that the day of the "homer" seems to be disappearing. As one indication, visiting teams are winning with more frequency than they used to.

Even if the officiating were perfect, however, the other problems would remain. The schedule, for instance. With exhibition games added to the regular season, teams play 100 games every year, and a team that gets into the championship playoff series can be playing between 120 and 130 games.

Added to that is the stress of bunched games in different cities. Because teams can't always get into their arenas exactly when they want to and because owners like to keep road games as close together as possible to cut down travel and hotel costs, it is not uncommon to see a team playing four games in five nights, all in different cities. That kind of schedule guarantees that players will be tired and playing less than their best a good part of the time. I wish I had a nickel for every time I've gone to a game and watched the players sleepwalk through the first half.

That kind of schedule can also affect the outcome of the season. As an example, in the 1972–73 season, the Warriors were making a good run at the Lakers just before the All-Star break. In their last game before the break, Barry twisted his ankle. It couldn't have come at a worse time. The Warriors had eight games in nine nights after the break, two of them against the Lakers, and with Barry limping, lost seven of the nine. Before anybody knew what had happened, they were ten games back and only went through the motions the rest of the season.

After the rigors of the regular season, teams in the top half of the NBA (or, more accurately, 8 of the 17) extend their season into the playoffs, and thus have a chance to be considered champion of the entire league.

The playoffs are a farce for several reasons. The main reason is they allow too many teams in. In baseball, only division winners get into the playoffs; in football, only division champions and the two best runners-up in each conference, a total of 8 out of 26 teams. But in basketball, the mediocre sometimes survive; Atlanta made the playoffs in 1972 without even winning half its games, and thus could have won the whole thing.

Nothing that bad has happened, but it's questionable whether the best team always wins. Injuries are too much of a factor. In 1972, the Knicks lost to the Lakers, at least in part because Dave DeBusschere was hurt and Willis Reed hadn't recovered from his knee problem. In 1973, the injury problem was reversed: John Havlicek could hardly raise his right shoulder for most of the Knicks-Celtics series, and Jerry West pulled a hamstring muscle early in the Lakers-Knicks championship series. The result—a championship for the Knicks.

By that time, I hardly cared, because the season had gone on for so long. Obviously some people still do care, because the playoff games draw so well, and owners always justify them on that basis. But I contend that the playoff games draw at the expense of regular season games.

Go back to the example I used earlier, of the Warriors and Lakers in the second half of the 1972–73 season. The Warriors were out of the running for the championship but far ahead of third-place Phoenix and almost guaranteed a spot in the playoffs. They relaxed, coach Al Attles experimented to find his best combination and they played under .500 ball for that half of the season after the All-Star break. And the fans stayed away in droves, knowing they could see the Warriors in the playoff games when they'd be trying to do their best again. I suspect that happens often, particularly among people who have limited money to spend on games. Why watch meaningless regular season games when the playoffs will soon start?

The regular season games are often meaningless, too, because of the terrible imbalance in the NBA. Consider the 1972–73 season: at the top, Boston had an .829 percentage and Los Angeles and Milwaukee both .732; at the bottom, Buffalo and Portland were .256 and Philadelphia, after struggling under the .100 mark most of the season, finally made it all the way to .110, a whopping 59 games behind Boston!

Even worse is the fact there was only one season-long race in any of the four divisions, that matching Boston and New York in the Atlantic Division. Chicago made it a little hot for Milwaukee in the Midwest Division and Atlanta for Baltimore in the Central Division, but Milwaukee and Baltimore both pulled away late in the season to win comfortably.

The playoff situation was even more clear-cut. The playoff teams could have been picked after the first month; in not one of the four divisions was a third team ever close enough to challenge for the playoffs.

That kind of imbalance hurts everybody, not just the weaker teams, because even the top teams have trouble drawing a crowd when Buffalo and Philadelphia come to town.

There have been plans considered to balance the competition, and there is some precedent for this: in 1965, both the Warriors and the Knicks got two draft choices right off because they had been so bad the year before. For the record, New York took Bill Bradley drafting first and Dave Stallworth No. 4; the Warriors' choices were Barry, No. 2, and Fred Hetzel, No. 3.

The plans being considered—they were first brought up at the All-Star break in 1973—varied, but they would all allow for clubs to draft players from another club's roster. One plan would allow teams to freeze eight players, and every team would have a chance to draft from another team. Another plan would allow the nonplayoff teams to draft from the playoff teams and would allow only six players to be frozen on a playoff team's roster.

From the standpoint of balancing competition, the second plan makes much more sense because few teams are so deep they have quality players beyond the first eight; making the rest available wouldn't be doing any favors to any team.

Basketball is a game which can be evened up in this fashion because one or two players can make a big difference. The classic example is Milwaukee. The Bucks were dead last until they got Kareem Abdul-Jabbar, who made them a playoff team. When they then added Oscar Robertson in a trade, they became league champions.

But because of the curious laissez faire attitude owners have in other areas, one wonders if anything will be done to balance competition. The merger which seems pro basketball's only salvation has, for instance, been held up because owners don't want to share gate receipts, as Sen. Sam Ervin has insisted they must. And yet, sharing the gate receipts would be a great thing for the NBA because it would reduce some of the advantage New York, with its 19,500-seat arena (usually sold out, too) has over clubs like the Warriors, which can fill only half of a 13,000-seat arena.

The logic seems inescapable, but the owners resist it. I'm afraid the patient is terminal, doctor.

15
.
Fixed Games: How Did The Jets Win In '68?

Early in my career as a *Chronicle* columnist, I wrote two facetious columns during football season about the strange results of games in the NFL. I'll never make that mistake again. From past experience, I should have known you don't try to get subtle with a sports audience, because most fans can't even spell the word. Many readers thought I was saying that games are fixed and to this day, no other subject comes up more often in my mail. Most of my correspondents are convinced professional games are fixed, particularly in football, and they usually have examples to prove their point.

It is an easy enough supposition to make because there are some strange happenings in pro games. During the '72 NFL season, for instance, the San Francisco 49ers were upset by Buffalo; Kansas City was upset by Philadelphia; Oakland was upset by Denver. In every case, those games looked as if they should have been taken off the betting board.

In the '73 NBA season, Boston had the best record in the league, yet they lost to New York in the second round of the playoffs. The Golden State Warriors, who had won only one of six regular season games with Milwaukee, beat the Bucks in six games in a playoff series. Then, the Warriors, who had split six regular season games with Los Angeles, lost to the Lakers in five games—one of them by 56 points!

Who can figure it? Certainly not the fans, nor the coaches. But, not the gamblers, either.

There are a lot of reasons I don't believe professional games are fixed, and none is more persuasive than the fact it would hardly be worth it to an athlete.

Consider the two biggest scandals in this country's sports, the 1919 "Black Sox" and the college basketball fixes. In both cases, the athletes needed the money. The White Sox were notoriously underpaid, and thus easy pickings for somebody who promised them big money. The college basketball scene is always a likely target, because the fixers are often dealing with kids from the ghetto who have neither the money nor the background to resist temptation. Even a youth who thinks he can make a lot of money in the future finds it difficult to resist the immediate temptation when he has very little now, particularly since he can see that somebody is already making money from his efforts.

The financial structure of professional sports, however, certainly discourages any thoughts of throwing a game. There is simply too much money to be made legitimately through salaries and endorsements. Even offensive linemen are getting into commercials now, and all of this would be washed away if an athlete were found guilty of taking a bribe.

There are, of course, inequities in the salary scale. But the athletes the fixers would have to reach are the stars, who are making a great deal of money and who would have to be extremely stupid to risk throwing away the possibility of even more for one quick payoff—especially since that payoff is often not delivered. Neither the Black Sox nor the college basketball players got much money from the gamblers.

And even if the fixers could find such a stupid athlete, it would be difficult to find any others, and you would need more than one. Obviously, the first man you'd go after if you were fixing a football game is the quarterback, but a quarterback who was obviously off his game might find himself on the bench. The fixer couldn't risk that. There is no advantage to fixing a game that might come unstuck.

Baseball, of course, is a different matter. The pitcher is so important that he alone might make the difference. But there is relatively little betting on baseball during the regular season, compared to football, because there are such turnabouts from day to day, and even then, the pitcher might not be enough; even if he gave up eight runs, his teammates might score nine. (And he too might well be yanked long before that.)

What, then, is the reason for the startling results in pro sports? Emotion, I think. There is usually less difference than it seems between the best and worst in pro sports because nobody who is playing professionally is a bum, except relatively. Thus, a team that is playing its best can beat a better team that lets down, and it is easy for the good teams to let down.

I mentioned earlier the Kansas City loss to Philadelphia during the '72 NFL season. I talked to Bill Richardson of the Kansas City *Star* about that a couple of weeks later. "When the Chiefs watched game films of Philadelphia," Richardson told me, "they felt sorry for the Eagles." They played that way the next Sunday. Presumably, their pity disappeared when the Eagles won.

Emotion can make the difference in that type of game, between otherwise poorly matched teams, and it can also affect the play of teams in big games, causing them to play very strangely at times. For a couple of specific examples, try the Kansas City Chiefs in the '69 AFL championship game and the Baltimore Colts in the third Super Bowl.

The Chiefs were as high as a team can get for that championship game against Oakland, because the Raiders had made a habit of beating them in the big games over a three-year period, and that very excess of emotion almost cost them the game. What is most remembered about that game is the fact that Daryle Lamonica hurt his hand and then threw interception after interception in the second half. What is seldom remembered is the fact that the Chiefs kept fumbling the ball back after every interception. They were so eager, they couldn't hold on to the ball. It was an incredible performance on both sides of the field, and it became obvious that it would not be a case of who won the game but who lost it. Eventually, the Raiders made more mistakes than Kansas City, and the

Chiefs won it. In the press box, a lot of writers made bad jokes about how neither team wanted to win and play Minnesota, but the next week in the Super Bowl, a much calmer Kansas City team methodically destroyed the Vikings.

The third Super Bowl is the game most often cited by those who are sure the fix is in. Baltimore was a 17- or 19-point favorite, depending on which betting line you subscribed to, and yet the New York Jets won, 16-7. It didn't make sense. The Colts had gone 13-1 in a tougher league and had annihilated Cleveland in their title game, 34-0; the Jets had been 11-3 and had just edged by Oakland, 27-23, in their championship game.

The Colts were very emotional for the Super Bowl, too emotional. Joe Namath had talked all week about what the Jets would do to the Colts, and some of the Colts had lost their cool. Lou Michaels even got into an argument with Namath in a restaurant during the week. By game time, the Colts were so keyed to get Namath, they made Joe's job easy. The Colts blitzed more than they would have normally because they were so eager to show up Namath, but one of Namath's assets as a quarterback is his ability to read defenses. When he spotted the Colts' blitz, he simply checked off and sent Matt Snell storming past the onrushing linemen and linebackers for big gains.

There was another reason for the strange result, one which comes up more often than you'd think in big games: the teams were simply misjudged. Baltimore was not as good as most people thought, and the Jets were a lot better. Basically, the Jets were better because of Namath, who is in a special category as a quarterback. The Colts had seen nobody like him all year. It was easy enough to see where fans, sportswriters and oddsmakers had gone wrong. The NFL did seem much stronger than the AFL. After all, Green Bay had won easily in the first two Super Bowls. But it was an off year for the NFL, and Baltimore was not the dominant team Green Bay had been.

The NFL bias still prevailed the next year, when Minnesota was made a 13-point favorite over Kansas City, apparently because the Vikings were an NFL team. But the Chiefs were far superior, as an objective comparison of the personnel would have shown before the game. They won, 23-7, and even those who had thought the Jets were lucky to win the previous year conceded that Kansas City was far the superior team in this game.

Old prejudices die hard, however, and the carry-over from the NFL superiority bias is still with us. For Super Bowl VII, though the American Conference had a slight exhibition and regular season edge in interconference games, and though Miami was undefeated, the Dolphins were a slight underdog to Washington. They made a mockery of those odds, of course, winning decisively, despite the misleading 14-7 margin.

What about the regular season games when teams seem to be trying to lose, by fumbling away touchdowns, by throwing interceptions, by making strange calls? A fan wrote me once with what he thought was a specific example of a fixed game: a Ram-49er game in which both teams seemed to be trying to lose. Roman Gabriel seemed to be ignoring open receivers and throwing to covered ones, and the 49ers kept fumbling near their own goal line. My correspondent thought that could not be explained by coincidence.

It can, though. Football is not an exact science, despite those silly Xs and Os the coaches love. Runners do not always hit the right hole or receivers run the right patterns. Balls are dropped that should be caught, and passes are tipped into the hands of defensive backs playing out of position. Quarterbacks and coaches are engaged in a guessing game, trying to anticipate what the other team will do. Sometimes they guess right, sometimes they guess wrong, and that is usually the difference between a bad call and a good one.

To use a specific example again, this one from the '70 American Conference championship game between Oakland and Baltimore. Early in the game, the Raiders advanced to the Baltimore 40, mostly by running the ball. Quarterback Daryle Lamonica then went to the air, throwing long, incomplete passes. On third down, he was sacked and put out of the game with a pulled muscle. The Raiders lost the game, 27-17, and though they were in it until the closing minutes, many thought Lamonica's injury was the turning point of the game right there.

In the press box, most writers thought Lamonica's calls were stupid, and I have no doubt that around the country, fans who had bet on the Raiders were convinced Lamonica was trying to throw the game, because the right call in that situation was obviously another run.

But was it? Not necessarily. The Raiders at that time (they have since modified their strategy) believed: 1) You pass so you can run; and 2) When you get to the other team's 40, you go for the end zone, instead of trying to move slowly but steadily downfield.

If they had continued to run the ball, the Colts might very well have adjusted their defenses to stop the run, leaving the Raiders still out of effective field goal range and faced with a third down situation that forced them to pass, with the Colts knowing a pass was coming. By throwing on first down, they hoped to catch the Colts keyed for the run and, as a matter of fact, they nearly did. A pass to Fred Biletnikoff at the goal line which was just a fraction too long would have been the touchdown the Raiders were seeking.

So much for smart and dumb calls. It is easy enough to second-guess after the play has failed, but the quarterback must make the call in advance. In that situation, it's a little naive to assume he's either stupid or crooked, or both.

There are other physical reasons for what seem to be strange plays. From the stands and press box, football seems like a chess game, but it is not. Quarterbacks must make split-second decisions on where to throw the ball with 270-pound defensive linemen bearing down on them. Quite apart from a natural concern for their bodies, the quarterbacks face another problem: Often, they can't see past the linemen, and it does no good for a receiver to be wide open if the quarterback can't see him.

We expect too much of athletes, and I am as guilty as anybody. Because they are physically gifted, we expect them to do their best on every play and in every game, and that is not possible. All of us have days when we can't do anything right. We spill coffee, we stumble going up stairs; even fitting a key in a lock is a major problem. Athletes have these days, too, and they have to play on some of them. No athlete can explain why he can do something right in one game and, under nearly identical circumstances, do it wrong the next time.

Specifically, again. In the second half of Super Bowl VII, Bill Kilmer threw to Clifton McNeil for what would have been a first down at about the Miami 30, which would have given the 'Skins a chance to get in the game again. Kilmer had time to throw, McNeil was open and it was a pass Kilmer has thrown and completed countless times. This time, Kilmer threw behind McNeil, incomplete.

Things like that happen, and that's what makes sport so interesting, that lack of predictability. It is not a case of the fix being on, at all. What's that? You don't believe me because you absolutely know of this game where the quarterback had a receiver wide open in the end zone but threw instead to a covered man and . . . .

16

.

Athletes And
The Self-Discipline Myth

It always amuses me when coaches, particularly football coaches, talk of the need for self-discipline and the way sports produces leaders. That has been one of the rationales for sports since God knows when—the old argument went that the battle of Waterloo was won on the playing fields at Eton—but if there was ever any validity to that argument, it has long since been lost.

In fact, sport produces followers, not leaders. I still remember when the original student demonstrations started at the University of California and football coach Ray Willsey bragged that none of his players were involved, possibly because he had nothing else to brag about at the time, Cal's football fortunes being at an all-time low. He should have been ashamed of that, because it proved there were no leaders on the football team, nor even any players who were thinking for themselves. The Cal student body, whether in favor of the demonstrations or opposed to them, was fervently aroused over the issue, but on the football team, passivity reigned. That was no surprise, because the system encourages reliance on others, usually coaches, for ideas and the very patterns of life. Conformity is the desired goal, and conformists are not leaders.

Teamwork is important in sports, more so in some sports than others. Obviously, a football team cannot win if one lineman decides he wants to block in one direction and another lineman in another, and the team concept is legitimate in that context. Unfortunately, many coaches carry it much further.

Hank Stram of Kansas City, for instance, has always attributed much of his success to the fact that his team projects an image of togetherness; on the road, they wear team blazers. ("They look like a bunch of mechanical men," scoffs Oakland Raider tackle Art Thoms.) But other teams have been successful without this kind of regimentation. The Raiders, for instance, have all sorts of hair styles and dress. Billy Cannon used to wear dirty blue jeans on road trips, and Thoms has been known to wear a T-shirt advertising "Acapulco Gold" on the front. None of this has seemed to hurt their play on the field.

The concept of team unity is generally ridiculous, anyway, whether it's in appearance or reality. The Oakland A's won a world championship in 1972 while fighting with each other, their manager and their owner. Even in their great moments, they were unhappy. After Vida Blue saved their championship win with four innings of relief, he and starter John Odom almost fought in the dressing room because Odom thought Blue had made the "choke" sign in talking to him. It wasn't any better in 1973. Joe Rudi complained because he was benched—apparently at Charlie Finley's order—and Reggie Jackson sounded off when he was given a day of rest he didn't want. Significantly, these complaints came as the A's were making a run at the American League West lead.

Baseball is such an individualistic sport that team unity is seldom a factor, but even on a football team, unity is a much overrated virtue. Daryle Lamonica is such a loner that virtually the only friend he had with the Raiders after he was traded there in 1967 was another quarterback, Cotton Davidson. There was, in fact, so much antipathy between Lamonica and the rest of the team in those years that a story made the rounds that Lamonica and Cannon had had a fight, variously reported as happening in the locker room or an airplane. The story had no basis in fact, but Lamonica never pretended that he wanted any friends on the team. "I want respect, not friends," he said on many occasions. "I might have to kick some ass in the huddle, and I don't want to have to worry about friends." And thus, in the first three years Lamonica was with the Raiders, the team was 13-1, 12-2 and 12-1-1.

Later, as Lamonica started to suffer injuries more and more, George Blanda got his chance to shine, particularly in the miracle year of 1970. That galled Lamonica, who muttered to friends that Blanda was simply taking advantage of the situation. "The teams are geared to stop me, and George has a different style. That throws them off." It was a valid point.

Blanda tried to downplay the rivalry, but he obviously enjoyed his late-career success and was more popular with his teammates, though he often relieved them of money in the card games on airplane trips. But whatever quarterback was at the helm, the Raiders continued to win.

By 1972, a third quarterback—Ken Stabler—had entered the already chaotic quarterback situation. Obviously at Al Davis' request, Stabler started the season opener in Pittsburgh. When he was ineffective—and unlucky—Blanda came in, but could do no better. Finally, Lamonica was sent in for the fourth quarter and got the Raiders three touchdowns in a gallant, though insufficient, comeback. From that point, Lamonica was back as the starting quarterback, while Stabler seethed on the bench and debate continued in the press and among the Raiders themselves as to which quarterback should be starting. The result of all this dissension? The Raiders were 10-3-1 and won their division for the fifth time in six years. Stabler became the starter in the fourth game of the '73 season, once more forcing the unhappy Lamonica back to the bench, and the Raiders again won their division.

You would think examples like this would at least make coaches wonder if team unity is all that important, but it doesn't. Most coaches even decide what players should eat and wear, and how close they should cut their hair and when they should go to bed. The idea of a curfew should be repugnant to any athlete; unfortunately, there are only a few who truly rebel. Those who violate it usually do it as a little boy would break a rule his parent has made, just to see if he can get away with it.

Can you imagine what would happen if a bank decided that its employees must go to bed at 11 P.M. every night and sent a boss around to check? That bank would have to close its doors in a minute. But virtually every football team, from the high school through the pro level, does that. Even a team as relaxed about other aspects of discipline as the Raiders insists on a curfew.

The idea is that if the coaches don't check on the players, the players will be out drinking and screwing all night long, without being conscious of the effect they'll have on the team the next morning. And, undoubtedly, some would be, because they've been treated as children all their lives. If somebody else makes decisions for you for many years, you don't start making your own overnight.

The system is, or should be, humiliating for coaches, too. My wife was appalled when she made a trip to San Diego a few years back and talked to Diane Spencer, wife of offensive lineman coach Ollie Spencer of the Raiders. Diane could not even sleep in the same hotel as her husband, and she had to wait until he was through tucking players in at 11 P.M. before they could go out to dinner. It may or may not be a coincidence that the Spencers' marriage broke up a couple of years later.

It seems to me that the curfew system is self-defeating. Because athletes are not forced to exert self-discipline off the field, they do not develop it on the field, either. In tight spots, they look for help from the sidelines. Undoubtedly if the curfew were abolished, there would be some who would take advantage of that and ultimately hurt their game performances. But those types of athletes are hardly the ones you want to rely on in a game, anyway, and it might be best to weed them out beforehand. That would leave those who had the emotional maturity to take care of themselves, which would seem to be preferable.

Tommy Prothro tried to bring some sense to this whole system when he was hired to coach the Los Angeles Rams in 1971. Practically his first act was to abolish the curfew in training camp, which horrified other coaches. Unfortunately,

Prothro failed to win a divisional title in two years, though not because he had abolished the curfew, and he was fired. It will be a brave coach indeed who tries abolishing the curfew again because, in pro football's mind, the linkage has been firmly made: no curfew, no title. By now, everybody has conveniently forgotten that the one big problem with the '72 Rams was a quarterback, Roman Gabriel, who could throw effectively only about every third game. The lack of curfew had no effect on Gabriel.

Prothro's problem illustrates another facet of the football business. An intelligent and well-rounded man, Prothro tried to approach coaching a pro football team with the same maturity he approached other problems. Unfortunately, he extended this thought of maturity to his players, who didn't deserve it. Specifically, he thought to tell them the truth: when they played San Francisco, he told them they were playing a good team and had to play their best to win, which they did. When they played Denver, he told them they were playing a weak team. The players took that to mean they didn't have to play well against teams like Denver, and so they lost several games they should have won. It seems incredible that a professional athlete, whose livelihood depends on playing well, has to be encouraged to do so, but as we have seen, athletes are not accustomed to making any important deductions for themselves.

But even if a coach is justified in assuming that he has to make all the on-field decisions, it remains incredible that he thinks he should have the power to decide how short a player should wear his hair. And yet, the majority of coaches feel that way.

Certainly, there is no reason to think that hair has any effect on an athlete's performance. There have been some quite good teams whose players have had short hair, and some quite bad ones with the same attribute. Hank Stram's teams at Kansas City have all been short-haired, but when Ed Khayat tried the same approach at Philadelphia, the Eagles continued to be the losers they've always been. Sparky Anderson guided a team of short hairs to the '72 National League pennant, but he lost the World Series to the A's, who looked like a throwback to the old House of David teams.

Playing ability is more important than hair length. And yet, the idea persists among coaches that short hair has a significance far beyond appearance. There was an article in May, 1973, in "Texas Coach," by Tony Simpson, head football coach at a junior high in the suburbs of Houston, which delineated some of the worst aspects of the hair code business in sports. Simpson's article contended that long hair on boys and men is the sign of a "sissy" and should be banned from American athletic fields: "It is time that American coaches stopped allowing themselves to be personally represented by male athletic teams and individuals that look like females." He continued:

> Only in the animal world is the male designed to be most attractive or the prettiest—for example, the male lion has the mane, the male peacock has the feathers. This is normal in the animal world only. However, a male with long hair is cute, he is pretty and he is sweet. If the coaches of America would grow long hair like their athletes, we might be able to scare the Russian and Chinese Communists to death with our lack of masculinity.
>
> It should be pointed out here that the only reason males are free to look like females and their coaches are free to permit this is because we had real men that were not cute, not sweet and not pretty with courage and sense enough to kill our enemies on battlefields all over the globe.
>
> If common sense indicates that long hair on a man is a disgrace, let's stop compromising our common sense by allowing it. A good hair code will get the abnormals out of athletics before they become coaches and bring their 'loser' standards into the coaching profession.

Simpson said keeping his hair short is a sign of male discipline. "Without self-discipline and respect for authority, you have an uncontrollable problem among the youth with drug abuse, crime and sexual perversion. And this describes the U.S. in 1973."

He said a woman who wants a man with long hair is not a "real woman in her soul."

> But the American male youth—and many not so young—wear their hair long simply because they know the female will like it. These so-called males are in submission to the warped norms and standards of the females who like to set the dress and grooming standards for their mousy husbands, their pantywaist boyfriends and feminine sons.

161

It is hard to know where to start with this nonsense except to point out that a lot of men who have accomplished some good in this world have had long hair, starting with the obvious example of Jesus of Nazareth.

Sports has been the backwater of society in the hair issue, and it is enough to make us all despair. The story is hardly new; on every level from Little League to the majors, it keeps popping up. Eventually, I think reason will prevail—Simpson "resigned" as coach shortly after this article appeared—but it's ridiculous that all hair codes haven't disappeared long before this.

Usually, the hair and dress issue is only a symbol for a larger issue beneath. When coaches and officials try to enforce their outmoded hair and dress codes on younger athletes, they are really worried that long hair and flamboyant dress are symbols of revolt, that an athlete who could decide to wear his hair long might think he could make other decisions for himself. This is abhorrent to most coaches; like the colonial rulers in under-developed countries, they want to retain the status quo.

The point on which the hair-dress conscious coaches all founder is their inability to detect the difference between reasonable rules and those based only on personal prejudices. Hair styles have nothing to do with performance; it is all a matter of styles in society, and nothing more. Coaches wear short hair because that was the norm as they were reaching adulthood, but Jesus Christ had long hair, George Washington wore a powdered wig and Abe Lincoln had a beard. No doubt, Simpson would not have any of them playing on his team. Short hair has become such a fetish with some that it has been observed that anybody with short hair who wears a Brooks Brothers suit can get away with almost anything, which may be why it took so long to uncover the Watergate gang.

Along with this idea of short hair goes the curious notion that "masculinity" is synonymous with force. Simpson gives himself away with his talk of "sissies," which is his obvious code for homosexuals. We have all known coaches and physical education teachers like this, who are determined to promote their idea of masculinity at the expense of their charges. Long hair means softness, i.e., femininity, and thus must be discouraged; it is a sexual fantasyland.

In truth, it is at least as important for a boy to learn tenderness as toughness. I submit that masculinity has nothing to do with learning how to beat up on somebody but has everything to do with learning to be gentle and considerate with a woman, with being loving to a child and even with learning to cry at great moments of sadness or joy. Simpson and his kind would never understand that. His obsession with masculinity makes me wonder. A man who is secure in his masculinity does not feel the need to talk about it.

Even in relatively nonviolent sports, toughness is sought after among coaches and managers. Billy Martin, manager of the Detroit Tigers, often tries to provoke a fight with the other team to get his team stirred up, and woe to the player who does not come off the Tiger bench to get in on the fight. Conformity reigns again. In spring training, 1973, Giants manager Charlie Fox let it be known that any player who did not participate in a team brawl would be fined. Team unity again.

Football coaches seem especially prone to this kind of talk because football, with its armor plate and simulated war conditions, is so often treated as a proving ground for men and boys. Supposedly, a football player proves his courage by going out on the field and hitting other players. Yet, this actually has nothing to do with courage; it is simply a personal attribute. Some men like body contact and some do not, and the ones who like it are the ones who gravitate to football. If blocking and tackling are signs of courage, how do you explain the terror with which football players usually watch the approach of a hypodermic needle?

Football players are courageous when they play with injuries, but in many cases, they are pulled along by a combination of their teammates' enthusiasm, the excitement which acts almost as an anesthetic, and the unmentionable—drugs. When football coaches talk about the necessity for courage and self-discipline, they are talking errant nonsense. True courage and self-discipline would enable players to buck the conformist thinking of their coaches; I know no coach who wants that.

On the college level, the philosophy of toughness is probably best exemplified by Woody Hayes of Ohio State, who makes a point of coaching in shirt sleeves on the sidelines in cold weather, as if to say the weather can't affect him. It is no coincidence that Hayes' players are generally like robots, discouraged from any personal initiative or self-discipline.

Hayes and his pupil, Bo Schembechler of Michigan, are fanatics on the subject: football to them is a game of infantry, of foot soldiers, and they carry it to the extreme. It is no wonder that Hayes admires Gen. George S. Patton; he thinks the same way. Players are mere pawns in his grand strategy. (Parenthetically, it should be noted that the one chink in his strategic armor is passing. Like many another infantry general, he has never believed in air war, and his teams neither throw well nor defend well against the pass. If everything else is relatively equal, always bet on a good passing team against one of Woody's.)

Hayes' and Schembechler's approach to the game is best shown by their trips to the Rose Bowl. In the belief that winning justifies everything, both virtually locked up their players. Schembechler even took his players to Bakersfield to practice for one Rose Bowl, and Jack Tatum once told me what it was like in the last Rose Bowl he played in, for an Ohio State team that was regarded as perhaps the best in collegiate history—until it lost to Stanford.

"I wasn't terribly upset because I felt I played well," he remembered, "and I didn't think we were going to have a great game. There were a lot of players who were very unhappy with the coaching staff, and they couldn't forget that and go out and play the way they would have otherwise. There were a lot of things that disturbed us. For one, we came out a day early because we were told that would give us more time to relax, but we just got off the plane and went right out onto the practice field. We had a predominantly senior team, but the curfew was 10 o'clock every night. We asked them to make it 12 o'clock for at least a couple of nights, but they wouldn't do it."

Fortunately, as Simpson noted in another context, the times are changing. Even Hayes modified his approach before the '74 Rose Bowl; he gave his players some freedom, and they won. Coaches with different ideas are getting into the profession and are inevitably changing it. One such is Mike White. As an assistant at Stanford, White was responsible for much of John Ralston's success because he persuaded Ralston that short hair, dress codes and unreasonable curfews had no place in college football. Stanford, a marked underdog both times, beat the tight Ohio State and Michigan teams in back-to-back Rose Bowls.

Ralston went on to coach the Denver Broncos and White, who had his choice of either Ralston's old job or the one opening up at Cal, opted for Cal, his alma mater. In addition to the problems any new coach faces of changing the system (old coach Ray Willsey was very conservative; White believes in a pass-oriented system) White has had additional problems because Cal has been on NCAA probation.

As a result, White had a very disappointing first season, winning only three games although his team finished strong with a dramatic win over Stanford in the closing seconds of the Big Game. White has not been a miracle worker at Cal, but I think he will ultimately be a winner, and, more importantly, he is bringing a breath of fresh air to the college game. He has ideas whose time has come.

Mike has imagination, and he also has a verve and enthusiasm he is able to transmit to the athletes. More important, he has moved with the times. He is from the awful, passive, crew-cut era of college sports, graduating in 1958 when athletes—and students—did as they were told, no questions asked, but he understands that today's athlete is much different.

"Today's athlete will play just as hard for you as a guy 20 years ago," says White, "but you can't get him to play by coaching the same way they did in 1910. The Knute Rockne stuff doesn't go any more."

White does it by treating players as individuals, being aware of their problems and their needs, not hassling them about dress and haircuts and seeing that they get their diplomas. One of the first things he did when the Bears convened for practice before their opening game in September, 1972, was to abolish the curfew. He let the players regulate their own conduct, and he had no problems.

White does not downgrade the importance of collegiate football—"We're the one thing that can pull the entire university student body together"—but he has not lost his perspective. "We should be an integral part of the University," he says. "I'm a teacher, and I want to show our faculty that there is a place for sports in the college curriculum, that we do have a contribution to make."

I think White is a forerunner of a movement that will eventually wash such as Simpson and Hayes out to sea, never to be mourned by a thinking man. And eventually, coaches may be able to talk of self-discipline for athletes and really mean it.

17

·

Little League:
Over The Hill At 13

The women's lib movement reached even into Little League baseball in the spring of 1973, and the Little League people reacted with their usual stupidity in two separate instances in Mill Valley, California and Ypsilanti, Michigan.

In Mill Valley, a suburb of San Francisco, 10-year-old Jenny Fulle wanted to play Little League ball so badly, she even wrote to President Nixon. It's questionable that the President ever saw the letter—it came just as Watergate was really heating up—but Jenny did get a reply through an official of the U.S. Office of Civil Rights in Washington, D.C. Jenny, addressed carefully as "Ms. Jenny Fulle," was informed that the office was "preparing guidelines to handle this type of discrimination." That, of course, is bureaucratese for admitting that nothing has been done, nothing is being done and nothing is likely to be done in the foreseeable future.

Jenny seemed qualified to play Little League baseball. In a physical fitness program at her school, she threw a softball 140 feet, less than the winning throw of 175 feet but better than a number of boys. Her mother, Donna Fulle, scoffed at the notion that Jenny might be shocked by locker room language. "There isn't a word a boy can use that 10-year-old girls aren't familiar with."

Asked why she didn't want to play baseball with girls, Jenny said, "Girls are expected to play with dolls. We don't have that much experience playing baseball, but that doesn't mean we can't. I haven't played with dolls since I was seven years old." Her mother added that Jenny hadn't worn a dress in at least two years. Her footwear wardrobe consisted of a pair of well-worn hiking boots.

"If I'd been lucky and born a boy," said Jenny, "there wouldn't be any problem. I agree with most everything I know about women's lib."

When 360 Mill Valley boys paraded behind a martial band for the opening day ceremonies, Jenny sat impatiently behind the backstop. "It makes me mad," she said. "There are a lot of girls who want to play and lots of boys who want us to play. It's just that most girls are afraid to ask."

She conducted a poll of her fifth grade class to see how they felt about girls playing baseball. Of 16 boys in the class, she said, only 3 objected and they "are the tough boys who show off in front of girls. What would they do if a girl got into Little League and did better than they did?"

What indeed? She's on to something there. With that remark, Jenny cut directly to the problem girls and women face in competitive sports. It is a lot easier to understand the male chauvinist attitude in sports if you start from that point. Sports have been an extension of the male ego, a method by which a boy can show off his muscles to an admiring girl. It is a crushing blow if she turns out to have more muscles.

But Jenny, despite her battle, couldn't play Little League baseball. The Marin league authorities were fearful of losing their charter from the national organization. They were right to worry about that; in Ypsilanti, Michigan, it happened.

The Ypsilanti Little League had a 12-year-old girl, Carolyn King, on one of the teams. Carolyn had not yet played a game, and the Ypsilanti league officials had hoped to persuade the national organization to drop its rule against girls competing before she played. But before the league season started, the national organization revoked the Ypsilanti charter.

But in this instance, Little League had overreached itself. Ypsilanti city manager Pete Caputo barred the Little League from using any of the city's baseball diamonds until the league drops its discriminatory practices. Caputo's action was exactly right (it was later upheld in the courts): Little League does not own the fields on which it plays and thus exists only through the the forbearance of the communities involved. Under those circumstances, it takes considerable gall for the national organization to be ordering people around as it does.

A similar action then took place in Mill Valley, though too late to get Jenny in for the 1973 season. The Mill Valley city council, at a standing-room-only meeting, voted, 3-2, to tell the national Little League that its local teams won't be able to use city playing fields in 1974 unless girls can play. (Ironically, one of the negative votes came from woman mayor Jean Barnard.)

Representatives of both the Marin Chapter of the National Organization of Women (NOW) and the American Civil Liberties Union (ACLU) upheld Jenny's position at the meeting.

Fred Hurvish, an ACLU attorney, told the council that it is unconstitutional for a city to provide exclusive use of public facilities to groups that are discriminatory. And, he said, Boyle Park, with the only two city baseball diamonds in Mill Valley, was used by the Little League all day Saturday and most week-nights, and thus other groups were prevented from using it.

The Little League publicity mill is second only to the NFL, as any columnist knows, and immediately the publicity men began churning out material to indicate that their antigirl rulings had nothing to do with chauvinistic attitudes (oh, of course not!) but were simply a medical necessity.

"We have medical facts to back up our conclusion that it would be improper for girls to play Little League baseball," said Dr. Creighton J. Hale, vice president of the national organization. "It is a physiological fact that a 12-year-old boy and a 12-year-old girl do not have the same attributes that are required to compete. Medical evidence precludes them from competing. A girl is more likely to suffer a broken limb because of the difference in bone structure. Muscle fibers are stronger in the boy than in the girl. The reaction time for a girl is slower."

Little League's concern for the health of girls is certainly touching, but the study is a curious one, because other medical studies have come to the opposite conclusions.

George Solomon of the Washington *Post* interviewed Dr. Stanford A. Lavine, an orthopedic surgeon and the team physician for the University of Maryland. "I can see no medical reason why a girl of 12, or younger, cannot compete in baseball with a boy of comparable age," Lavine said. "If anything, girls mature much faster than boys because their growth line flows sooner than boys'."

Dr. Clayton L. Thomas, the Harvard consultant on human reproduction and a member of the United States Olympic Medical and Training Services committee, reported that the vast evidence finds that prior to puberty boys are taller but girls and boys are equal in weight, strength and reaction time.

As its answer to all this, Little League was trying to form a separate girls' league for softball—for "safety's sake." The idea of playing softball instead of baseball is probably a valid one for both sexes at that age, because a softball is obviously less dangerous than a baseball, but to restrict it to the girls' league is obviously patronizing and just another example of the old attitudes.

Little League would be a good level on which to approach the idea of girls competing because those who want to would be physically equipped to handle the competition, and there would be more girls physically qualified at that age than at older age levels. Having girls in the program might also teach the boys a valuable lesson: there are other ways of impressing girls than by baring your muscles.

Having girls in the program might also effect a much-needed change in the emphasis in Little League. Too often, it is now thought of as a training ground for future big league ballplayers, and it is true that well over a majority of big leaguers are Little League graduates. But any program on that level should concern itself more with teaching good sportsmanship and the sheer joy of playing than with developing physical skills in a small minority.

One time I was talking to Joe Kapp about the organized junior sports programs; we were in agreement that they were largely a waste of time. At the time, Joe's son was nine and on a

Little League team. "He goes out to team practice and is bored for an hour," said Joe. "Then he goes off with his friends and has fun playing for hours."

This goes to the basic fault of all these junior programs, whether they be Little League or Pop Warner League or whatever: organization. These programs are all aimed at fitting the adults' needs, not the children's; the adults, not the boys, compartmentalize sports. Whatever caused adults to think it necessary to form léagues and teams and precise standards? It is the playing of the game that should be important, not the keeping of statistics and records. Youth should be a time for experimentation, of trying different sports and different positions and of playing with different friends, instead of being tied down to one group.

It is always easy to overglorify moments in your youth, and I am as susceptible as any to that. But I don't recall feeling deprived as a youth because I didn't have a fancy uniform, or a specific time when I could play ball. When I was a kid, we just played. We used whatever was available. That might have been a school playground or a vacant lot or a big backyard or even a street, but we played.

Our equipment was seldom first-rate. (I remember getting for my birthday a rubber covered baseball that disintegrated within about 30 minutes of the time it was first used.) Usually, we played with a baseball that had long since had the cover knocked off and was covered with friction tape to protect the core. Remember those? It was absolutely impossible to throw a curve with one of those, but we survived.

The important thing was that we had fun. It may seem necessary to adults to have the right equipment and the proper uniforms and some kind of coaching, but it is not that important to the kids. The kids are deprived of something important: anticipation. When you have uniforms and organized play at nine, high school, college and professional ball hold no special lures for you. There is no way of telling how many kids quit baseball early because they have simply grown tired of the overly organized aspects of the game.

There was another important aspect to our games: everybody played. Some were chosen ahead of others, and I can remember those agonizing moments when the captains looked right past me to pick kids on my right and left, but we all played. That is more than you can say for a lot of the Little League programs. There are some leagues where all the kids have to play, and there are some managers in leagues where there are no such requirements who make certain that everybody plays. But there are altogether too many instances where reserves just don't play at all, because the coach has to win.

Again, that is an adult-instilled attitude. Competition is fine; it is the very essence of sports, and life, and something the kids enjoy. But there is great confusion among adults between competition and winning. Kids need to be taught to be satisfied with doing their best, but instead the emphasis is on winning, because the adults need to compete vicariously at the expense of the kids.

Sometimes, when I inveigh against Little League, I feel it's a little like picking on a cripple. It's a natural target. The cast of villains is familiar—the coaches who don't know the game, the umpires who don't know the rules, the mothers who scream at the umpires and managers and players. Oh, yes, especially the mothers. It is very comforting to stand aside and laugh at these people. We could never be like that, of course—so coarse, so unfeeling, so stupid.

Until, that is, our sons become old enough and we are dragged, willy-nilly, into the program. For the awful truth about Little League, the one thing we hate to admit, is that those people are you, me, your neighbor, your brother, even, dear God, your mother.

The people involved in Little League are good people, basically. Most of them are dedicated, earnest, well meaning—and they have produced a monster. Why? Mainly because the whole program was conceived and has been carried on with entirely the wrong set of values.

It is, as I said earlier, too organized for comfort, and the organizational pattern is bad. It starts while the school year is on, which makes it both superfluous and a nuisance. There is certainly no need for an additional recreational program during the school year. Then, precisely when the program is needed, in midsummer, the Little League season is over for all those boys except the ones on teams which make the playoffs.

That might be five percent of those competing during the regular season; it might also be less.

There is one reason for ending the season in July: it is necessary to have playoffs building up to the Little League World Series. Of all the things that's wrong with Little League, that probably tops the list.

It is hard to say who is worse off when the playoffs start, the boys who don't make it or the boys who do. I'm inclined to the latter, because it is in the playoffs that the whole business really gets blown out of proportion. Unless you have witnessed the phenomenon first hand, there is no way you can believe the adulation that adults give to a 12-year-old boy who can throw a fastball by other 12-year-old boys. Even on the local level, boys are spoiled by this kind of attention. Can you imagine what it must be like for those who make it all the way to the Little League World Series? Frightening.

This adulation doesn't last, of course. We have all known pitchers who were overwhelming in Little League because they matured faster than their contemporaries but who fell back in later competition when others catch or surpass them. How would you like being a has-been at 13? There are adults who still look back at 14 strikeouts in a six-inning game at the age of 12 as the high point of their lives. That's great, too, isn't it?

Postseason play also fosters the idea that winning is everything, that a manager should try to develop his best team rather than give everybody a chance to play. And it puts intolerable pressure on the boys so adults can have the opportunity to make fools of themselves. A boy will pitch and lose in the World Series and cry for an hour. This is almost criminal.

I would hope that communities will start to take a long look at the Little League programs and ask themselves if they are really worth it. As they stand now, I don't think they are. Ideally, any form of baseball for youths should have these components:

1. It should be open to both sexes.

2. It should be played through the summer, instead of starting during the school year.

3. It should be run by the recreational office of the city or town, and it should have its games during the day and during

the week. This would discourage parental attendance, which would lower the pressure level and enable the kids to discover and experience the fun of playing instead of being indoctrinated with the necessity of winning.

4. It should be possible for all to play, instead of only the best.

5. It should restrict postseason competition to, at the most, a playoff between adjacent leagues or communities.

Obviously, the national Little League organization isn't going to consent to these ideas, because they take away its raison d'être. But that's the idea. More and more, communities are starting to break away from the national organization, and that's all to the good. If programs are administered locally, they can do a better job of adjusting to changing situations and supplying what is needed for that community without being subject to rigid ideas and the pressure brought on by a national organization.

18

.

A Better Idea For Intercollegiate Sports

In David Wolf's excellent book on Connie Hawkins, *Foul!*, he tells of the time when Hawkins was being recruited by college basketball coaches. The story is worth recounting as an example of what college athletics really mean.

Hawkins was then being taught by Nathan Mazer, head of the English department at his high school. "The first day they worked together," wrote Wolf, "Mazer gave a reading test and an IQ test to the young man 250 colleges wanted as a student. Connie's reading level was seventh grade. His IQ was 65: low-grade moron."

That did not discourage any college recruiters, of course, because Hawkins had great basketball ability. They figured they could get him through school by tutoring him well and scheduling him in basket weaving and its many variations.

Nor is this a unique or even unusual occurrence. Every year, there are probably hundreds of such cases. There is no way of measuring the exact number because most of the cases are only whispered about, but you get a general idea from the high percentage of athletes who do not graduate from college.

In his first year with the Oakland Raiders, I talked to offensive tackle Bob Brown, who took an understandable pride in the fact that he had graduated from the University of Nebraska, through no fault of the athletic department. "They wanted me to play football and that was the end of it," said Brown. "They set me up with a faculty counselor the first year and he had me signed up for 12 units a semester. I didn't know any better then [Brown came from the ghetto area of Cleveland and admits that he was far below average in academic skills at the time] so I went along with it. But at the end of my freshman year, I sat down and figured there was no way I was going to graduate in four years taking only 12 units [an average of 15 was required]. So, I made out my own program. I had to take a lot of extra units to make up for that first year, but I made it in four years."

Brown is an exception in more ways than one. He fought his way out of the ghetto on his own, and he has a physically comfortable life today. A lot of athletes, particularly the black ones, don't make out that well. Coaches and college presidents bend the rules to get them into school and they bend the rules to keep them in, but they make no effort to educate them.

In college sports, rules are made to be broken. The NCAA is supposed to be a watchdog and does catch a few: in 1973, for instance, it caught Southwestern Louisiana State in a whopping 115 violations, and Oklahoma was forced to forfeit its football wins of the previous year because somebody had falsified the academic record of a freshman player. But these only scratch the surface, as everybody knows.

A case I am personally familiar with surfaced in 1971. The University of California was put on probation because Isaac Curtis (and another player, Larry Brumsey, who soon dropped out of intercollegiate football) had failed to take the 1.6 test in the spring before he entered the university. The test was designed to predict a student's performance in college: if he did not score at least 1.6 (C-minus) on the test, he was not eligible for intercollegiate athletics unless he first went to junior college. The rule has since been banned by the courts for good and sufficient reasons.

Nobody but the NCAA knows for certain the exact violations of the rule in the Cal case, since the documents were not made public, but from what I understand from those close to the case, Curtis was advised not to take the test by an assistant coach.

There are several things that should be understood about that case. First is the school it involved. I am convinced that the NCAA has a particular grievance against Cal because it was at Berkeley that the student demonstrations first started. The NCAA, whose officials all have the crew-cut mentality of the 1950s, is convinced that student demonstrations are the root of of all our society's problems.

Second is the fact that at the time the violations were first made public, Curtis was carrying a B average at the university, far beyond what the 1.6 test required. This would seem to make the issue a dead one, but it obviously wasn't to the NCAA, which pursued it with great zeal.

Third is the school's athletic record in recent years. Cal has not been to the Rose Bowl since 1958. Its '71 NCAA track championship (taken away because Curtis competed on the team) was its first. In basketball, Cal had won the '60 national championship under Pete Newell but had been under .500 in all the games played since. If there was anything the school authorities needed to be punished for in sports, it was ineptness, not cheating. It seems a little difficult to believe that Cal was cheating and USC and UCLA were not, though the southern schools had dominated football, basketball and track on the conference and even the national level in that same time.

The NCAA move put the Cal authorities in an impossible bind: either they suspended Curtis and punished him for something that was not his fault, or they played Curtis and took an indefinite NCAA suspension (later extended to 1975) and thus punished the other players, who would not be eligible for any postseason play.

Cal decided to take the suspension and let Curtis play, which he did in his junior year. In his senior year, he transferred to San Diego State, where he was moved from running back to wide receiver and played well enough to be drafted by Cincinnati on the first round of the college draft. (In a similar situation involving running back James McAlister, UCLA suspended the athlete and remained in the NCAA's good graces—but, of course, UCLA had a national championship basketball team to consider.)

Significantly, in the Curtis case, all the wrong people were punished. Though Curtis was not suspended, he felt the pressure all year of being one of the athletes who had caused the school to be put on suspension, and it was that pressure which caused him to transfer. Football coach Mike White, not at the school at the time of the violation; Dave Maggard, named athletic director after the event; and all the school's athletes, none of them involved in the case, suffered. Meanwhile, the assistant coach who was involved moved on to another school, without any punishment. That is always the way it is—the innocent are punished and the guilty go free—which is why our system of intercollegiate athletics is a farce.

It is basketball in which the most flagrant violations occur, because of the nature of the sport. You need far fewer players to be a contender in basketball than in football, and one player can mean practically everything. Joe Namath doesn't help you if you don't have support for him, but Bill Walton makes a team a contender even if he's playing with four cripples. So basketball coaches, whether they be knaves or decent men, are forced to break the rules, to get that one player who can make the big difference. The best players are promised money, girls, anything. Once in awhile—Walton being the best example—these boys are from solid enough homes that they can maintain their perspective in the face of all the temptations.

Usually, they are not, however, because basketball is the city game, the ghetto sport. Imagine what it is like to youths who have never had anything in their lives. Suddenly, they are taught that their basketball skills are marketable. They are brought to college to play basketball. If they are academically deficient, and they usually are, the recruiters don't care; they can always find meaningless courses and cooperative professors to make certain the athletes stay eligible.

Sometimes, the story has a happy ending, and the athletes go on to make a lot of money in professional basketball. Too often, it does not. Something happens along the way; perhaps a player takes money to shave points. Why not? A coach, a respected man in his community, has already taught him that rules don't apply to good athletes. Even if they don't shave points, they can get in trouble. Hawkins was kicked out of school and banned from the NBA because he was approached by a gambler. He lacked the education and verbal skills to satisfy his interrogators that he was innocent, and our society is quick to punish the inarticulate.

Usually, the players simply aren't good enough to make it in pro ball, so they go back to the ghetto and a bleak future. They haven't learned anything in college that would help them get a job; basket weaving isn't much in demand these days. And pimping and numbers running are the only profitable occupations in the ghetto. The blacks know all this, and the pressure for success weighs far more heavily on them than on the white players.

Such pressure contributed to the '72 incident in the Minnesota–Ohio State game when, with only seconds remaining and Ohio State leading, 50-44, the Buckeyes' Luke Witte was kneed in the groin by Minnesota's Corky Taylor, starting a free-for-all. It was a natural outbreak for a player coached by Minnesota's Bill Musselman, who preached that defeat is worse than death.

When ugly incidents like this occur, the athletes are punished, but there is seldom an attempt to get at the cause of the problem. The coaches who broke the rules are not punished, nor are the college presidents who want teams that will make their schools famous, nor the alumni who demand winners before they will contribute to the building fund. Those who do not learn from history are doomed to repeat it.

There are other excesses in the collegiate athletic programs. Athletic scholarships are the traditional means of acquiring athletes for the programs, but nobody has yet devised a satisfactory method of dealing out the scholarships. Some conferences limit scholarships, but that never works, because coaches always find ways to get around the limits. Gary Shaw, in his excellent book about football at the University of Texas, *Meat On the Hoof,* tells how:

> An integral part of spring training was "shit drills." These drills were for the purpose of running guys off—making them quit. . . . There was a practical reason. The conference rule was that at any one time a school could have only the money equivalent of a hundred full scholarships. . . . From 1961 to 1964, Texas gave 207 full scholarships. Since Royal could legally have only a hundred on scholarships, over half this 200 plus had to give up their scholarships for Royal to stay inside the conference limit.

The "shit drills" were designed to cause such physical punishment (they always featured players colliding after running some distances at full speed) that players couldn't continue. As such, they worked. "Those drills," wrote Shaw, "started with 45 players and after three weeks of 2½-hour drills each day, only 5 were left, and they weren't part of the original 45."

The NCAA, in its infinite wisdom, found a way to end this punishment in early 1973: the organization simply made scholarships a one-year grant, and gave schools the right to renew them or not, at their discretion.

"The coach needs protection," said Walter Byers, head of the NCAA. "It had gone too far on behalf of the kids."

At least, Byers was honest about it. No more of this nonsense about building character. If the player doesn't measure up, his scholarship is taken away. Thus, schools don't have to worry about "shit drills" but can get on with the real business of inter-collegiate sports, which is building a team for the alumni.

"No, there is no guideline for renewal requirements," said Byers. "If the student-athlete has a complaint, he can take it to the school's scholarship committee. Hell, he can always transfer."

The arrogance of that statement is rather breathtaking, but it's standard NCAA. The organization obviously regards the athletic scholarship as a contract which can be terminated by the school at any time. Forgotten is all the pretty rhetoric about how athletic scholarships help boys get through college who would not otherwise be able to afford it. If they can't cut it athletically, get out. This shouldn't be surprising to those who have followed college sports, and particularly the NCAA's supervision of them. The idea is to protect the colleges, not the individual.

All the recent moves support that idea. An additional game was added to college football schedules, for instance, so that more money could be raised. Freshmen were made eligible for varsity sports, though that hurts most freshmen athletes, because freshmen teams could then be reduced or completely eliminated. And the whole emphasis on the program for the really big time schools is to discourage competition; only the very gifted are allowed to compete, and the competition is limited as much as possible to the revenue-producing sports.

The only solution, I think, is to abolish all the codes and artificial restrictions and make only a distinction between the professional schools and Ivy League–type schools, allowing each school to decide for itself which road to take.

The Ivy League is the only major conference in the country in which student-athletes are predominant. In the other major conferences, the difference between schools is of degree, not kind. There are, to be sure, more premed majors on any given Stanford team than on a USC team, but the good players are usually aiming at a pro career. In recent years, the only good Stanford player who spurned the pros was Jackie Brown.

In the Ivy League, there are no athletic scholarships as such, though athletic ability is (as are musical ability and political ability) considered in giving scholarships. The emphasis is on sports as part of the educational system. The quality of Ivy League sports is, of course, quite low compared to other major conferences, but it makes no difference because the schools are evenly matched. A Harvard-Columbia game is more interesting, for that reason, than a Cal-USC game.

Since intercollegiate athletics is so expensive—especially for teams which have been consistent losers—it would make sense for a lot of schools to go the Ivy League route. For the rest, honest professionalism would seem to be the best. It is hard to pretend that most of the big time schools are not professional now. The only significant difference between USC and the Oakland Raiders is that the Raiders pay better. Sometimes, even that distinction is blurred.

The professional schools could hire their athletes openly and not pretend to make them go to class. As it is now, athletes are steered into easy courses that hardly advance their education so they can stay eligible. Under this system, athletes could go to any class they wished, but they wouldn't be required to go to any class and their grades would have no bearing on their eligibility. Some might even find they liked to try the tough courses, knowing they wouldn't be penalized for it.

The athletes would be paid a living wage, though nothing like a professional one, because they would be playing college ball only to gain the necessary experience for pro ball. This is happening now, though few like to admit it.

Thus, the hypocrisy of the present program would be swept away. No longer would it be necessary for coaches to lie, cheat and steal, or to talk about building character at the same time they are breaking the rules themselves and encouraging athletes to break them, too. I would think the coaches would welcome the chance to be honest men again.

19

•

Racism, From Aaron To Ali

As Henry Aaron drove for Babe Ruth's career home run record, his mail got ever more abusive. The secretary, Carla Koplin, who was assigned to handle it said, "I wish he wouldn't read it." Some of it was simply the same kind of thing that Roger Maris had to face in 1961 when he went for Ruth's season home run record: some sports fans, especially the older ones, do not like to see their old-time heroes diminished, and they feel that breaking Ruth's records sullies him somehow. This kind of thinking led commissioner Ford Frick, the great equivocator, to put an asterisk after Maris' record. But a lot of the heat Aaron got came simply because he was a black man chasing a white man's record. The mail he got increasingly started off: "Dear Nigger." There was at least one anonymous death threat if he broke Ruth's record. "It bothers me," said Aaron. "I have seen a President shot and his brother shot. The man who murdered Dr. Martin Luther King is in jail, but that isn't doing Dr. King much good, is it? I have four children, and I have to be concerned about their welfare."

None of that should surprise anybody. The racism of the modern fan lies in most cases scarcely below the surface, and sometimes it is not even that deep. I know every time I write favorably about a black player for The San Francisco *Chronicle,* I will get a certain amount of unsigned—yes, always unsigned—mail which starts out, "Nigger Lover," and goes downhill from there. Often, readers misinterpret to fit their own needs. When I criticized Willie Mays, some were happy to assume that it was because he was black, though I had taken pains to indict Mays for his unwillingness to stand up for his fellow blacks.

Virtually the only mail I get supporting Charlie Finley has been because of Finley's attitude toward black players, which often seems like that of the plantation owner to his slaves. (Of course, this is Finley's general attitude toward all employees, white, black or in between.) There was no question that Finley's side of the Vida Blue dispute was popular with white fans, and there was also no question that Blue's race had much to do with that. A white pitcher asking that much money could be forgiven; a black pitcher could not be.

It seems very difficult, even now, for whites to accept blacks in sports as simply human beings, and the reverse is sometimes also true. A black reporter from Washington wrote after the 1973 Super Bowl that there were many blacks playing in the game and few writing about it. It was his thesis that black athletes talk honestly only to black writers, and thus very little that was written about black athletes by white writers was valid. You've probably already guessed his solution: more black writers and radio-TV newsmen. Can you imagine what he would have said if somebody had proposed an opposite solution—to bring in more white athletes?

This is just racism in reverse, of course, and it does nobody any good. It's nonsense to say you need the same skin color to get a story from an athlete. There are always going to be some athletes a writer gets more from than others, but that depends on the whole personality, not just one attribute. Two examples: I can talk far more easily with Tom Keating, who is white, than Tommy Hart, who is black; I can also talk much more easily with Gene Washington, who is black, than I could with Billy Cannon, who is white.

The need for more black newsmen is obvious, but the cause is not served by this kind of talk. Nor is it served by those who are only marginally qualified and who often bluff their way into situations because of their skin color, who go around filling the air with "brothers" and hollering discrimination whenever they, or any other blacks, are criticized.

I ran into that situation myself in the spring of 1973 when I wrote a column critical of the Warriors' Cazzie Russell. A black radio newsman was in the Warriors' dressing room that night, telling Cazzie he was the victim of racism and harassing any white writer who tried to talk to a black athlete. I doubt that Russell himself believed that, because he's not stupid, but it's annoying. The black newsman was interested in furthering his own career, of course, not Russell's or the other blacks on the team. He would love to set up a black-white division because it would limit his white press opposition, and he cares little if that exacerbates the already-existing racial tensions.

In the best of all possible worlds, we should be able to treat black and white alike. That millennium may never be reached, but failing that, we should at least be willing to live and let live; it should not matter whether an athlete is black or white or yellow or brown if he does the job. But it does matter to a lot of people.

When I wrote about the Russell incident, I got letters from white fans who thought I was saying there should be fewer blacks in sports; either I was more obscure in my writing than I thought or they weren't paying attention, because I didn't intend that at all.

That blacks should be limited to a certain number in sports is a favorite theme song of a lot of white sports fans. In a sense, the blacks have brought this on themselves by demanding quotas according to their numbers in other fields. But it would be stupid to contend that this is the main reason for the whites' demands in sports. The bigots wouldn't want blacks at all, and they simply seize on any argument that's handy to advance their cause.

Owners are quite conscious of this, and they bow to the fans' wishes partially by limiting the number of blacks on a team, though not often any longer the number on a starting team, because that proved to be self-defeating. Blacks know they must be better than a white player to stay around; there is probably no team anywhere in professional sports which would not make the decision in favor of the white player if a white or black is battling for the last spot on the bench. Blacks are starters or nothing, generally.

Of course, owners, managers and coaches also use the fans' attitude as an excuse. There is seldom much effort to educate the fans because those in the hierarchy feel the same way. Almost 30 years after Jackie Robinson broke the color barrier in major league baseball, and at a time when Southern politicians even carefully avoid the word in public, baseball coaches and managers often use the word "nigger" to describe their ballplayers in private conversation.

It is still generally true that teams room black athletes together and white athletes together but seldom mix the two. If there is an odd number of blacks on the team, one of them will get a room to himself. This results from a blindness on the part of coaches and managers to the fact that there are some blacks who are closer to whites on the team, because of their own background, than to other blacks. On the A's, for instance, Reggie Jackson and Joe Rudi are very close; Jackson was also very close to Dave Duncan—he cried when Duncan was traded to the Cleveland Indians. Jackson, of course, is black, and Rudi and Duncan are white.

Most of the theories about black participation in sports have been proved wrong along the way, but that hasn't stopped white management from entertaining other myths. Once, it was said that blacks could play the other positions but did not have the courage to become baseball pitchers, but Bob Gibson certainly disproved that; Gibson pitched his way out of an inning after his right leg, the one which supported his weight when he went into his motion, had been broken.

Some thought there would never be a good black tennis player, but that was before Althea Gibson and Arthur Ashe. Like golf, the other "country club" sport, the only thing that stops blacks from becoming proficient in the sport is their lack of opportunity to play it.

Blacks were once eliminated from consideration for the "thinking" positions in football, like quarterback or middle linebacker, But Willie Lanier certainly proved that a black can play the latter position. That great black quarterback still hasn't arrived, but that is due to a number of reasons—ability to play other positions, lack of coaching in college—totally unrelated to intelligence. (The intelligence of quarterbacks is much overrated, anyway. It is intuitive knowledge that is most important. Frank Ryan was much smarter than either John Unitas or Joe Namath, but Unitas and Namath were more adept at reading defenses.)

When blacks started playing baseball, there was a definite quota system. At first, only one was allowed, and some clubs resisted even that for quite a while; the Boston Red Sox didn't get their first black, the otherwise undistinguished Elijah "Pumpsie" Green, until 1959. Then, they had to be the "right" kind of blacks. No "uppity" blacks were allowed. Jackie Robinson had to hide his combative personality when he first started with Brooklyn, and the Yankees were reluctant to bring up Vic Power because he was too flashy a ballplayer. They traded Power and brought in Elston Howard, who was smart enough to say only the right things and act only the right way. Nobody would ever accuse Howard of being too flashy, and thus he survived with the Yankees. Then too, it was understood that there could never be a majority of blacks on the field at a time, because the fans would count them and stay away. But the Dodgers broke that rule and everybody survived. It is no longer worthy of mention when a team has more black starters than white, but attendance has increased in baseball, football and basketball since blacks were allowed in.

Basketball is the only major sport with more than 50 percent blacks throughout the league, but the sport is moving ahead in spite of itself. Because of its majority of black players, basketball has been the pioneer in black coaches, and along the way, a couple of more stereotypes have been broken. It was whispered that blacks weren't smart enough to coach, but Bill Russell came along and coached the Celtics to championships. It was feared that whites wouldn't respond to a black coach, but Al Attles has coached the Warriors—a team which has had as many as four white starters, two of them Southerners—and there have been no racial problems.

It took some guts on the part of Red Auerbach to name Russell as his successor. In one way, Russell was the logical man to coach the Celtics. He had been the dominant figure in the sport and his team won 11 of 13 NBA championships while he played. But Russell is very much his own man. He does not believe in taking a back seat to anybody, which necessarily offends those who believe blacks are inferior. Making him the first black coach was comparable to making Jackie Robinson the first black baseball manager. But nobody seriously thought of making Robinson a manager because he was too outspoken.

Even as a player, Russell criticized his former coach, Phil Woolpert, of having racial stereotypes when Woolpert was coaching the great USF teams of the mid-50s. And when he was named coach of the Seattle SuperSonics in the spring of 1973, he referred to racial discrimination in Boston when he was a coach and player there.

"I had what was to me a very traumatic experience working in Boston, and there are some scars left," Russell said. "Boston is probably the most rigidly segregated city in the country. When I went there, I felt they had a code of conduct—first for athletes and another for black athletes. For example, one of the writers, about the second year I was there, told me he didn't think I was a good enough person to be playing with the Celtics."

Russell said one year the Celtics signed their top draft choice, a black, "and on the front page of the sports pages it said that would make four black guys on the team and the city of Boston wasn't ready for that many blacks on one team. And so I asked the writer about that and he said he meant nothing personal about it.

"In Boston, we won 11 championships and after the last championship, all I could hear was that there were too many black guys on the team."

This all happened in what is probably the most advanced, in racial matters, of the major sports. Baseball and football are worse and hockey, of course, is a white man's sport. (Which may be why the Bruins, when they were losers, outdrew the champion Celtics in Boston.)

For years, Frank Robinson has been the logical choice for the first black manager. He is intelligent and competitive, and he has proved his managing ability in the Puerto Rican Winter League. And yet, there are a lot in baseball who have disliked the idea of Frank Robinson managing a team; the very people who admire Billy Martin for his aggressiveness dislike Robinson for the same trait, because his skin is a different color. There has always been vague talk about Robinson "proving himself" by managing in the minors. Alvin Dark, whose playing virtues were similar to Robinson's, started his managing career in the majors. Dark, of course, is white.

Pro football isn't any better. There are plenty of black players of stature who would make good head coaches, but as far as I know, none have been seriously considered. Most club managements think they are making a big move when they hire a black coach—to talk to the black players, of course.

That's the situation in the team sports, but the classic case of racism in sports remains that practiced in an individual sport, boxing, against Muhammad Ali, née Cassius Clay. It is sad, because Ali could have been the greatest boxer of all time but fate and man conspired to make his career a case of what might have been. Only for a brief period was he allowed to show what he could do at his best, and there was nobody else even close.

He was so much better than anybody else he could tease and torment those who had offended him—Floyd Patterson, Ernie Terrell—by cruelly carrying them for several rounds and inflicting further punishment before knocking them out. During that brief reign, he may have been the best boxer-puncher the heavyweight division has ever seen. Certainly, he was the most entertaining. The ring was his stage, and he was a master performer. His style irritated the purists because he violated some basic rules. He carried his gloves too low for one thing, and he pulled his head back to slip punches instead of blocking them or ducking them. By all rights, that should have left him open and vulnerable, but it did not, because he was so fast, he could make up for his fundamental errors—just as, in another sport, Willie Mays made his own performing rules.

Outside the ring, Ali was a great promoter, talking constantly to all who would listen and some who would not. He made up poems to predict what he would do in the ring, and he often hit his predictions right on the nose. In the ring, he was a delight. He would dance away from his opponents, taunt them and dare them to hit him; they could not, because he was so much faster. He was a delight to watch, and a breath of fresh air in a sport which needed it.

It would seem that such a presence would be welcomed, but it was not. Boxing, traditionally a sport for the economically underprivileged part of society, was more open to blacks than other sports, but the attitudes of those in the sport and those watching it were hardly enlightened.

In the early part of the century, heavyweight champion Jack Johnson had scandalized white America by his actions while he had the title, and the actions of black heavyweights since then had been very different, of necessity. The most-admired black champion was Joe Louis, who was quiet and self-effacing to the point of obsequiousness.

Ali, then Cassius Clay, was of a different mold: he was uppity. He kept predicting he would win and talked about being "The Greatest," and he was never servile to whites. Unlike Johnson, he did not go with white women, but he did everything else wrong, as far as a lot of white sports fans were concerned. Sonny Liston, who had served time and seemed never more than a step and a half away from prison the rest of his life, would properly punish Clay, thought many fans, and he was reviled when he lost twice to Clay, under suspicious circumstances. Patterson was the "white hope" when he fought Ali, because he had the proper self-effacing attitude which Ali lacked. And when Ali finally fought Joe Frazier, the rooting interest often broke down along racial lines, though both were black. The black fans mostly rooted for Ali and a lot of whites rooted for Frazier, as they had for Liston earlier, to punish Ali.

When Clay joined a Black Muslim group and changed his name, that was the last straw for many white fans. He had to be punished, and a way would be found, sooner or later. Eventually, Ali supplied the method for his own punishment by refusing to serve in the Army.

The name change irritated a lot of whites beyond all reason. The same people who would not have thought of calling Sugar Ray Robinson by his real name, Walker Smith, or Jersey Joe Walcott by his, Arnold Cream, could not bring themselves to call Ali anything but Cassius Clay. To me, it was a simple matter of human dignity: a man has the right to be called whatever he wants to be called. A lot of people were not willing to grant Ali that dignity. (Not only whites, either—Frazier always called him "Clay.")

Then, Ali made the mistake of refusing to go into the Army and saying he had no quarrel with "them Viet Cong." In a surfeit of self-righteousness, boxing commissions took away his title because he would not serve. The action was unquestionably unconstitutional because he had not been convicted of a crime, but the commissioners were interested in protecting the reputation of boxing, a sport-business that is notoriously gangster infested.

In retrospect, it would have been nice if the President of the United States had shared Ali's disinclination to fight the Viet Cong, instead of dragging us further and further into a dispute that was none of our business.

Ali's decision came at a time when a lot of respectable people were beginning to question the wisdom of the Vietnam War, but nobody got the abuse he did. Because Ali belonged to the Black Muslims, many scoffed at his claim of being a conscientious objector. Yet, you have to concede that his decision was one of principle, because he could certainly have avoided combat by serving in a Special Services unit, as athletes have usually done. Instead, he chose a different course and fought it to an eventually successful conclusion, but it was a Pyrrhic victory. He spent twice the time in exile that he would have served in the Army, and he must have known that this would happen.

When Ali was finally reinstated, he was not the same fighter he had been. An athlete who has been away from his sport for a year often has great trouble returning; Warren Wells, who caught 36 touchdown passes in three years for the Oakland Raiders, could not make the team after he had been imprisoned for a year. Ali had been away for four years. He was still quicker afoot than any other heavyweight, but he was no longer uncatchable. When he fought Frazier, he could not fight in the style which had made him so successful earlier. He had to stand flat-footed much of the time and slug with Frazier, and thus Frazier won, though there is no question that had they met in Ali's prime, Ali would have won easily.

Typically, the loss to Frazier didn't stop Ali. For the next couple of years, while others were trying to rematch the two, he went everywhere, fighting everyone, while Frazier was ducking him and fighting nobodies like Ron Stander and Terry Daniels until he ran into an unexpectedly stiff George Foreman punch.

But though Ali kept interest alive in the heavyweight division by default, it was not the same. He struggled with fighters who wouldn't have belonged in the same ring with him earlier, and he had his jaw broken by the nondescript Ken Norton. Racism had once again claimed a victim, and we were all the poorer for it.

20

.

Are The Olympics Really Necessary?

More and more, sports are being used as a political vehicle—by both ends of the political spectrum—because they have the attention of the world. Nowhere is this more obvious than in the Olympics, though those in charge continue to pretend that it is above politics.

Adolf Hitler tried to use the '36 Games as a background for his racial theories, though that exploded in his face when Jesse Owens won four Gold Medals. In 1968, led by Harry Edwards, who is now a professor at the University of California, American blacks threatened a boycott, throwing the American Olympic team plans into utter confusion. In the end, the official boycott was called off—Lew Alcindor/Kareem Abdul-Jabbar conducted his own unofficial boycott with the basketball team—but Tommie Smith and John Carlos demonstrated the black power salute on the victory stand, which got them thrown off the team by an uptight U.S. Olympic Committee.

In 1972, the political controversy centered around the Rhodesian team because of Rhodesia's racial policies. The International Olympic Committee thought it had solved the dilemma by calling Rhodesia a British colony, which was a transparent fiction. When the black countries threatened to pull out, the IOC buckled under the political pressure and expelled Rhodesia from the Games.

Though the Summer Games, because of their wider scope, have more often been involved in politics, the Winter Games have not been left alone, either. Denver was awarded the '76 Winter Games, but environmentalists in Colorado led a successful fight to back out of sponsorship of the Games.

Mexican students sought to use the Olympics as a forum to protest inequities in their society in 1968, but the Mexican government discovered a way to quell that rebellion: soldiers were ordered to shoot the rebels. The government feared that too lengthy a protest would have forced cancellation of the Games, which were to be used as a showcase for Mexico, and reasoned correctly that the student deaths would soon be glossed over. Those attending the Games seemed to give little thought to the price that had been paid so the show could go on; the Mexican Games were hailed as one of the best in Olympic history.

But nothing captured the imagination as did the assassination of the Israeli athletes by Arab terrorists in 1972 at Munich. Given the stature of the Olympics, this kind of violence was predictable, but it horrified everybody. As they expected, the Arab terrorists got far more publicity than they would have even by hijacking airplanes. They were wrong in thinking the publicity would help their cause, but they could not be expected to understand that in their demented state. They should have never been given an opportunity like that.

To the eternal shame of all those concerned, the '72 Olympics dragged on to their conclusion, despite the deaths. They should have been ended immediately. That they were not proved that, to those concerned, the playing of games was more important than the loss of human life. Stopping the Games would not have brought any of the dead back to life, but human decency required the gesture. It was startling that the "Olympic ideal" was more important to some than human dignity. Yet, it was almost to be expected. I was surprised there was even a temporary halt, because it would have been more in keeping with Avery Brundage's philosophy to ignore the carnage and insist the Games must not be delayed.

Brundage, the former president of the IOC, is a special case. To his mind, the Olympics have always been more important than anything, and it is easy to pillory him for that. But he is not alone. One syndicated columnist, so long concerned with the playing of games that he has lost his perspective, suggested that because Tel Aviv airport was not closed when Arab terrorists killed people there, the Olympics should not be stopped, either. This is errant nonsense, equating what is real and important with what is not. Obviously, you cannot close everything and head for the bomb shelters because terrorists have struck; just as obviously, you can stop those things which are not necessary. The Olympics, despite all the pomp and fanfare, are surely in the latter category.

Others were determined that the terrorists not be allowed to kill the Olympic ideal. There was really no need to worry: the Olympic ideal was killed years ago, and some of its most ardent supporters were to blame. It has remained only as a myth. The ideal was killed by those who emphasize nationalism in the Olympics, which means virtually everybody; it was killed by those who have used the Games to promote political philosophies; it was killed by those who talk piously of peaceful competition while encouraging, actively or passively, killing outside the arena. Let us not forget that while our team was competing in the Olympics, we were dropping tons of bombs on Vietnam, nor that the Spanish Civil War was on during the first German Olympics, in 1936, and that Italy's conquest of Ethiopia had just been concluded, nor that the Korean War was on during the '52 Games. So much for the idea that by competing peacefully on the athletic fields, nations would forswear competition on the fields of war.

The Olympics as a symbol are dead. They remain only as sporting competition and spectacle, important enough in that context but not all-important, as their more fervent supporters think. It was a grand concept, an Olympic Games which would bring people together, but the concept does not match the reality. The only way to save the Games is to destroy them. As they exist now, the problems are insuperable. And, so what? Who needs the Olympics? The athletes? They benefit as much from the smaller international meets, which do not cause the problems the Olympics cause. The countries? Get serious.

The Olympics are very welcome to those who have the construction contracts. Beautiful buildings are erected in the host country, for no purpose. Only occasionally is something built which can be used after the Olympics are gone.

The basic concept of the Olympic Games needs to be examined, because it is a concept which is inevitably driving a further wedge between the haves and the have-nots. There is, for example, the emphasis on building. Brundage always liked to move the Games around so that more countries would build magnificent new structures, but there are a couple of serious objections to that. One is that, even if a country can afford it, building huge athletic structures is a waste because the problem in modern life, particularly in this country, is that too many people are willing to watch the best instead of trying the games themselves. Participation should be encouraged, but the Olympics discourages it because the Games are open only to the very best. There are far more professional athletes in this country than Olympians.

And the cost of the structures, particularly to poor countries, is overwhelming. The facilities Mexico developed for the '68 Olympics were beautiful, but in Mexico City today you still cannot drink the water and the streets are lined with beggars who lack even the very minimum of food and clothing. What benefit did Mexico derive from the Olympics to compensate for that? How much better it would have been to divert that money to combat illiteracy and poverty.

As this is being written, there is some question whether Montreal can afford the '76 Summer Olympics. Montreal Mayor Jean Drapeau, in pushing his city before the IOC, had assumed financial help from the rest of Canada, but the rest of Canada was not all that eager to help Montreal, a French city in a country which has a majority of English-speaking citizens. Aside from the French-English conflict, there was reason for Canadians to wonder what it would do for them to have the Olympics—besides increasing their taxes.

In Colorado, before the voters brought government officials and Chamber of Commerce boosters to their senses, the people were faced with these thoughts, as written by Sam Brown Jr. in the *New Republic:*

Are The Olympics Really Necessary?

1. No government has ever made money on the Winter Olympics.

2. The Squaw Valley Winter Olympics in 1969 had, to early 1972, cost the taxpayers more than 13 times the original optimistic estimate of $1 million; the cost had risen to $13.5 million.

3. The '68 Winter Games in Grenoble, France, has cost $250 million, of which $50 million was paid by taxpayers. At the time of the article, the city was still heavily in debt and local property taxes had risen 125 percent!

Because costs had risen steadily and because an Olympics in Colorado would have had to be spread out much more than at Grenoble, it would have cost fantastic sums to put on the '76 Games at Denver.

This is best put in perspective by comparing the cost of the Olympics with other items in the Colorado state budget, with figures again supplied by the *New Republic* article. The money allotted to build the bobsled and luge course was four times the annual state budget for air and water pollution control; the cost of the speed skating facilities was seven times the budget for handicapped children; and the ski jump would have cost 75 times the amount spent on the control of venereal disease the previous year. This, I submit, is scandalous, and the Colorado voters eventually agreed. Faced with the huge sums that would be needed and the very possible harm that could be done to the environment, they voted down the Olympics, showing what I suspect is the first sign of a dissatisfaction with the Games that is certain to spread.

For an event which is supposedly amateur, the Olympics are very solidly based in money. It costs money to put them on, and it costs money to compete. The Winter Games, in particular, are a rich man's activity. Even in countries like this with excellent winter sports facilities, it costs money to get to the areas and it costs money to buy the equipment and use the facilities; thus, these sports are almost entirely the property of the rich and upper-middle classes. A ghetto boy may make the U.S. track team, but you won't see him skiing in the Olympics.

The Olympics started as and have remained in may respects a sport for the aristocracy. Look at the list of events in the

Summer Games; do you think you will find many poor men and women competing in the equestrian events?

Many of the Olympic officials, like Brundage, are rich men, which explains their cavalier disregard for the amount of money required of countries and competitors. And even those who do not have money have a strange attitude toward reimbursements: in 1972, the U.S. Olympic Committee would not pay expenses for the athletes at the track and field qualifying meet in Eugene, Oregon, even when Olympic coach Bill Bowerman arranged for a commercial tie-in that would have paid all the expenses.

If the Olympics are to be continued, several changes should be made immediately. Nationalism should be discouraged, instead of encouraged. As it is now, the Olympics officially promote individualism, but in fact, they promote strong nationalistic feelings. The Games start with a parade of the country's competitors under their own flag, which leaves no doubt in anybody's mind what is happening. Though no official team standings are maintained, the United States and Soviet Union have always kept their own totals, usually on standards which would best boost their own totals while holding down the other's, and the totals are printed in the country's newspapers.

There is no way to stop this entirely, but a good start could be made by eliminating all team sports, which would promote individual competition. Separate competitions could be held in the team sports, as they are now in the World Cup of soccer or in tennis's Davis Cup. This would have the concurrent value of reducing the number of athletes in the Games and thus the emphasis, which would make it less likely they would be used for political and terrorist ends.

Setting up permanent sites for both Summer and Winter Games would eliminate all the senseless building of structures which are seldom used after the Olympics are gone. The Winter Games should be established in a resort area, such as Innsbruck, Austria, which could be expected to benefit from having the Games, and the Summer Games should be put in an area which would meet the requirements of housing and athletic facilities and perhaps security as well.

And, finally, all the nonsense about amateur codes and professionalism should be eliminated by simply throwing the Games open to any who want to compete. The Games are supposed to be strictly amateur, but even Brundage must realize by now they are not. To call any of the Communist athletes amateurs is to make a mockery of the facts. There is no professional sport in Communist countries, so athletes have jobs, but they are token jobs which leave them free to compete as long as they are able in their specialties without worrying about the support of their families.

In European countries, winter sports have more importance than in our country, so skiers in particular have made quite a good living while remaining technically amateurs. Brundage, though quite willing to close his eyes to Soviet professionalism, was constantly enraged because of the obvious commercial tie-ins that European skiers have. He ruled Austria's Karl Schranz ineligible during the '72 Winter Games, though it would have required a Solomon to explain how Schranz's case differed radically from others.

Although the United States has clearly suffered in its competition with the Communist countries because of this outmoded amateur code, Clifford Buck, president of the U.S. Olympic Committee, said in 1972 that if the pros were allowed in the Olympics, "That will be the end. The man who competes because he loves the sport would never have a chance against one who spends his entire life working to perfect his professional skills." Buck's statement overwhelms one with nostalgia, for it is exactly the kind of thinking that prevailed around the turn of the century, when amateur sports were the only thing a gentleman would ever play and golf pros had to enter country clubs by the servant's entrance.

The distinction between amateur and pro, even in this country, is so blurred as to be meaningless. Tennis officials finally had to admit that in setting up a division of players who could compete in amateur tournaments and yet take prize money from professional tournaments. Is a college football player, for instance, an amateur because he does not get a salary or a pro because he accepts money in the form of an athletic scholarship? Is a skier an amateur or a pro if he gets money for endorsing a product? Is a Communist athlete amateur or pro when he gets paid for a job which he leaves to train for his sport?

The difference, usually, is in the amount of money; there are few gentlemen athletes any more, in this country or elsewhere. An amateur is one who gets less money (usually, though not always) than a pro, and has to take it under the table.

Track and field is the best example in this country of the kind of hypocrisy supposedly amateur athletes have to practice. Prior to the starting of a professional tour in early 1973, the only track and field competition was in the amateur meets and no athlete, after college, could afford to hold down a full-time job and yet have enough time to practice and retain his athletic proficiency. So, athletes took money under false pretenses. One long-accepted practice was for athletes to accept money from promoters for trips they never took. An East Coast athlete, for instance, would be given money for two plane tickets from his home to Los Angeles and San Francisco. Then, he would buy one ticket, and stay in California in between meets and pocket the difference. There were other methods, too, some of them as simple as just taking cash from promoters and never reporting it. The officials of governing bodies like the Amateur Athletic Union were content with this system because it gave them control; if they wanted an athlete to compete in a meet that he wanted to skip, they could always threaten to take away his amateur standing, and they always had plenty of proof on hand.

Obviously, this is far removed from any honest amateurism, and eliminating the artificial barrier between professionals and amateurs would make the Olympics honest, if nothing else. That would be the prime advantage, because there would be relatively little difference in the competition, since most professional athletes would stay with their sports rather than compete in the Olympics. It's unlikely, for instance, that Kareem Abdul-Jabbar would leave the Bucks in midseason to play for the U.S. team in the Olympics. But at least he'd have the chance if he wanted it.

Eliminating the concepts of professional and amateur in the Olympics would also eliminate one of the basic inequities of amateur sports: an athlete is a professional in Olympic sports if he plays another sport or even coaches. The justification for the rule is that an athlete can gain an unfair competitive edge by turning professional, but it doesn't work that way. As just one example, Jimmy Hines was a sprint champion in the '68 Olympics and then played pro football; as recently as 1972, he was with the Oakland Raiders. Can anybody seriously argue that playing football has enhanced Hines' ability as a sprinter? In fact, it probably seriously hindered him, because frequent tackles eventually slow the fastest man and lack of practice makes it impossible for an athlete to compete on his previous level. It is even worse for coaches, because they seldom have time to work out as they should.

Making all these changes might make it possible for the Olympics to return to their original purpose. Otherwise, I think they're headed the way of the dinosaur.

21

·

Athletes:
The Spoiled Class

It is one of the ironies of the sports world that many fans would do almost anything for their athletic heroes, while the men they idolize dream of nothing more than a world without sports fans. Without sportswriters, too.

It is not so surprising when you think about it. Most people, locked in jobs that bring them no fame beyond the next desk, imagine it must be wonderful to have people cheering you and recognizing your name and face when you are in a public gathering. Athletes, though, have always had this kind of treatment and they see the other side. They don't like the boos, or the criticism in the papers. Sometimes they don't even like straightforward statements about their life, true or not. Reggie Jackson told me he didn't like the fact that I had said in a magazine article that he played around and that was one of the reasons his marriage had ended in divorce. He didn't deny it; he just didn't like to see it in print.

Far from being pleased that others look up to them, some athletes resent it. Sal Bando, captain of the A's, complained in an interview for *Sport* magazine because he was expected to set an example for young fans, though that hardly seems an un-reasonable demand for an athlete on a championship team.

The fact is, to put it simply, athletes are spoiled. The problem is that an athlete has been treated like a Crown Prince through-out his formative years. The adulation starts early, with the junior league hysteria, and never abates. By the time an athlete becomes a professional, even a marginal one, he has been wor-shipped for at least 10 years. He has been a star in the junior leagues, a star in high school and a star in college. The individual who can keep a proper perspective of himself in this situation is rare indeed. Athletes are so spoiled by the time they become professional, they do not even realize they are spoiled. That isn't to say they can't be pleasant to be around; many of them are excellent company. But they expect special treat-ment because they have always had it.

The situation is becoming worse, instead of better. Minimum salaries have been raised to a comfortable level and maximum salaries are ridiculous, and athletes have come to expect this as their due. Athletes relate to other athletes and simply don't understand that their situations are much better than many others. Once I was talking to Jackson in the A's dressing room as he was writing out checks. "I'm trying to live on a budget," he said, "of $30,000 a year. That isn't easy for a major league ball-player." I sympathized as best I could, not having been faced with quite that problem myself. But I knew what he meant: living on the scale that Reggie Jackson thinks is demanded of him—whether it is or not—is expensive; $30,000 a year is indeed a stringent budget in those circumstances.

But what neither Jackson nor most athletes comprehend is that the people they're talking to aren't making that kind of money. I'm sure it would have shocked Reggie to realize that I wasn't making $30,000 a year, and he would never think that the majority of the fans watching him at a game would never reach that kind of yearly salary. When Reggie thinks about money, he thinks in terms of his friend Dick Allen, who was making $225,000 a year at the time. Thus, at $75.000, Reggie figured he was underpaid.

It isn't just the salaries, either. Athletes complain because their meal money on the road is only $18 or so a day—they are unaware that the fans who read their complaints would consider themselves very lucky if they had that kind of allowance. The pension plans are very cushy, and the fans cannot understand why athletes threaten to strike to get even more; nor can they understand, in football's case, why the modern athletes freeze out the sport's pioneers.

As in all such sweeping generalizations, there are exceptions to this rule. Usually, they are athletes like Ben Davidson, who didn't play football until he was in junior college, didn't start more than half the games for his college team in his senior year (though he later found himself billed as the "former Washington All-American") and didn't become a star until he was a pro. By the time he did get fame, with the Oakland Raiders, he could handle it.

Warrior guard Jim Barnett is another exception. At every level of play, Barnett was told he wouldn't be able to make it at the next level, and he never had a chance to become complacent. Barnett is even more of an exception than Davidson because he is truly unconcerned about the money he makes. He offered to take a 10 percent salary cut if all other players would do the same because he was genuinely concerned about the future of pro basketball. He also talks about going to Europe for a couple of years and playing basketball there, though that would entail a considerable financial sacrifice. He is regarded as a flake by his teammates, the fans and opposing players because of the zany things he does (such as stopping to talk to sportswriters or fans while the action is going on), but he retains a refreshing attitude towards everything that happens to him. At the same time, he realizes his teammates do not always share his attitudes.

"We bought a house," he told me once, "and I was really excited about it. It was the first house I'd ever owned. I told Rick (Barry) about it and he said, 'Fucking houses. They're all just a lot of work.'"

Barry's attitude is more typical than Barnett's, by far. I admire Rick in many ways. He is the total professional, playing his best for whoever is his current employer, and he has a drive that has made him the best despite the obstacles placed in his way. But he is spoiled. He takes for granted his $150,000 home and the fancy clothes he wears and the special treatment he gets wherever he goes. He could not understand when he came back to the Warriors why people called him greedy because by current professional basketball standards, he was not overpaid.

Money is probably the biggest difference between the athlete of today and 20 years ago. There are other differences. Some of them are trivial, as in hair and dress; some are more serious, like the disaffection that led George Sauer, Dave Meggysey and Chip Oliver to drop out. But money is the one that cuts across the attitudes of all athletes.

Athletes like Barnett, for whom the game is first and the money second, are now very rare. Present-day athletes are true professionals and very interested in the size of their paychecks. That is not to say they don't enjoy playing, or that they do not play their best; I wouldn't care to argue that paying a man less will make him do better. But at the back of an athlete's mind now is the realization that a successful career can mean financial security for the rest of his life. "I'm very good at counting," says Davidson. "When I retire, I want to count the receipts from my apartment house, my bars . . . ."

And most athletes go after the money with a zeal which borders on ferocity. They share one attribute with J. Paul Getty: there is never too much. They will compromise any principles they might have just to get a little more, as is obvious every time you turn on the TV and see them in commercials. Some of these commercials are well-done, but most of them are horrible violations of good taste. The worst I ever saw was that gasoline commercial with Tom and Nancy Seaver a couple of years back, where Nancy was driving to three different stations to get gas and Tom was explaining to her that she needed only to drive to one.

The commercial insulted the intelligence of those watching and those participating, and I winced every time I saw it. On the mound, Seaver has a great deal of real pride in his ability, but off the field, pride is something easily discarded if it makes him another dollar. After the '69 Mets' World Series win, he even advertised his services and the services of his wife for personal appearances. You'd think he'd be embarrassed, but he obviously does not embarrass easily.

The money that can be made, on the field and off, has made athletes much more independent than they used to be. Five years ago, the thought of a players' strike would have been incredible. No longer. We have seen pro basketball players defy their league commissioners and stage an all-star game themselves—without, it should be added, any reprisals.

Their independence shows on the playing field, too. There is still a lot of the traditional practice by the numbers, but it is decreasing, from necessity. Athletes no longer simply do as they are told; they are asking why, and the answer had better be good or they might just quit.

This has come as a terrible shock to a lot of older coaches and managers. They played in an era when nobody ever questioned a coach's order; now, it is being done with increasing frequency. Coaches who can explain why something is being done will be successful in the years to come; those who cannot are in trouble.

Call it the generation gap if you wish, but the generations are very close. A coach can be out of touch at 35 if he has not moved with the changing times. Some coaches and managers do not realize that a problem even exists. Others recognize the problem intellectually but are stymied emotionally. They cannot bring themselves to change their approach. Others, and they will be the successful ones in the years to come, know there has been a change in attitude and have moved to accommodate it.

An exaggerated example of the way the athlete's mind works these days is provided by Bob Brown, the sterling offensive tackle of the Oakland Raiders. Brown is half little boy, half calculating businessman. The little boy in him demands special treatment; the businessman has elevated his salary into levels generally reached only by those manning the glamorous positions of quarterback, wide receiver and running back. Brown is spoiled, no question. If he feels he isn't properly appreciated, he lets you know. When the Raiders ran mostly to the side away from Brown during the '72 season, he told reporters he was unhappy about that, even though the Raiders were winning, and that (and a desire to renegotiate his contract higher) caused him to say in the spring of 1973 that he wanted to be traded.

Despite his status as perhaps the best offensive tackle in football, Brown has moved around, from Philadelphia to Los

Angeles to Oakland. The Raiders were very cognizant of his temperament, as an incident from '72 training camp illustrates. Raider coach John Madden was angry because the names of waived players had appeared in the papers. (The Raiders are obsessed with secrecy, and it is never more apparent than in their treatment of waived players during training camp; even when such as Billy Cannon are cut, they try to pretend it didn't happen.) At a press conference after the afternoon workout, he answered every question with a surly, "I don't know." Finally, one reporter asked him why Brown had not worked out that afternoon. Madden immediately went into a detailed explanation involving Brown's off-season knee operation, his current problems with the knee and his worth to the team. Obviously, Madden knew Brown would not be happy to have reporters speculating on his absence and wanted to give out plenty of information.

This kind of independence is not limited to football. I already mentioned the independence of pro basketball players. It is the same in baseball, largely because of the disappearance of all but a few of the minor leagues. Once, baseball players spent years in the minors. Maury Wills was 27 and Hoyt Wilhelm 29 before they went on to exceptional major league careers. Now players jump right out of school. Burt Hooton played only a part of a season in the minors after college and pitched a no-hitter in his first year in the majors; David Clyde came directly from high school to the Texas Rangers. With players moving so quickly into the majors, they cannot be threatened with demotion to the minors. Nor is it a valid comparison when they are told they should be happy with their traveling arrangements because they are so much better off than they'd be in the minors; they have not spent enough time in the minors to know or care about conditions there.

The changes in structure have improved virtually every sport you can name. Athletes eat better, sleep better and have better coaching and equipment; in addition, the high salaries attract more good athletes and give them an incentive to stay in condition. Thus, they are bigger, smarter and less likely to dissipate their talents than their predecessors were.

The facts are indisputable. Baseball is much better than it was in Babe Ruth's era; in 20 years basketball has come so far as to make George Mikan, the "Player of the Half Century," as outmoded as the dinosaur, and football—well, would you like to figure where a good pro team could play Bronko Nagurski now?

But, though that works to the fans' advantage and should bring them closer to athletes, the reverse is true: athletes and fans are drawing ever further apart. As the emphasis on sports grows, athletes become more spoiled and fans more idolatrous, and neither can understand the other. One fan, though conceding the truth of a critical piece I had written, wondered whether I should have written it. "Athletes are the only heroes we have to look up to when we are young," he wrote. "To bring out these truths might make the young people cynical about the chance they have to emulate these characters. Wouldn't you like kids to look to a false John Unitas rather than a real Dennis Hopper?"

It's true that kids look up to athletes. Joe Kapp told me that when he speaks to groups, "If I ask them who wants to be President, I might get one hand up. But when I ask them who's going to play for the 49ers, they all raise their hands."

But kids can handle the truth, usually a lot better than their parents. If you tell your son that his favorite athlete is really a despicable human being, chances are he'll say, "Oh . . . Can I go out and play with Billy?" The real problem is that athletes are idolized at least as much by adults as kids. It is not kids who make up booster clubs; it is not kids who buy season tickets for football games; it is not kids who wait at airports to greet athletes returning from a trip; it is not kids who buy lawn mowers because Jack Nicklaus (who probably hasn't used one in 15 years) says one brand is the best.

I've seen some incredible things traveling with the Oakland Raiders. I saw one man who had shaved the forehead of his dog and imprinted a Raider emblem on it, for instance. I've seen fans rush up just to touch players, or to grab the tip ends of Ben Davidson's moustache. This kind of hero worship makes it easy to understand why athletes are spoiled. When they don't get such treatment, they think something is terribly wrong. The A's, for instance, were embittered when nobody called them to speak at banquets for $500 a shot after they became World Champions. The next year, they criticized the Oakland

Coliseum for not being more colorful, they complained of nonexistent chuckholes in the outfield or of their parking arrangements, and they moaned because more fans weren't coming out to see them. Childish, but typical.

The matter of attendance was especially crucial to the relationship between the A's and their fans. The players could not seem to understand that the rising prices had priced much of their natural following out of the park (Oakland has a heavy black population, and many of the affluent whites have fled to the suburbs). At the same time, in common with other athletes, they complained of the need to sign autographs or make other necessary good will gestures.

It is all inevitable—not only in Oakland but everywhere—and it is also sad. Fans and athletes are locked in a symbiotic embrace, but neither can understand the other. They were cast in their roles when they were about 10 years old, the one group worshipping and the other group worshipped, and neither can escape. It is only one more example of what happens when sports are so overemphasized.

22

•

Jack Scott:
One Of The Good Guys

Jack Scott doesn't seem to be a person who would scare anybody. His general appearance is professorial, his manner courteous, his voice mild. And yet, Scott has incurred the wrath of college coaches and athletic directors, the National Collegiate Athletic Association and Spiro Agnew.

With enemies like that, he can't be all bad.

Scott is a former athlete—a sprinter at Stanford—but he has shaken loose from the traditional jock viewpoint, and this has scared a lot of people. Operating out of his Institute for the Study of Sports and Society in Berkeley, he expounded what seemed to be radical ideas about collegiate sports: that sports should be part of the college program and not a separate entity involving hired gladiators; that women should be part of the program; that athletes should not be barred from competition because of NCAA technicalities; that sports should exist for sports' sake.

At the same time, he also got an undeserved reputation as the primary influence for the antifootball books by Dave Meggysey and Chip Oliver which caused him to be attacked by Agnew at a University of Alabama sports banquet in the spring of 1972.

Agnew's attack proved one thing: he hadn't read what Scott had written but was relying instead on word-of-mouth information. As even a cursory reading of his books would show, Scott's approach is much different from Meggysey's or Oliver's. Their feeling is that collegiate and pro sports are monsters and should be destroyed. Scott's view is positive: improvements are being made, more will be made and the system is worth saving. In his first book, "The Athletic Revolution," he even gave equal time to the traditional viewpoints, printing speeches made by such as Max Rafferty, then state superintendent of schools in California. But most people—Agnew apparently included—didn't get beyond the title. As with Eugene Burdick and Bill Lederer's "The Ugly American," people lost the semantics battle because they made up their minds without reading the book.

Scott laughs at the idea that he influenced Meggysey and Oliver. "They're intelligent people," he says, "and they had these ideas before I even met them. I gave them encouragement when they were writing, but I don't agree with everything they wrote, especially in Dave's case. He's a lot more bitter than I am."

Scott's influence was felt through his books and the institute, and he had a good reputation among younger athletes and the younger generation in the media, but there were a lot of frustrations. His institute was run on a shoestring out of an old ramshackle house in Berkeley, and he ran into opposition with his classes. He tried to get football coach Ray Willsey to speak to his class (again, the effort to present both sides), but Willsey wouldn't take the chance; he knew he might look foolish.

There was also the frustration any theoretician feels: he had ideas which he wanted to put into practice, but others were making policy. Thus, when he got the chance to become athletic director of Oberlin College in Ohio in the fall of 1972, he took it. The results, so far, have been mixed.

Oberlin seemed to be ideal for Scott's experiments in athletic democracy. The college has a reputation for academic excellence and virtually none for athletic supremacy; nor is there any pressure from alumni to produce teams that will put Oberlin on the athletic map. Instead of giving athletic scholarships, the school operates on the Ivy League standard:

special talents are considered along with academic ability when scholarships are granted.

But even at Oberlin, there has been a startling resistance to Scott's ideas, particularly those pertaining to blacks and women. He was hired, for a four-year term, by a 5-4 vote of the Oberlin Faculty Council. A new council is selected each year and though no vote was taken the '73 council seemed antagonistic to Scott. The council eliminated a physical education faculty post, though the number of physical education majors increased from 2 to 40 in Scott's first year. Why this resistance? Well, Scott learned that white men, even those considered liberal, often talk one way and think quite another when it comes to race and women in sports.

"After the killings at Jackson State," said Scott in the summer of 1973, "the Oberlin faculty passed a resolution deploring the killings and also saying that we should do more for the blacks here at home. Yet, no blacks have been hired for the general faculty since then; it's been up to the physical education department, which has hired three. For the general faculty, it's been the same old argument, that there aren't any qualified."

The first move Scott made was to hire Tommie Smith, the former Olympian whose world records were overshadowed in many people's minds because of his black power salute at the '68 Olympics. Smith was made the track coach and assistant athletic director. "Our track team broke four school records the first year," says Scott.

Then, he hired Cass Jackson to coach the football team, the first black head football coach at a predominantly white college. It was less that Scott was trying to strike a blow for humanity than that he thought Smith and Jackson were the best men available.

"Blacks have been discriminated against for so long," says Scott, "that when you go out looking for the best coaches available, there is a large reserve talent pool there."

None of which mattered much to his critics, who suggested that he go slow on the hiring of blacks. Scott's response to this was to hire Patrick Penn, another black, as basketball coach for the 1973–74 season. Again, it was a move based on excellence: Penn's last two high school teams had won the Ohio state championship. Penn's age (37) was also a factor. "The rest of us are around 30," noted Scott, "and I want to show it isn't just the younger ones who have these ideas. You know that old idea that it's all right for youth to be radical but they get conservative with age. Penn's a little older, he's settled with a family and yet he's got the same ideas."

Scott says he's found the resistance to blacks surprising, but he's gotten just as much reaction to his program for women. He went to Oberlin with the specific idea of boosting the women's sports programs—"It's ridiculous that girls have to stop competing at 18 even when they're champions because they can't get scholarships," he said then—and he's followed through.

"When I came here, they told me that women weren't interested in competing in sports," he said. "I told them, with the programs that were being offered, I didn't blame them; I wouldn't be interested, either. When I came, there was a hard core of about 18 women who were competing in two or three sports. Now, we have over 50 competing in two or three sports and probably another 50 competing in just one sport. We had more women come out for the swim team than men."

The women's athletic budget had been $950 before Scott; for the 1973–74 school year, his second, the budget was increased to $6800. There had also been some other changes which irritated some people.

"Oberlin had a new $5 million gym," Scott says, "but there were practically no locker room facilities for women. So, we converted the faculty locker room into women's facilities. That irritated the faculty members because the facilities were a little nicer than the students' and they liked coming there. We didn't do it to irritate anybody, but we had no choice."

There was another problem: because the women's swim season ended a month and a half before their championships, Scott allowed the women to swim unattached in the men's meets, with permission from other coaches. "It's been traditional for ineligible men to swim in meets like this," he says, "so I didn't see any reason we couldn't do it with the women."

Some did, though. The Ohio Athletic Association officially censured Scott for his actions. "They told me," said Scott, "that the last time a woman had competed with men in Ohio college sports was in 1947. She had finished third in a state golf tournament and they admitted that was a blow to their egos. At least, they were honest about it."

Scott thinks, as I do, that having women compete in sports will have a residual benefit for men, too. "I think we'll be able to see sports as a human endeavor," he says, "instead of a kind of masculinity rite, and the pressure on men to win in sports will be relieved."

But the main thrust of Scott's arguments is that sports should be fun and open to everybody, as participant and spectator; he even dropped the admission charge to intercollegiate athletic events. "There will be those who want to be the very best," he says, "and we want to encourage that. But we don't want to get into a situation where only the best are invited to compete. College sports should be open to everyone."

The mossbacks got to Scott in January, 1974, forcing his resignation at Oberlin, but his ideas make too much sense to be shoved back under the rug. The future belongs to him.

23

·

A Few Thoughts At Random

Indianapolis 500

It is past time the Indy 500 was permanently put into mothballs. There is no longer any reason for it, on any basis. No other major sporting event is worse run than the Indy 500. It couldn't even get past the first turn in the '73 race, where ten cars were involved in a crash that was at least partially caused by a bad start.

"It was the most-ragged start I've ever seen here," said one driver, Dick Simon. "Cars were scattered all over. People were everywhere."

Another driver, David Hobbs, said, "We are supposedly the best drivers in the world and we can't even drive down the bloody straight."

There is nothing startling in this. It seems that every year at Indianapolis there is some complaint about how the race is run. There have been complaints about drivers passing on the yellow flag, about cars spilling oil on the track and not being ruled off. Once, a pace car even crashed.

The race once made sense from a competitive standpoint, for those who get their thrills watching cars go very fast, but the speeds attained now have turned the track into a virtual suicide run. One driver, Art Pollard, was killed in qualifying trials for the '73 race. Another, Swede Savage, died of injuries and burns suffered in a crash during the race. Even the spectators are not safe; 11 of them were hit by flying debris in the first-turn crash.

There seems to be no way even the best drivers can escape the crashes. Some of the best drivers in auto racing history have been killed at Indy. Pollard was certainly no reckless, youthful daredevil; at 46, he had been around long enough to recognize the hazards and was skillful enough to be able to avoid most of them, but at Indy, he could not. Drivers accept this kind of danger at the inadequate dirt tracks they sometimes run. It is quite another thing to be exposed to this type of danger at what should be the premier event. The basic problem is that the course was built for cars going 70 mph. Even the drivers admit their fear. When A. J. Foyt says cars are going too fast, you can be sure they are.

I thought for a long time that race fans were at least subconsciously drawn to races because of the thought a driver might be killed. Now, I think it is a much more subtle thing, that fans want to see drivers extend themselves to their very limits and stop just short of that point where they would go fatally out of control. There is no such thrill at Indy. The cars have all developed past that point; now only luck saves the drivers. The best or worst can go in a twinkling. What kind of sport is that?

What justification is there for this race? Need it be held so a couple of hundred thousand people can drink beer and cry over "Back Home in Indiana?" It used to be argued that races such as Indy helped promote development of the automobile, but nobody seriously makes that claim any more. The best way to develop something for the family car is on a test course where driving conditions can be simulated and scientifically controlled.

It is not even a good race from a competitive standpoint. The speeds are so great that a few seconds in time translates into a huge distance gap, and cars that are really very close in time appear to be far apart on the track.

Finally, there is the ecological argument. I think we are all beginning to realize what the American love affair with the automobile has done to our society, the damage it has done to the environment and the problems it has caused with our energy supplies. We should be discouraging the use of the automobile, not romanticizing and encouraging it. Events like Indy only further our problems. Back home in Indiana, indeed.

Golf's Appeal

More than once, I have wondered about the appeal of golf as a spectator sport, because it seems to have so much against it. You have to settle for watching only one part of the game. Either you watch the putting or the driving or the fairway shots; it is virtually impossible to see all three.

And if you're following Arnold Palmer, you don't even see that much. What you see are the backs of heads of other people following Arnold Palmer.

Moreover, the pro golf tour is composed largely of pleasant young men known only to bank tellers. We are still talking about Palmer, though he has not won a major golf tournament since approximately the time Johnny Miller was being potty trained, because there have been no young stars to take his place as a crowd attraction. The biggest stars on any tour are still Palmer and Jack Nicklaus and Lee Trevino and 100 other millionaires as anonymous as offensive linemen.

What is it then that accounts for golf's popularity? More than anything else, I suspect golf is appealing because it is so personal in a world which has become increasingly impersonal. We can identify with both the golfers and their problems. When you are at a golf tournament, you can walk right along the fairways with the players and sometimes even talk to them in between shots. The golfers' expressions of pain or joy are visible to the fans, and some golfers, like Palmer and Trevino, play to the crowds and exchange jokes with them. In Trevino's case, sometimes on the backswing.

There is another reason why the bond between fans and competitors is so close at a golf tournament: everybody knows the problems. We can all sympathize with Nicklaus when his approach shot is buried under the lip in a sand trap, because we have been there. Of course, he cannot approach the shot in the same way; somebody would surely see him if he threw the ball out of the trap.

The Bing Crosby tournament carries this personal approach a step further because of all the celebrities who play in it. It was the first, and is still the best, of the celebrity tournaments, and well over half the fans come because they want to see the movie and TV stars. You can, after all, see Rod Funseth at the Kaiser—if somebody points him out to you. At the Crosby, you over-hear some marvelous conversations. Generally, they go something like this:

"Lookit, Marge, there's James Garner."
"Oooooooh, and who's the tall fellow over there?"
"The program says it's George Archer."
"Who's George Archer?"
"You got me. I think maybe I saw him in a gangster movie once."

And let's face it: I go to the Crosby because my wife wants to see Glen Campbell, not because I want to see Nicklaus. It is golf's good fortune that it lends itself so well to this kind of approach. The personal touch is still the best.

The Drug Situation

In the summer of 1973, the NFL Players Association resisted very firmly the suggestion made by Rep. Harley O. Staggers that players submit to a urinalysis after games, and I can't blame the players. They're being made fall guys in a situation which is a natural outgrowth of our society.

Nobody who has been around a professional team doubts that drugs and pills are plentiful; the pills are sometimes even available to sportswriters with hangovers. And they are potent. I speak from experience. I took an "upper" one time when I was hungover and didn't come down from the ceiling for several hours. It was a frightening experience, and one I haven't repeated.

But this hardly should be a surprise in our society, which has become increasingly drug-oriented. Some drugs—like liquor—are so common, we think nothing of them. And examine the contents of your medicine cabinet some day. This is one of the basic problems between parents and their children. The parents tell their children they shouldn't be taking drugs, but the kids know their parents are taking them by the fistful, and they soon lose what respect they had for their parents' advice.

Athletes are largely from the group that grew to adulthood during the last 10 years, when the hallucinogenic drugs were becoming so common. Few see anything morally wrong with taking drugs. Add to this the factor of the competitive pressure of professional sports and the fact that athletes cannot afford to take time off except for the most serious of injuries, and it is no wonder drug-taking is so prevalent.

Even 50 years ago, it was hazardous for an athlete to sit down; Wally Pipp sat out a game with the Yankees because of a headache and Lou Gehrig replaced him for the next 2,130 games.

Now, that pressure is intensified because the emphasis on sports in our society and the incentive of the money that athletic excellence can bring produce so many more good young athletes every year. In that situation, an athlete with a minor injury would rather pop a pill or take an injection that will enable him to stay in the lineup.

The pressure to win is also a factor. An athlete can't afford to play poorly because he is feeling bad. Thus, more pills. Whether they help physically is another question, but athletes think they do, which may be just as important.

The owners and coaches have to accept their share of the responsibility, because athletes are not getting their pills and drugs on the sly. They are available right in the dressing room. The accepted practice has been to put out baskets of pills in the dressing room, labeled with obscene or scatological terms that fool nobody. Athletes are free to take as many as they want, and everybody in authority is thus given an out: asked if he has given an athlete pills, a trainer can honestly answer that he hasn't.

This kind of situation can lead to tragedy, as it has at least once, in the case of former San Diego Charger lineman Houston Ridge, who says he was crippled because of drugs allegedly prescribed and administered by a team trainer and physician. But owners and coaches still prefer to ignore the situation, hoping it will somehow go away. They are not very different in their attitudes from a lot of parents who wake up one morning and find they cannot ignore the situation any longer because their children can no longer function on any level.

Since the Ridge case (Ridge, by the way, settled out of court in 1973 for $260,000), commissioner Pete Rozelle has finally started putting some needed pressure on owners and coaches to stop the casual pill popping. If the owners and coaches want to, they can stop it; it will be interesting to see how serious they will be about stopping it.

Even more than that, we need an honest examination of the whole drug situation and an admission of the pressures that cause the taking of drugs. That, it seems to me, is far preferable to merely pointing a cynical and hypocritical finger at the athletes.

The Camera as Referee

It is remarkable that a sport which is the child of television, as pro football certainly is, should be so reluctant to improve itself by using the camera to supplement the officials. It is long past the time that the officials should have been subject to visual review.

Every season provides fresh examples of the need for an instant replay of officials' decisions. The best in 1972 was the Jack Tatum fumble recovery and runback for the Oakland Raiders against Green Bay. The television cameras made it obvious that MacArthur Lane never had possession of the pitchout, and the play should thus have been ruled a muff, which cannot be advanced, instead of a fumble, which can. Tatum went 104 yards for a touchdown and the Raiders won, 20-14, so the play was critical.

Supervisor of officals Mark Duncan admitted the obvious and added that if officials make too many mistakes like that, they are replaced. But he did not say what should be equally obvious: a recourse to the television cameras could prevent errors like that.

Pro football cannot afford such errors because the competition is too tight. At the top, there is very little difference between the four or five best in each conference, and an official's call can be critical. What would have happened if Green Bay had lost its division title that year by the margin of that Raider game? There is no reason for allowing a disputed play to stand simply because the NFL insists on maintaining outdated methods.

Obviously, there are drawbacks to instant replay. One is that you couldn't be certain of getting every play, no matter what; all the replays of the disputed Pittsburgh touchdown in the '72 playoff game with the Raiders proved nothing. But having just a couple of cameras in strategic locations would probably work in 90 percent of the cases. Think how many times television's instant replay shows a controversial play.

Also, there would have to be some limits placed on the review of films. If each play were reviewed, the Sunday games wouldn't end soon enough for the fans to watch the Monday night games. Perhaps each team could be limited to three calls a game; perhaps a team which challenged a decision that turned out to be correct could be penalized 15 yards. That would certainly eliminate any capricious carping by coaches.

Pete Rozelle has always been reluctant to use the camera in this way because it would reflect on the judgment of the officials, though he has no such reluctance in singling out erring athletes. Linemen who are caught holding are identified instantly.

I suspect using the camera would actually work to the officials' advantage. They would probably be right a high percentage of the time on disputed calls because they are trained to make these calls, whereas critical coaches and sportswriters are not. But whether this is true or not, the game should be bigger than the hurt feelings of any group of men. It is time the NFL quit pretending there is no problem, particularly since the solution to the problem is so close at hand.

The Designated Hitter

It was typical that the American League, after coming up with the most progressive idea in baseball in at least a decade—the designated hitter rule—managed to screw it up. The league seems to have a decided death wish.

The American League owners adopted the rule so quickly and with such limited discussion that they left two big loopholes and only one was plugged. The first, which was changed, allowed a manager to pinch-hit for anybody in the lineup, not just the pitcher, but that was modified to make only the pitcher dispensable in the batting order.

The league left one loophole, however, which substantially reduced the impact of the rule, not making it mandatory that the designated hitter bat ninth, in the pitcher's spot. As a result, managers have moved designated hitters all around the lineup. Some have batted them leadoff, some have had them hitting cleanup.

Used correctly, the designed hitter rule should add to the excitement of the game. It should give the fans something to look for and it should affect the strategy of the game. Used improperly, it does neither.

Obviously, it is not going to make much difference to the fans if the designated hitter bats high in the order. I saw one game between Oakland and Minnesota where Tony Oliva was batting fourth for the Twins, which is exactly where he would have hit if he'd been playing in the field. Probably, many of the A's fans didn't even realize Oliva was the designated hitter. All this really does is strengthen the batting order somewhat, by substituting a good hitter for a weak one. That's all right, but it doesn't go far enough.

If the designated hitter were batting ninth, it would force managers to change their strategy. How many times have you seen a rally start in the bottom of the order, only to end when the pitcher batted, futilely? Many times, managers will walk the eighth place hitter intentionally to get at the pitcher. Obviously, they'd never do that if a good hitter were coming up.

It's a shame the rule was misapplied because it has a lot of possibilities. It opens the game up for hitting specialists, which is not as much a departure from baseball tradition as some think. What are pitchers, after all, if not specialists? Most pitchers can neither hit nor field well enough to play anywhere else.

The designated hitter is a good rule because it adds offense to the game, which is what fans want. The purists talk about 1-0 games, but any team that depends on purists for the bulk of its audience is on the road to bankruptcy. Unless you have a truly overpowering pitcher like Sandy Koufax, most fans would much prefer to see those 10-8 games that baseball writers hate.

Moreover, the designated hitter helps the game without gimmickry. Unlike bringing in the fences or lowering the mound, this change helps only those who can take advantage of it. The weak hitters don't benefit, but the good ones who can no longer play in the field—Orlando Cepeda and Jim Ray Hart are outstanding examples—have had their careers lengthened.

Simultaneously, it helped the quality of the game by getting some good-hit, no-field guys out of the field, so they can't mess up more plays. It would be a far better game if people like Harmon Killebrew and Frank Howard had only to bat and never went out on the field.

The change also helped starting pitchers, though few had considered that before. Because there was no need to pinch-hit for pitchers in the American League, starters stayed in games they were trailing as long as they pitched well.

Oddly, though, as an example of the way baseball people cling to the past, American League pitchers continued to take batting practice before each game, though it was no longer needed. That's baseball.

Soccer's Friends

Perhaps no sport has been worse served by those who claim to be its friends than soccer. Convinced that all they had to do was open the gates, owners and promoters made about every mistake that can be made. It is a credit to the sport's resilience that it still lives after all that has been done to it.

Until 1967, there was only amateur soccer in this country. Then, emboldened by the sport's success almost everywhere else in the world, two leagues sprang up out of nowhere, fighting for what turned out to be a very small audience.

Owners made two assumptions: 1) That a large promotional campaign would get Americans enthused about soccer; 2) That the ethnic groups would support the game. Both assumptions were false.

The first assumption was doomed from the start. As anybody who has spent any time around any sport knows, the basic support for a game comes from those who have played the game in their younger days and know it well. Baseball fans are usually former baseball players and basketball fans former basketball players. Among native Americans, there was no similar background of interest or knowledge, and the rhythms of the game were strange to them. Team owners were, in effect, asking Americans to pay money to become educated about a game. Predictably, that effort failed.

The second assumption seemed more logical, but it wasn't. The ethnic groups did relatively little to support soccer in this country because they were convinced the soccer was inferior to what they had seen in their former countries. In most cases, they were right. So, they played the game themselves and seldom went to the professional games. The Oakland Clippers, champions of the North American Professional Soccer League that first year, were appalled to learn that the amateur games continued to be scheduled on Sundays, in direct opposition to the Clippers' games.

Many teams, including the Clippers, soon dropped out of professional competition. To fill the soccer vacuum, foreign teams were brought in to put on exhibitions. These exhibitions did more to harm the soccer cause than to help it. Often, star players didn't make the trips, and even when they did, they played at half speed because the games didn't count.

The worst offenders were the promoters, whose greed overcame their judgment. In 1972, for instance, when Santos of Brazil, led by the incomparable Pélé, made a tour of the United States, it was billed as Pélé's farewell tour. That enraged him, because he had retired only from national competition. The next year, he was back again, and once again, some promoters couldn't resist the temptation to bill it as a farewell tour.

Despite all this, I see hope for the game. I think soccer is an excellent game for kids because it doesn't depend on size, as football and basketball do, and it is not a rough sport. Probably because of that, it has a lot of support among those building youth sports programs and the rapid expansion of youth soccer should yield a reservoir of soccer fans in a few years.

And maybe then, it can break loose from the fatal embrace of its "friends."

24

.

The All-Boor Team

Unlike *Sports Illustrated,* I have never considered chess a sport, in the sense that football and basketball and even bowling are, but I am forced to make an exception in Bobby Fischer's case. Bobby's behavior when he won the world championship of chess in Iceland has earned him a spot on my all-boor team.

This is a team I started organizing long ago. It is dominated by baseball personalities, and you can draw your own conclusions about that. My cleanup hitter, of course, is Willie Mays, but he would be hard-pressed by Roger Maris, a man with a remarkably even disposition. Maris was such a sorehead in his great year of 1961 that he made Mickey Mantle seem saintly. Nevertheless, Mantle has also earned a spot on my team for the ease with which he ignored autograph-seeking kids.

A digression to another sport, football, would allow for the inclusion of Art Powell, who had a stormy and only sporadically effective career with the Titans (Jets), Raiders, Bills and Toronto of the Canadian League. Even in his good days with the Raiders, Powell was a pain in the neck because of his habit of telling the quarterback what to call. His best efforts, though, were usually saved for the postgame interviews, when he would complain that he hadn't been thrown to enough. After one game in Buffalo, when he made that complaint, a reporter consulted his notes and told Art he had been thrown 11 passes, 2 of which he had caught.

Pro football has also given us Duane Thomas—a man who simply gave up talking after his rookie season, whether to his coach, writers or teammates—and such boorish men as George Allen and Bud Grant as coaches. And college football has produced Woody Hayes, a considerable accomplishment all by itself.

But it is still baseball which has the real stars. Gaylord Perry, for instance. As a pitcher, Perry is near the tops, but his personality is near the bottom. He's smart enough to change his style when he goes out on the banquet circuit, and the fans love him; but his teammates know the real Perry. His Giant teammates were happy to see Perry traded in 1972, even though he went on to become the Cy Young Award winner with Cleveland.

Perry became unpopular with his teammates because he had the habit of questioning the official scorer on any borderline hit decisions, his opinion being they should be errors, which would not affect his earned run average. Willie McCovey, in particular, had to bear the brunt of Perry's criticism when games were lost on close plays. Gaylord also was willing to assume some of the burden of managing the Giants; he told manager Charlie Fox not to play Alan Gallagher at third or Willie Mays at first when he was pitching.

When Perry was appointed player representative for the Giants, he took that to mean he was sergeant-at-arms for the clubhouse. Once, he threw the son of a sportswriter out of the clubhouse because the boy, a teen-ager, had hair too long to suit Perry's tastes.

His expertise in other areas did not always go unquestioned by his teammates. Once he tried to tell shortstop Chris Speier where to play, and Speier told him in very direct language to tend to his pitching. It must have been a treat for the lip readers in the box seats.

Sam McDowell, a pleasant enough fellow when sober, also belongs in here because of his tendency to tell different stories to different people on different days, some of which he may even have believed himself. Sam will tell the most outrageous stories with a zeal that suggests he has convinced himself. I remember one occasion when he was pitching with Cleveland when he assured me that he thought the Indians had a great team and that he wanted to spend the rest of his career there. At the time, the Indians were dead last and McDowell had asked to be traded. With the Giants, his stories became even more fanciful. In spring training in 1973, he left a note in the box of one writer saying he was quitting baseball and assured others he had no intention of retiring. He didn't retire, of course.

During the '72 season, when I was making a trip with the Giants, Sam won a game in Pittsburgh on his reputation more than anything. He had a very sore arm and threw no more than half a dozen real fastballs the whole game, but the Pirates were apparently off balance and couldn't get to him. After the game, he told a Pittsburgh writer he had thrown 80 percent fast balls. He also said he had thrown 30 percent curves and 10–15 percent changeups. Must be new math.

When you get to managers and coaches, there is an embarrassment of riches. Just since they moved out of New York, the Giants alone have had Alvin Dark and Herman Franks, and nobody has ever topped Leo Durocher, who is in Bartlett's for his famous dictum: nice guys finish last. Nobody ever dared ask Leo how he would know.

Through the years, as players changed, Leo remained his irascible self. Ken Holtzman, traded by the Cubs to the A's at his request so he could get away from Durocher, described Durocher's style. "I think after a while, the Cubs were playing defensively because of Leo. For years, the Cubs were always last in stolen bases. Why? It wasn't because we had no speed, because we did have some guys who could run. I think it might have been because they were afraid to run, afraid they might get thrown out or picked off because then Leo would yell at them when they came back to the dugout."

My most compelling personal memory of Durocher came a few years back when the Giants and Cubs were playing an early season game at Candlestick. The Cubs lost that game, something like their seventh in nine games, and I asked what I thought was a reasonable question of Durocher: Do you plan any lineup changes in the near future? "A question like that, you should go to the back of the room," said Durocher.

The next day, he made some lineup changes.

Dark's most glorious moment came one year when he was manager and general manager of Cleveland and the A's were trying to trade for McDowell. A good Southern Baptist whose religion is supposed to keep him from things like swearing, lying or cheating on his wife, Dark told Oakland *Tribune* reporter Ron Bergman that he had not heard of any trade talk involving McDowell. Bergman had just talked to both Charlie Finley, who said he had been talking to Dark about the trade, and McDowell, who said Dark had told him he might be traded. As he had to in a situation which involved those three, Bergman wrote a story with a lot of "maybe" and "possibly" and "perhaps" in it, but the Finley-McDowell version later turned out to be the truth.

Franks was famed for his obscenities when asked any question at all, as he walked around the clubhouse with a minimum of clothing covering his unlovely body. Later, he claimed that his temperament was designed to take the heat off the players, but in fact it did just the opposite. Because sportswriters could not get a civil comment from Franks, they interviewed the players more than they normally would have.

If Franks had just been a hot-tempered man, his outbursts would have been understood, but there was evidence that he picked his sports. Like his favorite player, Mays, he was much nicer to more-prominent writers. He insulted the regular writers around the Giants regularly, but once made the mistake of swearing at Jack Mann, who was then with *Sports Illustrated,* before he knew who Mann was. When he learned, he tried to apologize.

Obviously, you cannot go with three managers for our all-boor team, but there is an out. We can put Dark at shortstop and Franks in the front office, since he had considerable influence in making trades when he was with the Giants. Franks helped persuade Horace Stoneham to trade Orlando Cepeda for Ray

Sadecki, and he also got rid of catcher Randy Hundley because he thought Hundley held his glove wrong!

Naturally, Howard Cosell would have to announce the games for this team, and any one of several New York writers would qualify to cover them.

And the owner for this magnificent collection? There can be only one choice: Charles O. Finley.

Index

INDEX

INDEX

INDEX

INDEX